The Culture of Knitting

The Culture of Knitting

Joanne Turney

B L O O M S B U R Y

LONDON • NEW DELHI • NEW YORK • SYDNEY

Bloomsbury Academic
An imprint of Bloomsbury Publishing Plc

50 Bedford Square	1385 Broadway
London	New York
WC1B 3DP	NY 10018
UK	USA

www.bloomsbury.com

First published in 2009 by Berg
Reprinted by Bloomsbury Academic 2013

British Library Cataloguing-in-Publication Data
A catalogue record for this book is available from the British Library.

ISBN: HB: 978-1-8452-0591-1
PB: 978-1-8452-0592-8

Library of Congress Cataloging-in-Publication Data
A catalog record for this book is available from the Library of Congress.

Turney, Joanne.
The culture of knitting / Joanne Turney.
p. cm.
Includes bibliographical references and index.
ISBN-13: 978-1-84520-592-8 (pbk.)
ISBN-10: 1-84520-592-8 (pbk.)
ISBN-13: 978-1-84520-591-1 (cloth)
ISBN-10: 1-84520-591-X (cloth)
1. Knitting. 2. Knitting—Miscellanea. 3. Knitters (Persons)—
Miscellanea. I. Title.
TT820.T92 2009
746.43'2—dc22 2009021990

Typeset by Avocet Typeset, Chilton, Aylesbury, Bucks
Printed and bound in Great Britain

In Memoriam: Dr Judy Attfield

Table of Contents

List of Illustrations

Acknowledgements

I would like to thank the following people and companies for their encouragement, advice, support, comments and generosity: Lisa Anne Auerbach, Sue Bradley, Barbara Burman, Sarah Dallas, Andy Diaz Hope, Kimberley Elderton, Rosemary Harden, Harriet Harvey, Rachel John, Marianne Jorgensen, Alison Kelly, Sharon Lloyd, Rachael Matthews, Althea Crome, Dr Lesley Miller, Janet Morton, Linda Newington, Mark Newport, Lindsay Obermeyer, Liz Padgham-Major, Lauren Porter, Celia Pym, Caterina Radvan, Freddie Robins, Clare Rose, Laurel Roth, Rowan, Sirdar, Adrienne Sloane, Arno Verhoeven, Shane Waltener, Gill Willis, Donna Wilson, and the countless amateur knitters who freely gave their time and opinions to this project. I would also like to thank the staff at the Knitting Library, University of Southampton, The Fashion Museum, Bath, and the Women's Library.

My special thanks are directed towards Bath Spa University for supporting this project, and to my wonderful colleagues at Bath School of Art and Design for their enthusiasm and encouragement. In particular I would like to thank Dr Rina Arya, Dr Jo Dahn, Alex Franklin and Robin Marriner for their assistance in commenting on work in progress and for their valuable suggestions.

My personal gratitude is also extended to my family and David, who have been a constant source of help and inspiration.

Introduction

Hand knitting, once a major British industry, has regained much of its former respectability since the days, not long ago, when it was described as a suitable occupation only for the aged and feeble minded.[1]

Knitting is big news. Suddenly, an activity associated with the elderly and infirm has become hip. Indeed, in a 2004 survey, the Craft Yarn Council of America expressed a 13 per cent increase in knitting participation of those aged 25–34.[2] In the UK, the yarn manufacturer Rowan estimates that over 11 per cent of the population regularly knits,[3] whilst the UK Hand Knitting Association estimates that in 2006, 475,000 people took up knitting in the UK and USA.[4] So, one might conclude that knitting is undergoing a revival. But has knitting ever really gone away?

Investigating predominantly hand knitting (although examples of machine-knitting and industrially produced knitting are included), this book aims to investigate not merely why knitting is so popular now, although elements of this are addressed, but the reasons why knitting has such longevity. Knitting, of course, is something everyone is very familiar with: it is everywhere. Often this kind of familiarity means that it defies discussion or contemplation – and tends to be ignored.

It is not just the ubiquity of knitting that stops people talking about it. It is generally understood as ordinary, unchanging, and what it represents and means is so culturally constructed and embedded that it is assumed there is nothing more to say. This is primarily because the meanings of – or the popular associations of – knitting are rather limited: old ladies, woolly objects, and the old-fashioned. This is not to say that these associations have no basis in reality. Some old ladies do knit, some knitted things are overtly woolly, and some knitted items defy the laws of fashion and are extremely 'ugly'. But this is only one way of understanding or approaching knitting, and there are many more.

This book investigates the cultural impact and meaning(s) of knitting and its development since 1970. The distinctly contemporary basis for this study is a deliberate attempt to move away from a historical appraisal of knitting, which seems to be the primary focus of many texts addressing the subject. This does not mean that the book is a-historical: it is extremely important to assess why and how knitting has been understood, performed and used over time. Such a historical backdrop is essential for an understanding of the here and now. But, it is also important to move on: to move away from the homely, the traditional and the gendered, which dominates much of the literature of knitting.

The period of study (1970 to date) is important in this respect because it is a period that encompasses a variety of significant developments in approaches to culture and society, which have a potentially huge impact on knitting. The impact of feminism, for example, led to a reappraisal of women's work, of which knitting and other needlecrafts were central. Feminist and queer theory went on to investigate the fluidity of gender, its presentation and display, which in turn led to significant re-evaluations of traditional binary gendered stereotypes. Additionally, knitting as (historically) an ordinary activity was open to investigation as a response to developments such as the new art history and the establishment of cultural studies in the 1970s, which enabled the reappraisal of cultural production and its meanings or readings.

The period encompasses changing attitudes to work and leisure resulting from large-scale de-industrialization, including a changing workforce and working patterns, an ageing population and a greater emphasis on leisure and consumerism. Many of these social and economic changes related directly to the construction of a 'new' femininity – women who worked, had families, engaged in consumerism, were educated, made choices and were seen to 'have it all'. The media embraced this new femininity as a new mobility, empowering women to throw off the chains of housewifery and become 'superwomen'. The changes occurring as a result of the economic shift from production to consumption were played out through the media portrayal of women, as well as in new products aimed at these 'new' women.

In terms of social and cultural history, the period offers a wealth of discourses that challenged established norms. Conflict in Vietnam, Watergate and ecological disaster encouraged new forms of mass political activism and alternative ways of living. Likewise, a trend to categorize consumers as 'lifestyle' shoppers classified social individuals as specific groups that went beyond groupings based on socio-economic classes. Similarly, the rise in multinational corporations and the circulation of global capital are of importance in an appraisal of the popularity of an activity that seems to exist outside these remits.

Throughout the social development and disparity of the period, knitting has likewise continued and developed. Many books about knitting, from a variety of perspectives, were published throughout the period, each offering an insight into techniques, styles, patterns and previously unrecorded histories, each offering new perspectives on the discipline, celebrating knitting as an activity that has its own history, techniques and motifs, and own audience. Although academic in conception, knitting texts frequently include patterns to make up at home, emphasizing the practicality of the discipline rather than focusing on critical modes of interpretation. This book aims to redress this.

During the period of study, knitting, although a discipline in its own right, has been utilized and manipulated by others, enhancing the potential of knitting as an

Figure 1 Knitted 'pineapple' tea cosy, 2007. The tea cosy epitomizes the domestic history of knitting as an aspect of women's dainty work and taste. The humorous pineapple theme fuses the homely and expected with the exotic and unexpected, transforming the ordinary and mundane into the unusual and amusing. But must knitting always be relegated to the kitsch and the banal?

interdisciplinary medium. Knitting is no longer only an ordinary, domestic practice but can be fine art, craft, design, film, performance and fashion, as well as a leisure pursuit. It can – and frequently does – make social comment, political statements and questions issues of national and global importance. As such, knitting has a multiplicity of meanings, purposes and objectives, is undertaken by a variety of different people, in different places and at different times. This book aims to address knitting in all these guises to survey and investigate the ways in which knitting has developed cultural capital, as well as the means by which knitting can be described as a culture.

Knitting is indeed a culture, but it is not monolithic. Not all knitters knit in the same way, using the same tools and equipment, or for the same reasons. Similarly, outcomes are not the same, nor are they for the same audience. In saying this, though, it is important to note that there are similarities, which emanate from notions of construction, and cultural and social understandings of what knitting is and what it represents.

This book intends to outline these sociocultural meanings and to address them from a variety of critical perspectives. The aim of such an investigation is to critique contemporary knitting practices and objects, but also to create a dialogue that questions some well-worn stereotypes. By assessing the literature of knitting, manuals, patterns, social and regional histories alongside testimonial discussions with artists, designers, craftspeople and amateurs, it is hoped that a contemporary analysis of the meaning of knitting now (and over the past thirty years or so) will be established.

It is also important to investigate practice and objects more critically in order to establish a language of knitting, which transcends hierarchical boundaries such as 'art', 'craft' and so on, merely because these classifications tend to dismiss knitting – i.e. 'It's only knitting'. Such marginalization from academic discourse negates this hugely popular, discursive, skilled and dynamic practice. To see knitting as a culture, with its own language, practices and so on is to empower knitting from the ties of other disciplines. This has been addressed through chapterization driven by critical theory, which aims to create a discursive approach to the subject, but also to eradicate the aforementioned hierarchies. So, each chapter is enhanced and addressed through the use of examples of practice and objects that otherwise would be classified as 'art', 'craft', 'fashion', 'design', 'ordinary' or 'amateur' practice.

What Is Knitting?

In its most basic form, knitting can be defined as the formation of a fabric consisting of vertical columns through the looping of a continuous yarn.[5] When performed by hand, knitting is produced on two or more needles that are either circular or sticks, which are used to loop, draw through and secure stitches as the knitter works back and forth. Based on two stitches, plain and purl (or knitting forwards and backwards), patterns and textures are created by adapting (and/or varying), omitting or working together stitches, twisting or turning yarns and/or the knitting, and by using different yarns, colours and so on. Although knitting is a relatively simple activity – the repeated looping and twining of yarn into a stitch – it is also remarkably complex. As one respondent noted:

> You cannot go to a class one day and expect to make a pair of mittens the next. It is a skill; it takes time. When I look at women in their eighties, I think I will never have their knowledge, I will never be as good as them – and I've been knitting for twenty-five years. I say to students that learning to knit is like learning a sport and a language at the same time: it takes dedication, practice and the combination of hand and brain. You can't just do it.[6]

This is the dilemma of knitting; it is seemingly simple – any fool can do it – yet it is extremely difficult, complex, involved. As the knitter and historian Montse Stanley acknowledged:

Knitting has an image problem. The reason, it could be argued, is that long ago knitting became the victim of its own success. The apparent simplicity of basic hand knitting is deeply ingrained in our collective perception. That knitting can attain high levels of complexity and significance once it goes beyond the beginner stage tends to be overlooked.[7]

An additional aspect of the problem in understanding knitting is its proliferation: knitting is everywhere. It is a constructed textile, so many of the things that are worn or surfaces that are walked or sat upon are knitted. Knitting therefore represents a democracy of objects and practices, so prolific, so mundane, that it isn't noticed: it's taken for granted. And, combined with the cultural stigma of the easiness of knitting, which belies its actual complexities and skill, knitting is overlooked.

Similarly, knitting has historically been a domestic practice; this means that knitting has been seen as largely undertaken in the home and is therefore both familial and familiar. This is certainly evident in popular conceptions of knitting – grannies in rocking chairs, clicking needles and fashioning yarn into garments. So potent is such an image that a recent advertising campaign for Shreddies, a breakfast cereal, has adopted the strap-line 'Knitted by Nanas' to add a humorous vein to the seemingly knitted wheat squares. Such familiarity breeds contempt. We see knitting as a site of nostalgia, a highly gendered relic from yesteryear that not only defies fashion but somehow deserves derision.

As a result, this book intends to make visible an aspect of textiles practice where the created objects are so prolific they are frequently ignored, taken for granted and in turn seen as 'not special'. Consequently, the investigation aims to question how the seemingly mundane becomes significant, how it can be talked about critically and the ways in which we can approach and understand marginalized creative practices. Due to the thematic constraints of this book it has been necessary to be selective in terms of global location: geographically focusing on knitting primarily in the UK and USA, but drawing examples from Europe and Australasia to offer a wider sense of contemporary knitting.

This text addresses knitting in all its classificatory guises (art, craft, design, fashion and ordinary objects and practices) and covers a broad societal and ideological sphere. Therefore it has been necessary and desirable to employ a variety of methodologies in order to extend more established approaches to the subject. It is deliberately interdisciplinary and borrows from the methodologies of anthropology, oral history, design history, cultural and social history, social geography, therapeutic studies and cultural studies. These disciplines have proved useful in assessing and uncovering the aesthetics, locations, contexts and reasons for knitting during the period of study. Equally, the language of the crafts has been of central importance to the study, primarily because the act of knitting is an act of craft. This is to say it is a learned skill: it is repetitive and is undertaken, in the main, by hand.

Oral history has also provided a framework in which voices hitherto ignored or marginalized can be heard. Interviews have been conducted with artists, designers and craftspeople in the UK, Europe, USA and Canada, as well as groups of amateur makers in the UK. Testimonies have also been drawn from the Mass Observation Archive (MO) in the UK to provide a comparative historical account of attitudes towards knitting. These two approaches intend to elicit responses that are both qualitative and quantative, enabling the expression of knitting in macrocosm and microcosm.

It is anticipated that the seeming disparity of the methodological approaches will both demonstrate and enhance knitting objects and practices, challenging stereotypes and preconceptions of what knitting means in the contemporary world. Likewise, each chapter adopts a different critical position. By addressing knitting from perspectives in discourses as diverse as feminism, postmodernism, psychoanalysis and post-Marxism, each chapter aims to demonstrate that theoretical

Figure 2 Fashion photograph, 1964. Fashion Museum, Bath. Courtesy of Bath and North East Somerset Council. The inherent stretch in knitted fabric enables it to cover and fit objects and people flexibly.

appraisal can help to unpick the intricacies of knitting within contemporary society.

This book cannot be reflective of everyone's experience of knitting, nor can it offer a definitive guide to contemporary knitting It offers a selective sample of new ways of seeing, new methods of critiquing knitting, without the constraints of disciplinary boundaries. Similarly, this book is not a blank celebration of knitting: it is critical and does question the language, literature and iconography of knitting, as well as the motives of knitters themselves. It is, however, intended to create an environment in which knitting can be valorized, recognized and discussed. The book therefore pays tribute to everybody who knits, whatever their skill level, intention or motivation, regardless of what they knit and for whom, whether they knit to make a statement or for the sheer pleasure of doing so – it aims to acknowledge their practice. Equally, the book proposes to raise an awareness of knitted objects, whether they are exhibited on catwalks, in galleries, on the bodies of small children, or stuffed behind the wardrobe, in an attempt to discuss knitting as a culture.

–1–

Knitting: A Gendered Pursuit?

When one first thinks of knitting, one thinks of women. Whether it's an image of old ladies clicking needles in rocking chairs, to hip young chicks knitting for peace or Cast Off's hand grenades, or remembering clothes that mothers, aunts or grannies have made, knitting is firmly gendered in the popular psyche. One reason for this is that knitting is largely a domestic pursuit; it is associated with the home and, by association, with women. This chapter will investigate the establishment of knitting as a gendered pursuit, briefly charting its conception as a gendered and leisured occupation and discussing the ways in which these conceptions have continued well into the twenty-first century.

Adopting a feminist approach to knitting, the chapter aims to establish a framework for the discussion of what has become ostensibly an activity or pastime for women as an expression of femininity. Referring to texts addressing gendered cultural and spatial divides, the chapter intends to reassess the meaning of knitting for women, and indeed men, assessing the ways in which both activity and object have not only been gendered, but also have challenged these restrictive models. This chapter therefore addresses knitting as an activity that has been marginalized (although never really marginal), investigating the reasons for this and the ways in which these issues have been addressed since the 1970s.

Feminism and Approaches to Knitting

> Dinner can be late, they say, stuff you, I'm knitting.
> So my house isn't tidy, stuff you, I'm knitting.
> So I haven't saved the world, lost 5 kilos, waxed my legs, stuff you, I'm knitting.[1]

Feminism has a long history dating back to the eighteenth century and the political writings of Mary Wollstonecraft, which developed into the Women's Movement in the late nineteenth century (suffrage and first-wave feminism). This chapter, however, is concerned with the waves of feminism developed in post-war society, concentrating on second- and third-wave feminism, which one might describe as women's liberation, and post-feminism. The purpose of this distinction is contextual and historical, positioning and juxtaposing philosophical and political thought as it emerges and finds a voice, with knitting and knitters from the

1970s onwards. Similarly, as knitting can be understood primarily as a form of popular culture, or everyday practice, the chapter aims to discuss the ways in which feminism informed mainstream activities.

Feminism is a political movement, which aims to challenge and overturn inequalities between the sexes. Feminists have argued that women have been historically socially negated and marginalized as a consequence of patriarchy,[2] a system which privileges and perpetuates male domination, understands women as 'the Other', and thus constructs and maintains their position as submissive. Although there are arguments amongst feminists[3] about what constitutes patriarchy and the specific site of women's oppression, there is a generally held belief that its axis lies with patriarchal society. Patriarchy derives from private ownership and became more defined during the nineteenth century with the rise of bourgeois culture, and is seen to dominate every aspect of daily life. Feminists have sought to redress this and reclaim women's position in history as well as critiquing their social, cultural, economic and political status. For example, the inequality of patriarchy is evidenced by distinguishing terms such as 'sex' and 'gender'; 'sex' is one's biological state, whilst 'gender' is a culturally constructed condition, which enables the continuation and validation of patriarchy. Feminism can therefore be seen as occupying an oppositional or marginal position, attempting to challenge and change that which is considered the 'norm'.

As a marginal or oppositional political movement, feminism, during the 1970s, became far more mainstream and widely accepted as a result of changes in legislation which promoted and protected gender equality: the Equal Opportunities Act and the Equal Pay Act were both initiated in the 1970s. The impact of such legislative change had a sociocultural impact, which transformed the ways in which women were represented and addressed in the media and in everyday life, and central to this were the dual themes of women's work and leisure, of which knitting can be seen as a part.

From a rather general standpoint, second-wave feminism views knitting as a sign of women's oppression, as a largely domestic task that takes up a considerable amount of time for little – if any – remuneration. Knitting is seen of one of many 'chores' that enslave women, bind them to the domestic environment and keep them occupied in mundane and lowly activities.[4] Similarly, knitting within the domestic sphere is a relatively mute activity; it is invisible labour, unseen and unrewarded, and as a consequence is socially and culturally deemed without value. Likewise, the economic position knitting had traditionally held within the home, as an extension of thrifty housewifery and of 'making do', further removed the occupation from the sphere of the monetary marketplace, firmly establishing its position as part of a 'woman's world' dominated by a moral economy. And, regardless, of the time taken, the skill involved or the creativity expressed, because of its locale and its sociocultural negated status, knitting can be viewed as an example of women's oppression. So knitting is a sign of women's work, domestic labour, of time spent on the familial (on others) rather than time spent on the self, or in a recognized, valued or rewarded occupation. One might conclude, therefore, that knitting was one of many domestic, repetitive chores, things that needed to be done to maintain the household.

Conversely, second-wave feminists have also investigated the significance of women's creative practice within the home, as well as exploring the relationship between men's and women's hobbies. These studies have concluded that there is no gendered difference in the significance, experience or pleasure in participating in such activity, and therefore studies have attempted to redress and valorize women's hobbies and creative domestic practice. Studies have focused on the ways in which women have been able to express their creativity through knitting, to find some mental space through repetitive activity, and although often throughout the twentieth century women knitted as a sign of thrifty housewifery, frequently they knitted things they wanted to, buying functional and cheap necessities that were 'boring to knit'. The editor of the feminist magazine *Bust* and founder and author of *Stitch 'n' Bitch*,[5] Debbie Stoller noted:

> Why, dammit, doesn't knitting receive as much respect as any other hobby? Why is it looked down on? It seemed to me that the main difference between knitting and, say, fishing or woodworking or basketball, was that knitting had traditionally been done by women. As far as I could tell, that was the only reason it had gotten such a bad rap. And that's when it dawned on me: all those people who looked down on knitting – and housework, and housewives – were not being feminist at all. In fact, they were being anti-feminist, since they seemed to think that only those things that men did, or had done, were worthwhile.[6]

Stoller makes the observation that one of the major successes of feminism can also be seen as a failure; it is contradictory, suggesting that if women are knitting they are bound by patriarchy, and if they choose to knit for pleasure, it is not deemed worthwhile and is judged and compared to male pastimes. Likewise, women have many more choices and success is now measured through women's ability to compete in traditionally male workplace domains whilst also maintaining the female roles of housekeeper and mother. Women now (theoretically) can do and be anything they want, yet they are still judged by masculine models of success, whilst needing to fulfil traditional roles. Within this multiplicity of roles, models of attainment and a constant media barrage of 'ideals' (i.e. Martha Stewart, Jo Frost, Nigella Lawson, etc.), successful contemporary post-feminist womanhood is competitive, challenging and ultimately impossible.[7] This is one of the key themes of post-feminism or third-wave feminism.

Knitting has undergone something of a post-feminist resurrection, and now seen as a public and social activity, which can encompass as much or as little as each individual knitter wants. Post-feminism or third-wave feminism is distinct from second-wave feminism as it understands gender as fluid, moving away from the binaries of male and female into an arena that is largely characterized by bricolage and identity formation. Such a position is possible as post-feminists believe that the aims of feminism have largely been met and that women, as long as they make some effort, can achieve or do whatever they want without the help of a man. This might be viewed as egalitarian, focusing on the individual rather than the collective, but the establishment of a multiplicity of roles and identities can be confusing. Similarly, as the expression of one's identity/identities is constructed through the consumption and display of goods, one might equally conclude that post-feminism is merely an aspect of capitalism (the freedom to consume) rather than the expression of personal or social liberty.

The relationship between consumption, post-feminism and knitting is significant because it has transformed the ways in which knitting is understood in popular culture. Primarily this can be seen as a move away from knitting as an extension of thrifty housewifery and chores towards one of personal pleasure, leisure and luxury. Yarn, for example, is promoted and displayed as indulgent and tactile, rich and luxurious, with price tags to match, distancing the product from any conception of thrift or poverty. Similarly, the popularity of knitting groups, which are primarily the domain of women, highlights a post-feminist belief that women have substituted romantic narratives with same-sex friendships and consumer goods, which allows women to have equality in relationships and exert their power in the marketplace, i.e. one needs to spend money on yarn, needles and maybe a pattern, but also on food and drink when knitting in a specific arena such as a bar or coffee shop. Also, post-feminism encourages women to spend time on themselves rather than on a man, so knitting for personal pleasure is indicative of this, especially when the item being knitted is 'useless'.

In recent years, the knitting for pleasure argument has been utilized by virtually all knitting texts, which have encouraged knitters to indulge and express themselves through the medium of knitting. Essentially, hand knitting now is a hobby rather than a necessity and as such is an indulgence, distanced from the world of domestic chores, therefore it is understood as a choice; whether that choice is gendered is dependent on the individual knitter, the choice of item knitted and the ways in which that knitting is socially and culturally received. Nonetheless, women who were involved with or lived through second-wave feminism find it difficult to reconcile pleasure with knitting, and the domesticity that still taints it.

The following sections in the chapter aim to address the ways in which knitting has been associated with femininity, domesticity and instruction for girls. As a contrast, gender issues will also be questioned in the case study, which will investigate notions of masculinity through cardigan-wearing in the 1970s and 1980s.

Familial Bonding

For many people, their first experience of knitting, and of learning to knit, is associated with family and the home. Often women learn to or take up knitting whilst pregnant, bonding mother with unborn child and fulfilling maternal urges for nesting and nurturing. Similarly, as a craft practice, knitting is a tacit skill passed from one person to another, i.e. it is much easier to learn though watching and doing than from a written or illustrated text. From this perspective, knitting is a relatively simple activity to teach young children as it requires discipline, but can also produce an outcome quite quickly.

Historically, children, particularly girls, were taught to knit by their mothers or grandmothers, and until relatively recently, this form of inter-generational sharing of knowledge was commonplace. Initially seen as a means of useful occupation, knitting was imbued with the concept of 'work' rather than leisure, as with embroidery, and had the dual purpose of providing an outlet for idle hands and a means of future employment. In the late twentieth century this was less the case and knitting, however potentially useful, was a means of creating bonds and relationships between female relatives.[8]

As an indicator of familial bonds, the forging and continuation of them, knitting can be viewed as connoting love, family and femininity. Like the family album, knitted objects, predominantly those produced between mother and child, are symbols of age, the acquisition of knowledge and development, and are often sources of embarrassment to the naive maker in later years. Kim Tucker, now retired and an amateur knitter, fondly remembers the sense of achievement that she felt when her daughter learned to knit:

> I taught her what I knew, but I thought she would never learn to knit. We spent hours and hours; everybody tried to teach her to knit and she just couldn't get the hang of it. I suppose she was about twelve before she finally got the sense to knit something, and she knitted herself a sloppy Joe jumper. And it was a great achievement, you know. It was in 'big wool' and on big needles, and she actually did knit something. From then on, she's never without knitting.[9]

This sense of pride is representative of a passing on of knowledge, but also of a shared interest that secures or provides the basis for a future relationship. This suggests that a passing on of a skill is representative of the transition from childhood to adulthood, a kind of rite of passage. The activities themselves are exercises in both bonding and learning, giving pleasure to both teacher and pupil, and are performed within the sanctuary, or controlled environment, of the home.

The exercises in craft-making experienced between parent and child or teacher and pupil are not just indicative of the making of objects or of the learning process that such activity dictates. These exercises in learning are also exercises in discipline, method and control. The development of motor skills, through method-ical and repetitive action, is combined here with the development and acquisition of social skills such as discipline and the engagement in the work ethic. As Ellen Dissanayake notes, craft-making is often associated with 'making special', and time and care spent in both the learning and the making of something is indicative of its value.

> Until very recently, 'making special' meant making with care, that is, taking pains and doing one's best. In an age that values unfettered sensuality, spontaneity, non-hypocrisy and letting it all hang out, it is good to be reminded that discipline and decorum have had an important place, not only for social control, but for indicating the value we attach to a thing.[10]

The pleasure of making, especially the shared making between mother and child, is intrinsically linked to sentimentality, or as Dissanayake suggests, 'making spe-cial'. Here, the artefacts of the young become both sentimentalized and symbolic to their parents through their marking a passing of time; they are souvenirs of edu-cational and creative achievement, or objects mapping personal landscapes, spa-tially and temporally.

Education

The most widespread way in which knitting entered the lives of the population, particularly women, was through education. Feminist art and design historians, such as Roszika Parker,[11] Pat Kirkham,[12] Christina Walkley,[13] Cheryl Buckley,[14] Penny Sparke,[15] and Barbara Burman[16] have all outlined the significance of needlecrafts historically in the education of girls, for both employment and leisure. Needlecrafts were seen as a means of teaching a 'useful' skill, but also as a means of instilling discipline and obedience. Craft activities as taught in schools therefore had a rich heritage, and were often determined by social and cultural definitions of gender, educational ability and future role in society.

Up until 1975, craft education in UK secondary schools was predominantly gender-based – home economics and needlecrafts for girls, and woodwork and metalwork for boys.[17] The 1975 implementation of the Sex Discrimination Act ensured that gender-specific subjects were outlawed. Therefore, all secondary school children were given a mixed art and crafts programme that consisted of small 'taster' courses – introductions to craft subjects, by discipline, each term. This was not ideal, as only limited time was available to teach and learn specific skills, although everyone, regardless of gender, was able to participate in a whole spectrum of crafts activities.

By the late 1970s, the disparity of subjects available and their viability in terms of life-long learning was being questioned by the government. For example, a speech given by the Labour prime minister, James Callaghan, in 1977,[18] criticized the education system for its failure to train school-leavers for work. Seen as unskilled professionally, personally and socially, school-leavers were deemed a threat to the British economy, and, following Callaghan's speech and the ensuing variety of white papers relating to the relationship between education and work, the result was the development of employment training schemes and a major over-haul of the education system.[19] The aims of a training-based education was to provide school-leavers with 'life' skills, to address the needs of 'new' industries, and to combat a vast rise in unemployment following mass industrial and civil unrest and the closure of much heavy industry.[20]

The employability of school-leavers and the education system's failure to meet the needs of industry continued as a priority under the new Conservative government. This theme was reiterated by Professor David Keith Lucas in the *Design Council Report*, in which he outlined the ways in which 'design' education (problem-solving and an understanding of the environment and man-made things) could improve the national economy, meet the needs of industry and improve the quality of everyday life.[21] The report, as one might expect, was full of the reformist zeal and heroic rhetoric, which had characterized the philosophies of the Design Council and its government-funded predecessors throughout the twentieth century.[22] The Design Council's definition of 'design' and 'problem-solving' as one and the same thing emphasized a modernist approach to design – as being both a noun and verb, which had characterized design education since the Great Exhibition (1851) and the publication of the art critic Herbert Read's *Art and Industry* in the 1930s,[23] which became a blueprint for design education and reform in the UK. This, along with a variety of contemporary investigations into the state of both the economy and education, contributed to the gathering of all craft disciplines in secondary schools under the umbrella subject of Craft, Design and Technology (CDT) proposed in 1977.[24] The uncomfortable cultural grouping of the terms 'craft', 'design' and 'technology' was an attempt to draw together what had previously been disparate activities, taught in different school departments, often with different cultures, aims and budgets.[25] The impetus to restore the relevance to the curriculum often forced unnatural links between subjects, for example knitting was compared to music and to computer programs because they all rely on patterns.[26] Consequently, generalized terminology was developed to justify the homogenization of variant activities, so that 'craft' was interpreted as

> concerned with the development of manipulative skills based on making and doing. This means that it is about the acquisition of skill and the application of techniques in order to produce well-designed artefacts.[27]

In turn, this approach was combined with new technology as a science of resources, materials and knowledge[28] bridged by the collaborative discipline of design, resulting in a simplification of all areas, whilst clarifying the overall aim of CDT: solutions to problems.

The Crafts Council[29] protested at what was seen to be the erosion of traditional craft skills in the curriculum,[30] commenting on the benefits both in terms of life skills and of well-being for all students, particularly the less able.[31] The Crafts Council's concern relating to the significance of craft in child development was rooted in educational psychology and was popularly exhibited in children's groups such as the Boy Scouts and Girl Guides, and television programmes such as *Blue Peter*, *Why Don't You*, *Magpie* and *How*, which all promoted the philosophy that the only way children learn is by 'doing'.[32] Indeed, this concern was not without foundation as 'craft' was removed from CDT and the subject now exists as a compulsory element of the school curriculum, for pupils aged 5–16, as Design Technology.[33] CDT notably prioritized woodwork, metalwork and ceramics, and although other crafts subjects, including textiles and needlework, were often available, they were the exception rather than the rule.[34]

The industrial emphasis of CDT indicated that the crafts, especially those associated with the domestic sphere, were less important or relevant to life-long education in the late twentieth century.

Similarly, the Crafts Council's emphasis on craft as 'art' was equally detrimental to traditional textile crafts such as dressmaking, simple embroidery and knitting – activities predominantly associated with 'leisure' or 'necessity'. These textile crafts were popularly seen as 'feminine', but were also associated with social class, boredom or thrift, and therefore ultimately 'domestic' – an image of craft that the Crafts Council was at pains to distance itself from.[35]

The low status of the crafts in relation to the world of contemporary work, combined with a low social status, effectively sealed its fate. Why teach needlecrafts in the 1980s when more women were going out to work than ever before, and also had families to look after, access to cheap, ready-made clothing and microwave meals,[36] and no time to knit or sew? These were skills for 'housewives' and girls were aiming to develop into 'superwomen'.[37] By the 1990s, home economics had been restructured completely and became food technology, re-emphasizing the priority of science and industry over the domestic.

Subsequently, the reduction in craft skills, including needlecrafts and cookery, has caused much media and public attention, often cited as part of a general moral, social and cultural decline.[38] The idea that craftwork is an expression of the self, of learning, and acts as a social leveller, is largely the result of a craft mythology developed prior to the 1970s. This is the 'craft as solace' syndrome, discussed by Christopher Frayling as the antithesis of the 'fine' crafts.[39] And this was the problem for knitting – that its practice was largely seen as 'out of step' with the contemporary world: it is not necessarily avant-garde, made by skilled professionals or undertaken as acts of political subversion and is therefore outside the remit of the Crafts Council. Equally, knitting was no longer necessarily a 'leisure' time-filler or an act of thrift, as a changing work culture and the reassessment of 'femininity' demonstrates, and such practices became understood as 'old-fashioned', and unable to meet the needs of – or have a valuable place within – contemporary society.

The diminished place needlecrafts have within the educational establishment has been addressed by the Canadian artist, Janet Morton, in a piece entitled *Femmebomb* (2004), a knitted cover for the Human Ecology building and four-storey former Home Economics building on the University of Wisconsin campus. Morton believed the faculty to be burdened with the history of the building; as something negative, domestic and outdated. Yet the faculty was one of the first places to admit female students in the Midwest, and was still full of young women. These female students were, as Morton comments, 'girly girls who wouldn't dream of coming to class without make-up and were completely different to the women I went to college with'.[40] The students appeared embarrassed by the feminist label, and the paradox and indignity struck Morton as amusing. In a quest to redress the stereotypes, she decided to both explore and explode them by utilizing techniques and technologies undertaken inside the building to express the building's exterior. The faculty buildings and surrounds became a tribute to needlecrafts, the buildings swathed in pink knit and the grounds decorated with crochet flowers. The hidden became visible, a stereotypical feminine expression of

Figure 3 Janet Morton, *Femmebomb*, 2004. School of Human Ecology building at University of Wisconsin, Madison, USA. Image reproduced with permission from the artist.

creativity and education, challenging perceptions of those stereotypes and their cultural production.

The real issue in relation to the restructuring of crafts practices in secondary schools relates to their relevance in daily life. If activities such as knitting and sewing were no longer relevant as 'life' skills and women were no longer interested in them, why did they remain so predominant in women's magazines and why did virtually all of the female respondents to the 1987 Mass Observation Autumn Directive mention their involvement in the practice of crafts on a regular basis?

Women, Knitting and Employment

Although the 1975 Sex Discrimination Act and the Equal Opportunities Act (of the same year) had a far-reaching effect in education, their impact in the world of work was less so. Even though by 1980 over 50 per cent of married women were in paid employment, the majority of these jobs were poorly paid, of low status and part-time.[41]

From the mid-1970s, women were encouraged to retrain and return to work through articles in women's magazines[42] and government leaflets. Access to employment was a government priority, but as industrial and manufacturing jobs decreased (in April 1981 unemployment in the UK had risen to 2.5 million), those in the 'new' service industries were being taken by women. This change in traditional and gendered employment roles was cited as the start of 'the crisis of masculinity',[43] and a consequence of the impact of feminism. The impact of de-industrialization had perhaps a greater effect on changing gender roles and the representation of women than legislation, offering women cleaner, flexible working and an image of mobility, which had not been seen since the Second World War.

The relationship between paid work and craftwork in the home is a recurrent theme in women's magazines from the 1970s onwards. The stance or approach taken was paradoxical – with craftwork presented as the ideal way in which women could earn money, work from home and set up their own business[44] combined with legal issues, 'useful' addresses and so on, juxtaposed with features exposing the exploitation of home-workers. These articles appeared between 1975 and 1985 on an annual basis, with craft as a potential business venture featured in the spring, and the exploitation of home-workers in the autumn. The regularity with which these articles appeared suggest that making craft as a means of making money was an issue that concerned readers during this period, but also indicates that women were not as mobile perhaps as the advertisements of the time suggest, with many still relying on home-based textile piecework as a means of income.

The magazines' representation of knitting as 'work' rather than 'leisure' is also significant, with women 'working' from home perceived as amateurs rather than professionals. The implication that a 'hobby' can make you money offered women who had never worked outside the home entry into employment with skills they already had, but at the same time reaffirmed knitting as an extension of thrift – 'making do'.

Indeed, thrift, a key component of women's magazines from their earliest days, remained a dominant feature, often in response to the national economic situation. In a review of the 1970s, acknowledging the 25 per cent increase in food prices in 1976, the introduction of decimalization (1971) and VAT (1973), huge increases in fuel prices and subsequent shortages, *Woman* concluded: 'The Retail Price Index rose inexorably. But women who shopped every week didn't need statistics – they found out the hard way.'[45]

Knitting as a 'thrifty' occupation or a means of saving money became the norm, with craft features juxtaposed with fashion spreads showing garments available to buy, noting differences in costs.[46] 'Readers' Offers' frequently included cheap dressmaking patterns where the magazine didn't offer garment-making features,[47] although the introduction of *Essentials* (1988), *Prima* (1986) and *Me* (1989)[48] saw the inclusion of a 'free' monthly dressmaking or knitting pattern and the cost of making it – the cost of the fabric/yarn, zip and buttons, as well as a projected time allowance for construction.

Femininity and Representations of Knitting

The publication of Shirley Conran's *Superwoman* in 1980 presented an image of women that was to be 'hijacked by the media'[49] to represent the 'new' woman who could 'have it all' (job, family, home, social life) and compete in a 'man's world' whilst retaining her 'feminine charms'.[50] Women's magazines started to recognize 'real' superwomen, and featured interviews with the prime minister, Margaret Thatcher,[51] the Northern Ireland Peace Campaigners and winners of the Nobel Prize, Jane Ewart-Biggs, Mairead Corrigan and Betty Williams, Anne Scargill, wife of Arthur,[52] the president of the National Union of Mineworkers, and round-the-world yachtswoman, Claire Francis.[53] Women's issues and campaigns were also emphasized, highlighting the 'one person can make a difference' ethos, as exemplified by the introduction of *Woman* magazine's 'Actionwoman' in 1974.[54]

The media emphasis on 'action women' and 'superwomen' found cult and stereotypical status in the televisual depiction of women, in particular in television programmes imported from the USA, such as *Wonder Woman*, *Charlie's Angels*, *Policewoman* and *The Bionic Woman*. In 1979, *Woman* magazine ran a feature entitled 'Superwomen … But Can They Cook?',[55] in which television 'super-heroines' were assessed in terms of their domestic skills and capabilities. The opening caption read:

They're great with guns, clever at karate, skilled at spying, lovely to look at – and we've all got the message they're the current Ideal Woman image. But what's the place of traditional women's skills in the all-action, all-glamour life? How do men – and women – think a superwoman should cope with the cooking? Would she leap twenty feet in through the nearest window to get to a kitchen sink? We thought we'd find out if the ideal superwoman manages all things well, all the time.[56]

The article's combination of chat, advice and recipes illustrates the general development of the aspirational, but fictitious, 'superwoman', i.e. cooking for 'Wonder Woman' is 'mundane' and to show her cooking for a boyfriend would be 'too subservient' – yet a recipe from Lynda Carter, the show's star, is included; 'Charlie's Angels' are described as 'high achievers in a tough male world who are also home makers', but the studio also mentioned that 'We frequently get the girls wet because they look so good in clinging costumes.' [57]

The disparity offered by the ideal – traditional, home-centred male fantasy combined with the high-achieving, competitive career woman – left women with an identity crisis, and one which, as the design historian Penny Sparke acknowledged, could be assuaged through the consumption of goods.[58] The role of women as consumers is distinct from women as producers in the home, now seen as the purchaser of a 'ready-made meal' rather than the cook, or buying a sweater rather than knitting one.

Lifestyle choices were not limited to commodities, as the 'Just Made It' craft section in *Woman*[59] demonstrated by featuring 'gifts to knit for all the family' – 'a knotted scarf for Auntie Annette', 'a comfortable cape for grandma', and 'a tweed tie for dad', which not only outlined the potential suitability of gifts for particular (typical) family personalities, but also emphasized the speed, ease and low cost of making each item. In this article, craft is offered as a 'cheaper' option to High Street purchases, and also as a viable one, by imitating the marketing techniques of the mass market.

The pre-packaging of 'taste' as an indicator of lifestyle choices seems to reflect a trend towards speed and convenience – perhaps a consequence of a time-conscious femininity in 'crisis' – but also indicative of wider cultural change such as widespread television viewing,[60] greater access to credit[61] and the development of a 'me' culture.[62] In relation to knitting, magazines embraced the 'quick-fix' DIY transformation, 'speedy' wardrobe updates and 'easy' home makes, continuing a tradition in women's magazines of emphasizing education and thrift,[63] but in smaller sections that demanded less skill and offered activities that could be undertaken in a shorter time and with fewer materials, yet would provide the maximum impact. The most notable examples of this appear in *Woman's Weekly*, the most predominantly craft-oriented of all the weeklies,[64] in which highly skilled, time-consuming craft projects were frequently replaced with simple, ready-to-sew dressmaking patterns or knitting pattern offers.[65]

Throughout the period of study, women's magazines seemed to undergo an identity crisis, shifting uncomfortably between 'traditional women's interests' to maintain a 'familiar' and 'friendly' feel[66] and not alienate an existing readership, and an active 'new' femininity, characterized from the 1980s onwards by the European-owned monthlies, *Essentials* and *Prima*.[67] The bridge between the old and the new manifested itself in a variety of ways, such as the introduction of less formal editorials, more 'real-life' stories and less knitting and fiction.[68] But most interestingly, craft projects, especially things to make for children, demonstrated this transitional femininity – the rag doll that has a 'fairy-tale' crinoline in its wardrobe alongside a jogging suit (an indicator of mobility),[69] and the dressing-up costumes include nursery rhyme characters (Little Miss Muffet; Bo Peep) as well as 'Wonder Woman'.[70]

Women's Work or Women's Leisure? Knitting at Home

Within the social sciences, feminists have questioned the relationship between women and activities undertaken in the home. Women's work is commonly

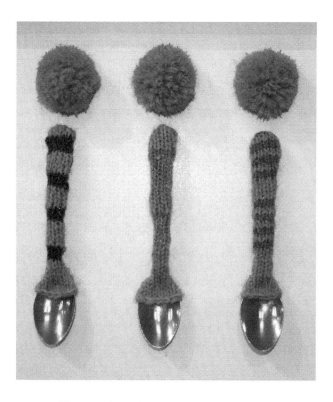

Figure 4 Liz Padgham-Major, *Just Encased*, 2007.

assessed as 'domestic', encompassing activities understood as unpaid 'chores' as opposed to other forms of work outside the home, which one would be paid for. Women's work can therefore be seen as diametrically opposed to other forms of work that are regulated and formalized, i.e. hours worked = money earned. This rationalization of work emerged as a consequence of industrialization, and women's production – and indeed women's leisure – became a site of discourse for feminist sociologists,[71] representative of the sexual division of labour.[72]

These themes have been addressed by textile artists in recent years. For example, Liz Padgham-Major's series of knitted covers for domestic objects, entitled *Just Encased*, draw attention to the relationship between women's work and women's leisure within the domestic sphere. In the piece, intricate covers for teaspoons outline the paradoxical juxtaposition of the beauty of women's creative practice and its ultimate futility. Likewise, *Home Comforts*, a knitted dustpan and brush, emphasizes the correlation and parity between women's work and leisure/pleasure within the domestic environment and its seeming invisibility. Padgham-Major states:

Figure 5 Liz Padgham-Major, *Home Comforts*, 2006.

I have deliberately chosen to work in a craft that is associated with women, domesticity and the home, and strive to take it out of context whilst highlighting and prompting the viewer to rethink their ideas about women and their role.[73]

Similarly, Janet Morton's knitted furniture and domestic objects, *Untitled* (2000), constructed from disused jumpers, draws attention to the home as a site of comfort, as well as of excess and misplaced sentimentality.[74] Morton's covered vacuum cleaner, plants and standard lamp etc. draw attention to notions of domesticity and the concept of 'making' a home, using techniques of thrift and craft synonymous with femininity. From this perspective the objects look 'cosy' and are 'cosies', questioning the constituents of domesticity, its values and its cost. The home contents have been subject to a 'woman's touch' and humorously play with

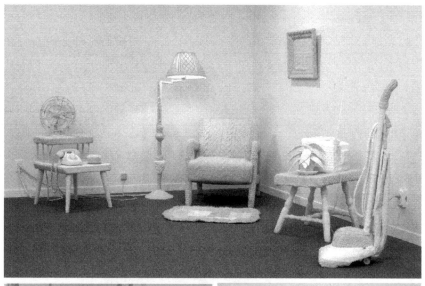

Figure 6 Janet Morton, *Untitled*, 2000. Furniture covered in leftover sweaters. Images reproduced with permission from the artist.

perceptions of women's taste, work and leisure, covering ordinary objects with previously discarded knitting. Domestic consumer goods have been subject to a personal touch, covered with signs of conspicuous leisure and domestic work. Each object is covered in cream-coloured knit, giving a homogeneity representative of the repetition of the act of knitting. Repetition here has been made strange, from which Morton creates a tableau of the absurd; a foray into a world of nostalgia and into the complexities of modern-day femininities.

For both Padgham-Major and Morton, the home becomes a site of discourse; it is both homely and unhomely, comforting and strange, an arena for work and leisure, and a platform for the discussion of women's domestic roles historically and now. In each example, women's work is exhibited, displayed and expressed, yet at the same time the medium conveys an invisibility historically attributed to women's creative practice and work within the domestic sphere. Yet in the work of both women, the praxis at which the invisibility of practice meets the desire to personalize is overshadowed by the underlying and undercover consumer goods, emphasizing the hypothesis that home 'making' is ostensibly about the display of one's wealth and taste through the consumption of goods.

Lifestyle Knitting: Gendered Pursuits

The home has been described by sociologists,[75] anthropologists[76] and design historians[77] as a site of consumption. Consumption in this respect refers largely to 'choice' – the arrangement and utilization of space and time, the display/use/disuse of possessions, and the meanings made and remade by these choices – the politics of domestic consumption.[78] Essentially therefore, if the home is a site of consumption, the manifestation of these acts evident in the consumption of goods can be seen as demonstrative of 'lifestyle'.

Lifestyle is most frequently seen as the result of a consumer society,[79] which in turn has historically been opposed to craft in its guise as 'solace in a changing world',[80] and knitting as part of an 'alternative lifestyle'. Although knitting exists as a commodity,[81] as do yarns and supplies, this section aims to investigate knitting as an extension of the female self when undertaken as a hobby.

In addition, the popular definition of knitting has acquired the stigma of the 'sentimental', a term frequently applied to the work, interests and taste of women. This section aims to investigate the aspects of sentiment embodied in knitting, in an attempt to valorize emotional responses and intent hitherto trivialized.

> I enjoy making silk purses out of sows' ears; of course sometimes they just remain sows' ears and are relegated to the bin. Then my youngest daughter says, 'Never mind, Mum, even Michelangelo must've had his off days', and of course the silk purses make very acceptable presents for birthdays or Christmas.[82]

This investigation is based on research undertaken from 424 male and female respondents (164 men and 260 women) who replied to Mass Observation Directive (MO) of autumn 1987 on 'regular pastimes'. The above quote is indicative of the responses – of the joy of doing – rather than the obtaining of a particular standard of skill, so frequently associated with craft disciplines.[83] Such comments also draw attention to aspects of knitting that allow women a creative outlet, one which is both – as the above respondent acknowledged – challenging and potentially useful.

The study initially outlines general observations of the responses and then investigates specific replies in greater depth. The aim of this approach is to survey the field of enquiry and then to address more specific and detailed responses in order to assess the 'meaning' of making in 1987. However, it is recognized that MO does not necessarily provide a general picture of knitting in the 1980s, as such an enquiry attracts specific kinds of people, in particular those interested in creative writing and history, desiring to 'leave a mark'.[84] However, MO provides a unique source of information in relation to 'ordinary' practices in daily life.

Figure 7 highlights the diversity of pastimes among MO respondents at this time. This diversity has been recognized by market researchers, who state that the lack of statistical research in this area is due to the disparity of hobbies.[85] The chart in Figure 7 shows that the most popular hobbies for both men and women are

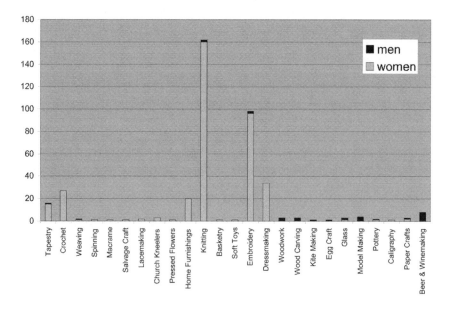

Figure 7 Chart highlighting the diversity of pastimes among Mass Observation respondents at this time. This diversity has been recognized by market researchers, who state that the lack of statistical research in this area is due to the disparity of hobbies.

reading and watching television. More contemporary statistical research has confirmed the continued popularity of these activities.[86] However, although there is no evidence to disprove the MO figures, it is important to note that the Directive specifically highlighted reading and watching television, with questionnaires specific to literary pursuits, and a 'TV Day Diary' commissioned by the BFI.[87]

An emphasis on 'passive' activities such as reading and watching television could perhaps imply a decline in 'active' hobbies such as sport, and craft activities such as knitting. However, there is little evidence of 'new' technologies replacing old hobbies, with only a few respondents mentioning the regular use of a video recorder, and none mentioning a home PC or computer games. This could be explained by the bias towards an older age group among MO respondents, as well as the relative newness of such technology at the time.

Figure 8 shows the division of craft activities undertaken by men and women. The gender split between activities highlights women as the dominant participants in textile crafts; men dominate woodworking. The chart also shows that significantly more women are engaged in craft activity than men, and this mirrors the findings of the literature of feminism, i.e. that women make things in the home.[88] The MO evidence demonstrates that over half of the female respondents knit as a

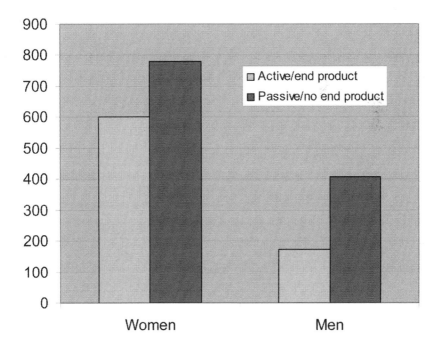

Figure 8 Chart showing the division of craft activities undertaken by men and women. The gender split between activities highlights women as dominant participants in textile crafts and men as dominant in woodworking.

regular pastime (160/260), with virtually all knitters stating that they undertake the activity whilst doing something else, such as watching television or listening to music or the radio. Respondents' statements include: 'Knitting is done at night while watching TV',[89] 'Knitting is also a hobby and I do this whilst viewing',[90] 'I sometimes knit in the evening whilst watching TV',[91] and 'Some nights I only do a little if the telly is more interesting; if it's an intricate pattern, I do more.'[92]

The repeated combination of knitting and television viewing indicated by the respondents seems to display a need for 'activity' while pursuing more 'passive' or less 'useful' activities. One respondent noted that 'I'd be very bored and depressed if I didn't keep busy',[93] while another stated: 'I tend to knit in the evening whilst looking at TV, as I feel sitting glued to the "box" is rather a time-waster, but if I am knitting I am producing something.'[94]

Whilst knitting is the most popular of craft activities, with embroidery second, many respondents engaged in more than one craft. It was largely stated that women who were engaged in decorative sewing, such as embroidery, also knitted and often made soft furnishings. This implies that home craftmakers were frequently engaged in making both 'practical' (garments, home furnishings) and 'decorative' items (tapestry, etc.). The predominance of knitting, along with an emphasis on 'practical' making, highlights the importance of home craft as a 'useful' pursuit. Similarly, 'making' instead of 'buying' jumpers, cushions, throws, blankets and so on indicates the role of home craft as an element of thrift.

However, although making may suggest economy, respondents indicated that craft was not a cheap hobby. One commented:

> Over the years though, these hobbies have become big business and likewise very expensive. We now have designer knits and tapestries, with big, glossy pattern books. The library's a good source of inspiration.[95]

The increased cost of craftwork was not limited to 'designer' craft kits and the impact of 'big business', but had also impacted on traditional 'thrift' crafts such as knitting. As one pensioner noted:

> I must add my family buys wool for my knitting, which I take up every time I sit down. I could not afford even the comfort of knitting if I had to buy it, my pension being only added to by £6.46 from PO Telephone where he worked for thirty years, with a break that made our pension nothing but a weight around our neck as I can get no DHSS help.[96]

The obvious distress felt by the above respondent in relation to her financial situation and her consequent inability to pursue leisure interests reiterates the relationship between wealth and leisure, as outlined by the nineteenth-century sociologist, Thorstein Veblen.[97]

Veblen's critical analysis of 'the leisure society' investigated the divisions between work and leisure in relation to social class. Quoting examples from history, and the distanced relationship between hand and brain (so commonly used to distinguish craft from art),[98] Veblen equated 'leisure' with non-work, or 'wasteful' pastimes, thus illustrating the commodification of time and its uses.[99] In relation to the pensioner's testimony, Veblen's theory observes how poverty excludes people from leisure, which can equally be applied to those living and working in the twenty-first century. The pensioner could not afford basic materials and therefore had to rely on the generosity of others or forgo her leisure pursuits – in the same way that more recent Marxist sociologists have commented on the exclusive properties of leisure within a de-industrialized 'leisure' society.[100] The increased commodification of craft materials, as recognized by the MO respondents, changed the economic implications of knitting from thrifty pastime to 'leisured' pursuit.

The rising cost of materials, kits and the like, along with a seeming change in the role of knitting at home, had little impact on the items produced or their purpose. Items for the home and family remained predominant crafts projects, closely followed by bazaar novelties or money-spinners. Few respondents made goods to sell for a personal profit; indeed, one respondent said: 'I am reluctant to make anything for anyone else as I wouldn't feel it would be good enough. Though some of the things I have made are admired by my friends.'[101]

The amateur status that characterizes the respondents' replies was indicative of the projects they chose. Use was frequently a deciding factor, either in terms of home decoration, family requirements or fundraisers. Embroidery, it was implied, had a 'limited' use (fire screens, cushions, footstools and pictures),[102] whilst knitting was 'useful' as long as family/friends wanted it. Other items made were 'gifts', 'bazaar goods' and charity items, such as knitted clothing for premature babies, which were donated to the local hospital.[103] The emphasis on item utility is qualified by a need for the maker to feel 'useful', or vice versa. A respondent lamented: 'When my youngest started to earn her own keep, I stopped making apparel for [her]. Not because I don't enjoy it, but the latest creation never got worn.'[104]

The enjoyment of making, as described by the above respondent, seems to be cancelled out by the lack of appreciation her making received. When, on the other hand, the item is seen by the intended recipient as 'desirable', the respondents felt differently, as another noted:

It's one of those pastimes where you go and lose yourself for a while; you are oblivious of what's going on around you, you dream of sun, sea, sand, peace, contentment, love … and what is more you are turning out a much appreciated sweater for half the price you'd pay in the shops.[105]

It seems that pleasure is inherent in making, but pleasure for the respondents is justified when their 'leisure' is being used in the pursuit of the 'useful', the familial or the domestic. 'Usefulness' is significant because it adds another dimension to the pleasure experience – it results in appreciation, thanks, and love and ultimately reaffirms the maker's position within the family. Making can be seen therefore as a means of inducing gratitude from others, which in turn is an acknowledgement or sign of the maker's identity within a group, family, community or wider world.

Whilst this may appear life-enhancing, feminist sociologists have studied the use of the domestic environment and analysed the division of labour within the home, concluding that the inequalities of the outside world are replicated in the home.[106] These studies confirm that women do most of the work on behalf of others within the home (housework/cooking/shopping/craftwork, etc.), with men responsible for DIY and car maintenance, thus reaffirming traditional roles.[107] Similarly, the division of the domestic space was seen as indicative of power relations within the home, with women having no space of their own.[108]

Respondents acknowledged this and those engaged in craftwork, particularly dressmaking, which takes up a great deal of space, bemoaned the logistics of their leisure activities. One stated:

> I would love a room of my own in which I could sew (maybe when the children have left home I will use one of the bedrooms). I would like to be able to sew and not have to pack it all away and clear up every time we needed the table for a meal.[109]

A male respondent, however, did not express the same need to 'clear up' after his hobby, or to return shared domestic space to its intended function:

> Having a utility room I am able to use it as a winery/brewery. There is always something quietly fermenting on the shelves. At the present time I have two-and-a-half demijohns (one-gallon fermenting jars) of home grapes popping their airlocks ... My wife appears to like the effect it gives her room although it looks untidy to me ... As I tend to leave my equipment around it looks more like a brewery than a laundry which is its proper function.[110]

The male respondent acknowledged that the utility room is his wife's 'space', yet he had left it cluttered with his hobby, which he observed was 'liked' by his wife. The alignment of the use of space with familial and gendered roles within the household is interesting here. The male assumes the utility room is his wife's because it is supposed to be used as a laundry, yet he sees the space as a suitable environment for his hobby – thus further dismissing women's activities in the home as familial chores. Under these circumstances it could be argued that knitting is a popular hobby choice for women because it demands no permanent space;

it is portable and can easily be picked up or put down, or away, as other chores intervene.

There is evidence of an element of sacrifice inherent in many of the respondents' testimonies.[111] (Pleasure and identity emerge as a response to the makers' relationship with others, making for someone else, and not taking up too much space.) Perhaps this can be viewed as an 'identity crisis'; the need for reaffirmation of identity as family structures change as a result of the ageing process. And, similarly, it could be argued that these women (and generally they *are* women) acquire a specific identity as a consequence of the adoption of traditional 'mum's' activities that, regardless of how enjoyable they are in themselves, are established and determined by traditional familial roles. Lifestyle, when applied to craft practice in these circumstances, can be seen as the correlation of the distinct areas of social responsibility, cultural background and expectation – a 'perceived' understanding of what women's leisure *should* be.[112]

The MO statements provide an interesting insight into the types of craft activities, the frequency with which they are undertaken and the significance of knitting in the lives of the makers. It seems that although respondents noted the increasing prices of craft materials, and the emphasis on making was shifting from thrift to leisure (which in many cases hindered or halted making), the meaning of making largely remained the same – as a means of identity-building, and also as a means of reaffirming that identity.

Patterns of Masculinity: Knitting Makes the Man?

Domestic craft activities have long been ascribed to the manifestation of conspicuous leisure.[113] Knitted (or embroidered) clothing for men was a sign of social status – a man who was wealthy enough for his wife not to work displayed this leisured status through the intricate work she produced for him. Similarly, a man who had knitwear in his wardrobe demonstrated an ability to participate in or afford leisure time and, by association, demonstrated his wealth and social status.

With the impact of paid holidays in the UK in the 1930s and the development of mass leisure, casualwear for men became not merely popular but essential. Demand for knitting patterns grew, and as a result knitting became an act of romantic love for a sweetheart or husband. Certainly, by the 1950s, girls were encouraged to knit for sweethearts as a means of showing commitment to the relationship and demonstrating potential housewifery skills. US teen magazines of the 1950s suggested that knitting was an antidote and solution to romantic crushes:

> I hope you'll not just sit and think about how nice he is. Do something! Go out and get that wool today, and cast on, you'll know knitting for him can be, and is, FUN. It not only whiles away your idle hours, but reaps heaps of results – gifts that stand up and say 'knitted with love'. And what could be better?[114]

The emphasis on knitting in order to get the attention of the object of one's affections is rather dubious; there is no evidence to outline how successful such an endeavour was or indeed how many young women were left broken-hearted and holding an unwanted sweater. What the advice offers, though, is the opportunity to catch a man through the articulation of domestic skills that may or may not show how she will perform as a 'wife', and the chance to take her mind from romantic daydreaming towards more useful employment whilst immersing herself in feminine domestic ideologies. This emphasizes that a woman must compete to ensnare her man by whatever means possible, which presents women as conniving and manipulative, situating the desired man as a startled and stalked deer, captured within the confines of a hand-knitted jumper. Such promotion of hand knitting as a symbol of romantic intent has been returned to recently under the banner of a 'new domesticity', with texts such as Judith Durant's *Never Knit Your Man a Sweater Unless You've Got the Ring* offering advice and knitting projects suitable for every stage of courtship, with projects intensifying as the relationship becomes more serious.[115] Knitting and romantic love appear to go hand-in-hand, with the knitted garment a gesture and token of love. Such a sentimental hypothesis seems to negate the proactive objective of the knitter: to purposefully stake a claim on another and potentially manipulate affections through the gifting of such a meaningful object. Such a garment may proclaim 'Made with love', but it also says 'You must love me because I made this for you', and as such is both loaded and problematic.

The manipulative potential of knitting was not only evidenced through gifting. Women were knitting for the men in their lives and were therefore shaping not only their wardrobes and what they should wear, but also the idea of what their men represented, what they would like them to be, whilst establishing an interpersonal relationship based on need and supply, i.e. men needed clothes, and women were providing them.[116]

As the popularity and demand for knitting patterns grew, so did the inclusion of male models wearing garments for home replication. One might assume that these images, primarily photographs, were part of the instruction, demonstrating what the 'made' garment should look like. However, as with all aspects of visual culture, representation was not merely of constructed garments, but of men. The men featured in knitting patterns were on display; they were subject to the scrutiny of women choosing patterns and therefore had to express aspects of masculinity that were comparable with the men for whom the garments would be knitted, whilst embodying what it was 'to be a man'. The male image was being consumed by women and used as a means of potential transformation: the ideal had the potential to be realized in knitted form.

Men in knitting patterns appeared somewhat embarrassed. Those featured were, until the late 1960s, ostensibly 'ordinary', either much older men or pre-pubescent boys, outside the remits of what could be described as 'desirable' or sexually alluring. The emphasis on the ordinary, models who were distinctly unglamorous and imperfect, highlights the ways in which masculinity was constructed and represented. Men were featured in active or creative leisure roles – painting, cycling, golfing, often in pairs, displaying engagement in a pursuit rather than passively modelling the knitwear. Similarly, their gaze never met the camera, which preferred to capture men looking into the middle distance, emphasizing a masculinity that could not be possessed, controlled or subjected to the gaze of another.

Men in these images were attempting to show masculinity as active, as an extension of camaraderie, and of 'men at leisure'. These were not images of men engaged in competition either in the workplace or sporting arena, but were men challenging themselves in less aggressive pastimes, and as such seemed somewhat out of step with other male representations. The images were constructed as 'natural': man in his leisure environment, captured unconsciously and fleetingly whilst engaged in a hobby or activity. Yet the models appear very self-conscious and as a result the photographs seem overtly staged. The over-construction of the images, combined with the pairing of males engaged in leisure pursuits, creates a sub-text that can be described as camp.

Knitting pattern photography exhibits camp styling through the overt and conscious posing, which feigns the natural and unrehearsed. It mirrors the theatrical, and combined with the coupling of two male models seemingly enjoying each other's company, creates a homosexual sub-text.

Questions surrounding the construction of masculinity dominate the superhero costumes knitted by the artist Mark Newport. For Newport, a figurative appraisal of the relationship between the masculine id, ego and superego as outlined in Freudian psychoanalysis is central to his understanding of masculinity. Driven by an interest in the role of contemporary fatherhood, Newport states:

> I started making the superhero costumes then because those are the people who have attained mythic stature for protecting others. And I chose knitting for the contradictions it gave to the image of the hero as a man of action, as well as to the costume because of the way a hand-knit garment, using the acrylic yarn I use, sags and droops. I chose the acrylic yarn with the knitting because it connects to the handmade acrylic sweaters my Mom would knit for me to protect me from New England winters.

Each costume is a knitted life-size replica of that worn by a comic book hero, articulating the presence of a superego. Yet each is displayed without a body, hanging as a lifeless shell, emphasizing the impossibility of filling or embodying such an outfit. Every garment is knitted by Newport, challenging the concept of suitable activities for men whilst highlighting the improbability and fallibility of knit for such garments: it stretches, shrinks in the wash, can unravel easily and is a sign of the imperfect. For Newport, masculine perfection is complex and impossible to

Figure 9 Mark Newport, *Self-Made*, 2004. Photo: Mark Newport, Bloomfield Hills, Michigan, USA. Image reproduced with permission from the artist.

achieve. Masculine concepts of 'protector' are merely a socially constructed costume and his heroic garments appear rather limp, testimonies to the frailties of the ego rather than focused saviours of the universe.

Like Newport's analogous sculptures bearing witness to the distance between the 'real' man and social perceptions of 'what men are', the camp nature of knitting pattern iconography can be seen as emasculating; not only are homosexual sub-texts alluded to, but men appear uncomfortable and embarrassed, and can be seen as vulnerable and without power. One might conclude that the knitting pattern is – as largely the domain of women – an expression of female power, and that the knitting of a garment by a woman for a man is an act of manipulation and control (as in the 'knitted with love' analogy), with the wearing of said garment an expression of complicity with the will of a domineering wife. If clothing 'makes the man', what happens to masculinity when women make his clothes?

CASE STUDY. Jocks and Cops: Cardigans for 'Real' Men

Masculinity, as discussed in the previous section as outlined in the iconography of the knitting pattern, is somewhat embarrassed. It is a masculinity that defies the gaze, is self-conscious and avoids any notion of sexuality. It is a masculinity that is emasculated, embracing the sphere of masculinity described by Naomi Wolf as 'the eunuch', the polar opposite of 'the beast'.[117]

Over the past thirty years, feminism and an increased interest in the representation of women throughout history has left a discussion of masculinity on the back burner. This has generally been attributed to the belief that masculinity is universal, or that it is something that is normal and therefore unquestionable. Of course, masculinity is not universal in the sense that it encompasses one all-embracing identity. If femininity (or the feminine) has its own identity, as has been proved, and it works in opposition to masculine identity, masculinity has to be defined to show the converse. Similarly, just as there is no single all-embracing or homogeneous femininity, masculinity is neither stable nor universal, even if it is presented as such. Certainly, gay politics in recent years has thrown the whole issue of masculinity and its constructs into question.

Cultural critics and theorists have alluded to the ways in which masculinity has been constructed as oppressive through the association with competitiveness, violence, aggression, power and strength. Paradoxically, this criticism reflects the way in which masculinity wishes to be defined as all-embracing and dominant. This powerful position allows the masculine to be sited as the core from which difference or 'otherness' is marked.

Masculinity had always been understood as a stable construct. Since the Victorian era and the sociocultural division of the sexes, masculinity had been sited as the norm, whilst everything non-masculine had been considered 'the Other'. Largely a response to the effects of the Industrial Revolution, colonialism, and to the ensuing developments in science, technology and the social sciences, white Western masculinity became the axis from which everything else was judged, marked and assessed. Masculinity, therefore, was imbrued with a sense of the right or true, whilst the non-masculine (and the non-white, Western masculine) was understood as somewhat deviant.

If masculinity is deemed 'normal', then the characteristics of masculinity can be seen as inherent in the ideology of white, Western culture. Masculinity became a sign of the dominant, powerful and rational prevailing culture. Effectively, the binary male/female became further segregated in binaries, with men associated with the city, the world of work and commerce, rationality, seriousness, hardness, strength and so on, with women understood as the polar opposite – countryside, home, irrationality, frivolity, softness, and weakness.

Such a sombre understanding of masculinity left little room for fashion and fashionable dress, as such a sartorial statement would be associated with frivolity or homosexuality.[118] This didn't mean that there was no men's fashion, or that men were subjected to sober cuts, colours and accessories, as seasonal changes were as frequent in menswear as they were in womenswear,[119] but notions of the peacock male were viewed with suspicion to such an extent that formal suiting dominated businesswear for much of the following century. It might be suggested that the real issue was the display of the body and the performativity of the self rather than the clothes themselves. If masculinity was demonstrated through the display of what was perceived to be a masculine identity, deviation from this might threaten the status quo and patriarchy in general.

This is not to say that masculinity was not displayed. Masculinity and the masculine body were promoted as a site of excellence, not objectified, but as an example of the peak of mind and body cooperation. The main format such imagery took was that of the sportsman, an example of prowess which demonstrated the ability of the mind to discipline the body.[120] Sporting activity involves mastery of the game or discipline, but also of the self over others. In sport there are winners and losers, and one can see this competition as embracing that of the duel, a fight to the 'death', man against man, sustaining injury along the way, and competitively consuming vast quantities of alcohol once the fight has ended. These are exercises in stamina, of excess and of pushing oneself to the physical and mental limit. Participation in sport expresses a sense of heroism and superiority, and the strength of the individual to gain mastery over the weakness of the flesh. In psychoanalytic studies, Michel Foucault discusses the significance of these images of 'hard', disciplined bodies, concluding that they demonstrate a phallic body, a body which demonstrates the ultimate masculinity, not only actual muscularity and strength but the triumph of the will over nature and pain. Masculinity is presented as a means of perpetuating the ideals of masculinity and patriarchy.[121] There is nothing sexual about these representations in their original forms (although any overt assertion of masculinity can be read as exerting a homosexual sub-text), and the body is exhibited as an extension of masculine ideals rather than as an object of desire. Although sexuality expresses potency and in turn power, these representations are devoid of the essence of the gaze, are not possessed or objectified by the viewer, and therefore are not submissive. Indeed, this iconology and iconography has permeated literature for young boys and men since the nineteenth century, conditioning men to believe that sporting prowess is both 'natural' and an expression of what it is to be male.[122]

Sporting male bodies are hard: they display taut, rippling muscles, demonstrating discipline and strength, developed and controlled by the will of the individual. These hard bodies cannot be penetrated, like armour, showing masculinity as untouchable and superior. Sporting (or hard) bodies are therefore signs of achievement, examples of a masculine ideal to be celebrated and emulated. From this perspective, it is difficult to correlate such excessive hardness and competition with the rather soft, fluid and innocuous cardigan, yet this garment has come to represent the everyday expression of contemporary masculine ideals.

Since the nineteenth century, knitwear, particularly knitwear for men, has been synonymous with leisure and, by association, sporting activity. Knitwear has an inherent flexibility: it stretches with and covers the body, offering warmth, protection and resilience to movement, and is therefore a perfect fabric for sports. It is also offers a contrast to less flexible forms of fabric construction such as weaving or bonding, offering a more 'relaxed' alternative. One might see this alternative expressed rather tenuously, spatially and culturally, and therefore knit becomes the fabric of choice for more relaxed and less serious pursuits such as those undertaken within leisure time.

The cardigan can be described as a waistcoat with sleeves, or as a soft knitted jacket, and as such imitates formal or business attire albeit in a more relaxed fabric and manner, originating and popularized in 1854 by the dubious hero of the Battle of Balaclava, Lord Cardigan, who wanted a less formal 'jersey' that could be worn without disturbing his hairstyle. Indeed, it is more formal than a sweater; a shirt and tie can be worn with a cardigan.[123] Therefore the cardigan is contradictory: a garment which is neither formal nor casual, suited perhaps to those unable to fully conform or participate in either area. Indeed, in popular iconography the cardigan is utilized as the workwear of the 'hip' but relaxed college professor, ageing in body and bohemian in mind, and the casualwear of the stuffy, overly formal man, for whom leisure represents a loss of control. The cardigan therefore becomes a sign of the maintenance of one's ideals and standards in awkward situations, a sign of comfort where there is none. This understanding of the cardigan refers predominantly to older men or men out of time, pace or place with the social environments in which they find themselves.

Since the cardigan's popularization within mainstream fashion for men in the 1920s[124] as a response to increasing mass access to leisure time and activities, the garment has been subject equally to fashion revivals and sartorial derision. As such the cardigan is often seen as 'the safe bet', and seemingly defies the laws of fashion. It is not a particularly 'manly' garment, as it satisfies none of the criteria that such a definition requires: it is not progressive, aggressive, challenging and so on, and although the wearer may well be comfortable in it, the garment is associated with impotency and an inability to feel in control of the situations one finds oneself in. It conceals the body as a shroud, has no structure and consequently slopes the shoulders, reducing the body to a soft, rather than hard and angular, form, and effectively weakens the physical stature of the wearer. In a cardigan, the body disappears and the wearer fades into the background: the wearer rendered passive. This study, however, investigates the significance of the cardigan in shaping attitudes about youthful, desirable and desirous 'new' forms of masculinity; the cardigan effectively comes out of the closet.

One might argue that new understandings of the constituents and representation of masculinity have arisen as a result of feminist analysis within visual and material culture alongside the impact of gay politics and queer theory,[125] which have questioned and challenged concepts of static 'natural' and gendered states of being. Similarly, changes within the economic landscape and consumer society, and concepts of 'lifestyle' have created new approaches to social and gendered groups.[126] As a consequence of the establishment of a multiple and fluid understanding of gender and sexuality, new forms of representation relating to gender identities have emerged. In relation to masculinity, these forms have been described as the 'new man'.[127]

The new man is essentially an advertising concept which aims to embrace contemporary and changing attitudes to masculinity, encompassing all of the elements of the 'old' man (fatherhood, provision, sporting prowess, competition, strength and so on) whilst exhibiting a connection with what one might describe as a 'feminine' side: traits of nurturing, caring, narcissism and the display of a sexualized body.[128] Within the constructs of the new man, the language of dress became a signifier of personal identity, communicating a sense of self through the consumption of goods and body display.[129]

This newfound self- and sexual awareness filtered into menswear during the period, particularly in casualwear. This was not really a wholly new phenomenon, yet the cardigan had never been a 'sexy' garment in menswear. In the 1970s and 1980s, this changed.

In the 1980s, the sporting male body, combined with a new man ideology, became part of the iconography of nostalgia. Drawing inspiration and aesthetic

Figure 10 Teenage boy wearing a sweater with the letter 'R' emblazoned on it. Photo: Nina Leen, Time & Life Pictures, 50702734 (RM) Getty Images.

from the rebelliousness of American teen idols such as James Dean (who displayed a sexual ambiguity), college-boy and working-class clothing became central to fashionable menswear and the construction of masculinity. The trend was encapsulated in advertising campaigns for Levi's 501s, Calvin Klein and Ralph Lauren, in which the mythology of 1950s Hollywood, demonstrated through the ephemera, music and images of Americana, became a contemporary consumer reality.

The popularity of a 1950s style, too, was sexually ambiguous. It offered a body-consciousness that was subject to the male gaze, objectification, and had been a mainstay of the gay male wardrobe for some considerable time; who was looking at whom? The emphasis on the male body as a site of consumption highlighted a male sexuality that was both narcissistic and an aspiration. In terms of clothing, this was demonstrated through the retro styling of the preppy and the high school 'jock', which incorporated jeans, penny loafers or suede shoes, T-shirts and college sports cardigans (letter sweaters), garments that show allegiance to a group through the use of insignia and motif.

The popularity of these cardigans in the 1980s can be viewed in two ways: firstly as a sign of stability, for group allegiance never really went out of style, and secondly as an expression of a new gym culture and body fascism, which was prevalent at the time. The clothing of the 'jock' essentially is clothing required for the performance and display of sporting prowess, demonstrating team belonging, and in an era in which heroism was marked by physical perfection and mastery of the body, sportswear expressed these ideals clearly. Such an overt articulation of male dominance was counterbalanced by narcissism, as many men who adopted these styles were not sportsmen, athletes and the like, but men who wanted to demonstrate their affiliation to such ideals whilst alluding to the potential rippling muscles beneath the garment.[130]

The styling reflected cultural and consumerist ambiguity, a desire to return nostalgically to a time of enthusiastic and confused adolescence, a desire to find oneself through imagery of the hero/anti-hero as neither innocent nor corrupt, fusing the traditional with the modern. In these representations, the 'college boy' and the 'jock' became synonymous with the transition from boy to man, a period fraught with danger, in which young men were encouraged to express themselves, explore their sexuality and make sense of the world around them.

Whilst the football cardigan or letter sweater became a sign of the past in the present, other cardigans exerted a clear sexual significance, overtly expressing the male as sex object, whilst simultaneously reinstating patriarchy. Although the football cardigan fused a contemporary nostalgia for a youthful masculinity with an ambiguous male gaze, other cardigans expressed an overt machismo that was urban, contemporary, aggressive and sexual.

In 1975, the American television cop show *Starsky and Hutch* was first broadcast. The show focused on two streetwise plain-clothes detectives from whom the show's name derives, who inhabited a fashionable yet seedy urban underworld, and aimed to bring the gritty realism of movie drama to the small screen. The characters were portrayed as aggressive, tough and competitive whilst upholding the law by whatever means necessary. Both Starsky and Hutch (Paul Michael Glaser and David Soul) were young, good-looking men, portrayed as womanizers, who were both sexually potent and sexy. Indeed, the men received fan mail from both women and men.

Plots centred on the characters' relationships and whatever crime they were investigating, and although women appeared, they did not figure in the narrative, occupying the positions of girlfriends or potential love interests. *Starsky and Hutch* adheres to the generic format of the 'buddy' movie, following the inter-personal relationship between two very different men, and as such annihilates women and reinstates the patriarchal order.

Starsky and Hutch were action men, both contemporary and competitive, and the iconography of the show focuses on cars and clothes, both indicators of speed, movement, display, acquisition and modernity. Clothing is particularly significant because it demonstrates that the characters are very much at home in their contemporary urban environment; they move with the times and they are comfortable in openly displaying narcissism as an expression of the self. The most emblematic item of clothing associated with the show was a large, belted, banded cardigan worn by Dave Starsky.

Whilst Hutch was constructed as sensitive, intellectual and cultured, and as a considered, tidy dresser, Starsky was undoubtedly more edgy, with a wardrobe that expressed his unkempt, fast-living and trendy character. The patterning on the garment – earthy-toned geometrics reminiscent of folk motifs, Aztec culture and 'primitive' societies – embodies a sense of the 'natural' man, a man in control of his environment (similar to the stereotypical cowboy), which perpetuates the patriarchal dictate of man's proper position of dominance. Here the man becomes the beast; able to disrobe at any moment, ready to fight, defend, capture and dominate his environment and become master of all he surveys.[131] Starsky, and his cardigan, embody the concept of phallic power, whilst simultaneously attracting admiration and desire from males and females alike. This cardigan is an unstructured, button-free and therefore unfussy garment, which could be put on or taken off very quickly. Yet the cardigan came to represent the ultimate modern man, tough, hard-working and hard-living, whilst consciously engaging in the display of the sexual self.

The Starsky cardigan is fastened with a belt, and as such offers sexual potential and readiness through the ease of access to the body through the garment: it can easily fall open and reveal what lies beneath. Reminiscent of a smoking jacket or bathrobe, the cardigan expresses intimate leisurewear for public consumption and display, extending to the wearer a sign of potency and sexual availability.

The cardigan proved extremely popular, becoming a fashion item and featuring in knitting patterns of the period, with one even featured in *Woman's Weekly*.

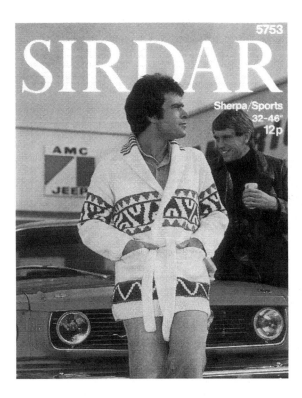

Figure 11 'Starsky-style' cardigan, knitting pattern, late 1970s. Courtesy of Sirdar.

Patterns featured models in action poses, either with or without a red sports car, gazing directly at the viewer. The distinct gesture and posing of the model show a clear understanding of the gaze (as distinct from knitting patterns of the past, which featured distant and rather embarrassed male models); these embrace concepts of both possession and the possessed. The models are assured in their environments and their clothes and with their sexuality. Directly referring to the TV show and characters, the patterns illustrate the commodification of the body, i.e. make the cardigan and transform your man into 'Starsky'. With men attempting to emulate the character's persona, and with women desiring him, the cardigan became a sign not only of identification, but of transformation and role-play. The cardigan enabled people, however tenuously, to make the fictional or the fantasy a reality, and male narcissism a sign of contemporaneity and desirability. Similarly, the conscious act of knitting such a garment for the man in one's life can be seen as a deliberate attempt to update home knits as well as updating the potential wearer. The transformation of yarn into garment can be seen as a process of transformation from man to ideal or 'new' man.

During the 1980s, both the football cardigan and the Starsky sweater became signs of a new masculinity, yet both garments were appropriated by women and became ostensibly 'unisex'[132] knitwear. One might conclude that this reappropriation of the garments is an expression of a move towards a more fluid or even androgynous performance of gender through fashion, yet this move was temporary. Masculinity may well have been feminized through dress, but the concept and constituents of masculinity had changed very little. For example, Pringle's traditional Argyle-patterned sweaters in muted pastel shades with pink and yellow,[133] soft, luxurious and hitherto a sign of conspicuous leisure and the wealthy, were reappropriated in the late 1980s and early 1990s by working-class men as a sign of affiliation to football teams and an aggressive masculinity of which violence and hooliganism was at the heart.[134] The mix of a seeming respectability with anti-social behaviour through knitwear and style in general created a climate in which masculinity could be both consumerist and patriarchal, negotiating concepts of masculinity on the surface whilst maintaining the status quo.

The cardigan has been a menswear staple for the best part of 100 years, and as a result can be seen as a design classic merely as a result of its longevity. Nonetheless, this does not mean that it is static, either in terms of design or meaning. As concepts of masculinity have changed, so too have the meanings of garments, particularly the ways in which they are worn and the attitudes such garments evoke. However fluid concepts and constructs of masculinity are, the ways in which masculinity is presented and represented largely return to established concepts of patriarchy, reaffirming a dominance and power, which, in a post-modern society, can be obtained and displayed through the acquisition of goods, lifestyles, signs and sartorial codes.[135]

Conclusion

Although it is possible to construct a feminist discourse surrounding the activity of knitting, such an analysis is fraught with contradiction. When a woman knits, is this an expression of her intelligence, creative ability and tenacity, or is she adhering to and reinforcing the conditions and values of a patriarchal society? It seems that knitting itself is not the problem, rather what one knits and its intention or purpose. For example, the knitting of a garment for personal adornment or bodily display, or knitting as a form of familial sacrifice, is ostensibly adhering to and replicating a patriarchal system; whilst knitting as a form of self-expression, for pleasure, or for a wider community benefit (as with knitting for charity) is not. Similarly, if one avoids stereotypical models in which women are perceived as consumers, rejecting mass-produced yarn, kits and a feminine ideology, women can equally distance themselves from patriarchy. One might also knit as a means of identification with a whole history of female knitters, making the act of knitting an expression of a solidarity and a continuation of a sisterhood.

Feminism, of course, has had a profound impact on how we understand women's creative practices such as knitting. Indeed, such approaches dominate an understanding of knitting both historically and in the contemporary world. Similarly, it is important to note that just as women are not a homogeneous group, nor is knitting or indeed knitters; knitting is not made by the same people for the same purpose at the same time, and this richness of practice and practitioners opens up an area of study which is both diverse and exciting. Nonetheless, as more men pick up needles and start to knit, gender boundaries and stereotypes continue to be readressed and challenged.

–2–

Knitting the Past: Revivalism, Romanticism and Ruralism in Contemporary Knitting

> Machines produce clothes more cheaply and quickly. But machines can't copy human hand work or create one-of-a-kind colours and patterns. Machines form stitches evenly and monotonously, with no trace of feeling. Every stitch in a hand-knitted sweater bears the traces of a time, a trip, a landscape; of persons, events, and thoughts.[1]

All knitting has a history. From patterns, styles and motifs through to techniques, objects, practice and execution, the development of knitting as a culture is rich in heritage and tradition. Indeed, it is this aspect of knitting that forms the majority of texts and ideas relating to practice, and without wishing to reproduce what is already in evidence in detail, this chapter aims to investigate why heritage and tradition are such a mainstay of an understanding of knitting today.

Within the literature of knitting, and this encompasses texts relating to both the practice of knitting and knitted objects, there is a pervasive language of Romanticism. Largely, this involves a rhetoric emerging from nineteenth-century discourses surrounding the effects and impact of the newly industrialized world, which questions the contemporary and idealizes that which is seemingly lost. This chapter intends to investigate the ways in which knitting within the late twentieth century (and beyond) has come to characterize a Romantic nostalgia, a dissatisfaction, and in some cases a rejection of the contemporary and a desire to 'revive' that which is near death.

By addressing the use and changes in motifs and styles of knitted garments and objects, as well as the ways in which hand knitting has been understood as part of revivalist traditions since 1970, this chapter will question the meaning of what can be described as 'heritage knitting' within everyday life. The term 'heritage knitting' is used here to describe resurrections in traditional styles, motifs and patterns, and their presentation, construction and promotion through the objects themselves and also through books, magazines and craft journals of the period. Taking a design history perspective, the notion of heritage knitting and its seeming centrality to craft revivals throughout the period of study aims to look at the ways in which the past is resurrected and its meaning to both producers and consumers. In addressing this subject, it is important to also uncover the ways in which

Romanticism and the cult of nostalgia inform and interact with the development of global branding and forms of capital within this period.

This chapter is constructed to address the main concerns arising from an investigation into the significance of the past for knitting; these can be assessed as encompassing two themes: influences and manifestations. 'Influences' refers to the iconography and iconology of the past, as well as art and design movements and philosophies that have permeated a contemporary understanding of knitting. Primarily governed by an appreciation of Romanticism and ruralism, these sections investigate themes of nostalgia, utopianism and the landscape. 'Manifestations' refers to the ways in which these influences are played out, both socially and culturally, through the themes of revivalism, reproduction and commodification.

The chapter starts with a historiography of nostalgia and revivals as a means of rejecting social and economic change through production, initiated by the Arts and Crafts movement and the socialist writings of William Morris in the nineteenth century. The Romantic zeal expressed by this mode of thought and its initiation through the resurrection of 'traditional' crafts practices provides a model for all subsequent attempts to redress social and cultural change through hand work. The chapter adopts a design history and material culture methodology, drawing from discourses in cultural studies that have concentrated on the meaning of the past in the present.

Knitting, and particularly hand knitting, has been subject to popular revivals, and although it is true to say that knitting has never really 'gone away', the chapter intends to question the increased popularity of both practice and objects over the past thirty or so years. What is it about knitting that makes it so ripe for revival, and why does it seemingly return with such veracity? In addressing notions of revivalism, the chapter also aims to establish how the combination of the past and the present can create a sense of zeitgeist as well as developing new and innovative forms.

The key themes addressed exemplify the notion that although specific types of knitting can be understood as revivalist inasmuch as they embrace tradition and notions of heritage, they also are socially and culturally conditioned and are therefore dynamic, changing to suit the needs of society (practitioners and consumers) at a given time rather than expressing a sense of the timeless and the static.

Arts and Crafts Beginnings: Romantic Longing

Much of our understanding of contemporary craft practices has its origins in the nineteenth century and the Arts and Crafts movement. Pioneers of modern design such as William Morris, who initiated the fusion of design theory and practice, saw the possibilities for design as a means for solving social problems. With such insight, the concept of 'design for society' was born and became a value system that dominated early twentieth-century design in Europe and the USA.

The Arts and Crafts movement had its foundation in Romanticism, a European movement in philosophy and the arts, which emerged in the eighteenth century as a response to the dominance of neo-classicism. Emerging amidst – and character-ized by – revolution, Romanticism focused on the experience of the individual rather than the collective ideals of society, personal emotional response and a pre-occupation with the past. The past was addressed with a sense of loss and nostalgic longing, but often the past was a constructed place of myths, legends, chivalry and harmony, which was created and recreated through literature and the imagination. Ultimately, the Romantics were interested in alternative states of being, tran-scending the self and escaping the confines of the body, which manifested in experimentation with narcotics, sex and the articulation of an inner vision as a means of escape, and the past offered an escape into a fantasy realm.

Morris's concerns for both design and society were immediate; the onslaught of industrialization had, for Morris and others within the Arts and Crafts circle, not only dehumanized labour through the factory system, and polluted cities and made them overcrowded (which had spread disease and unruly behaviour), but had also filled the world with ugly, mass-produced goods. Industrialization had, for Morris, created a social and moral decline, which in turn had led to a cultural slide: an ugly society created ugly objects. For Morris, the solution was clear, if not simple: to restore that which was lost and to recreate harmony, honesty and joy in life and labour that would impact on the world of goods.

Morris looked to the past for inspiration. Returning to a pre-industrial world, Morris found solace in the rural and medieval past, which encapsulated his socio-cultural solution. He believed this to be a simpler time, when everyone knew their place and man was able to work in harmony with his environment, materials and tools; this, in turn, would bring him closer to God. Of course, Morris's vision was utopian; he understood the past, as we all do, through contemporary eyes, and therefore his vision was clouded with a nostalgic yearning. He could never bring back the medieval past, however hard he tried in his workshops, but it was possible to revive the styles and ideals (albeit translated to suit nineteenth-century needs and sensibilities) of his chosen era.

What Morris offered, therefore, was not a resurrection of the past but an alter-native to the present. By reclaiming seemingly lost traditions, working closely with natural materials and motifs, nineteenth-century consumers could, for a price, align themselves with this vision of the past and assert themselves as bohemian connoisseurs of a prevalent Romantic style and ideology. Such retrogressive asso-ciations had a long-standing impact on the crafts, consigning craft to the 'simple life', ruralism, and offering solace in a changing world which continues to pervade a meaning of craft, and indeed knitting, into the twenty-first century.[2]

Establishing a Heritage of Knitting

It is possible to suggest that the past can never be understood as it was originally, and this is the main problem with notion of revival. Indeed, the past, as David Lowenthal suggests, is a 'foreign country'[3] and in order for it to maintain any form of relevance to contemporary society, it must 'speak' to the here and now: messages sent have to be received, lessons that could be learned have to be relearned, and alternatives to present problems – whether social, cultural, political, economic, stylistic and so on – should be presented in a manner that looks simultaneously backwards and inwards. Knitting is one area in which heritage and the role of the past in the present is manifest. As a craft, and specifically an ordinary or domestic craft, knitting communicates a tradition that is not merely gendered but is also vernacular, providing evidence of peoples and places that appear distant to the industrial or post-industrial urban contemporary world. This has been central to a popular understanding of knitting through texts, patterns and through the learning of it.

This too has been the focus within the literature of knitting, in which two main structural themes become evident: the history of regions and the cultural production emanating from them, and guides to patterns and 'how to' reproduce them at home.[4] These two components, in coexistence, presuppose that this is a harmonious match, with historical background and instruction entwined seamlessly. One might conclude that the academic interest in the subject is merely one part of a revised interest in knitting, as the inclusions of instruction and patterns offer the potential for both production and consumption of heritage knitting during this period, and therefore the reader as knitter is considered in each text. This assumes knitters are not merely interested in patterns, or indeed 'things to knit', but in history. However, the result of this approach is far-reaching; a linear history is created in which the knitter is positioned and so is, by participation in the completion of patterns, continuing the lineage of the discipline. The development of a written history, which cites examples of 'good' design to replicate, marks a significant move towards the validation of knitting as a discipline with its own history and heritage – a model that, like art history, charts the development from form to form over time. What is distinct from the art historical model is the absence of named knitters and an emphasis on innovation; in fact, the converse is true, with emphasis placed on a quest for historical accuracy and 'authenticity'. One might suggest that the fusion of these components situates knitting as a sociocultural and geographically specific activity, rather than an expression of the avant-garde, part of a 'there and then' rather than a 'here and now'.

Ruralism and Knitting: The Vernacular and the Landscape

The relationship between craft activity and potentially lost traditions was an established viewpoint by the 1970s,[5] linked to notions of the rural idyll, utopian visions of old England, Romanticism, and demonstrated in revivals occurring throughout the nineteenth and twentieth centuries. These representations were present in exhibitions of craftwork including the retrospectives of William Morris and the Arts and Crafts movement, which continued to promote craft as an alternative to consumer culture[6]:

> Where the style of he 1950s and the 1960s was built out of plastics, using man-made, chemically-based fibres for clothes, fabrics and furnishings, the style leaders of the 1970s made a fetish of the 'natural', the 'organic' and the home-grown; indeed to follow the range of handmade goods advertised in the Sunday colour supplements, on offer at the gift shops and galleries, or displayed at the home furnishers, one might have imagined that the economy had reverted to pre-industrial times.[7]

This form of retrogressive gazing similarly informed the relationship between craft, the rural and potentially lost traditions, particularly in relation to unemployment in the countryside, which had fuelled earlier government sponsorship (the Rural Industries Bureau etc.) and education projects organized by the Women's Institute.[8]

Indeed, much of the critical literature that highlights knitting as a continuation of vernacular traditions is driven by the Romanticism indicative of a past age. Craft objects and activities were interpreted as 'wholesome', 'untainted' by the modern industrial world of mass production, and therefore could be understood as a source of stability in an unstable world. The emphasis on comfort, on an alternative to everyday reality, in a non-challenging, non-changing aesthetic proved a significant element of the promotion of knitting and craft practices as a leisure activity, i.e. a 'relaxing' alternative to work, both comforting and home-centred. Indeed, the iconography associated with 'Victorianism' (rural and moral feminine pastimes) became synonymous with knitting as an activity and an object infiltrating High Street fashion styling through retailers such as Laura Ashley. Therefore knitting became part of an alternative to the contemporary and to the world of consumption, a contradictory position within the new and burgeoning heritage industry.

The portrayal of the rural as an extension of Victorianism can be understood as the reaffirmation and fusion of the binaries of nature and culture, with each sphere connected to specific activities, which in the contemporary era is most notably marked through heritage tourism and consumption. Geographers, sociologists and anthropologists have commented that the contemporary landscape or physical environment has been transformed as a result of and as a move towards mass consumption.[9] The sociologist John Urry, for example, draws attention to the ways in which the rural landscape has been managed and transformed to accommodate the landscape as a site of consumption through tourism and tourist goods.[10]

The consumption of the landscape is a direct product of Victorian Romanticism and associated rhetoric and definition. For example, Nicholas Green comments that the landscape was a social construction, encouraging its consumption as a vista, as one would in a painting, highlighting its distinction from the increasingly urban environment.[11] From this perspective, it is possible to suggest that the landscape embodies a sense of escapism and mythology distinct from everyday life. The Romantic landscape is wild and untamed, natural and organic, yet landscapes are constructed and managed to appeal to and service a tourist market that reinforces the ideology of 'landscape'. Indeed, as the Marxist theorist Henri Lefebvre has argued, leisure is merely a constructed antidote to work, which is just as alienated, organized and controlled as the daily grind.[12] Effectively, what is being offered is a simulation of a wild and natural environment which determines its consumption, referring to its history and perpetuating its mythology.[13]

As a heritage product, the landscape is consumed as an extension of a much wider tourist-led industry.[14] As tourism relies on the notion of escape – escape from the mundane world of work, and from reality – the landscape offers a foray into the past, particularly the pre-industrial past. Terms such as 'unspoiled' dominate the descriptions of place, creating an imaginary space for pleasure and relaxation which, combined with a menu of healthy outdoor pursuits,[15] offers tourists an opportunity to distance themselves from their sedentary contemporary lifestyles, returning to a mythological past where people 'made their own entertainment'.

This mythological landscape includes knitting on two levels: firstly as part of the iconography and iconology of the past, and secondly as a tourist object or souvenir. In recent years, knitting and other practices that express a vernacular sensibility have received attention from academics studying material folk culture.[16] The vernacular in these cases is demonstrative of an anti-modernist stance at the core of postmodern discourse, in which questions are raised in relation to the sense of a romantic nationalism represented in the production of the craft object and the object itself.[17]

The vernacular pertains to a particular combination of specific geographic conditions, including materials locally available, environmental concerns including skills, knowledge and local know-how, community beliefs and patterns of behaviour, as well as regionally specific history, tradition and symbolism. Crafts practice, due to a combination of tradition and the reinvention of that tradition as part of a postmodern nostalgia, exemplifies place over time. As Michael J. Chiarappa acknowledges:

> Vernacular crafts, by very definition, are affixed to cultural and historical considerations of local and regional – in short, objects supposedly deriving meaning from perceptibly bounded and inviolate historical, ethnographic and environmental settings.[18]

Vernacular crafts are interpreted here as material culture, ethnographic artefacts, recreated in the present to reaffirm regional identity either as (as Chiarappa believes) a Romantic affirmation of 'place' within a global community or, perhaps more cynically, as the creation and provision of local employment in the tourist industry through the production of 'regional crafts' as souvenirs. Here also craft is associated with loss and restoration, i.e. the loss of regional identity and/or vernacular craft skills, remedied and restored through the commodification of craft as souvenir.

> A Fair Isle jumper, like an Aran sweater or a Guernsey, is a classic, and the part-time knitters of the island have a limited production so there will never be a glut of genuine Fair Isle jumpers. The mass-produced copies, by the Scottish mills and the imported Fair Isles from Taiwan, although cheap, will never appeal to the purist who not only purchases a sweater but the tradition and history of many years.[19]

The significance of this resurrection of lost tradition is seemingly reiterated throughout the history of crafts criticism, and thus this perspective dominates and informs popular crafts practice. The craft gift or the craft souvenir emphasizes the notion of craft as authentic,[20] and the inclination to define the popular crafts as vernacular, and therefore potentially in danger of extinction, fuels a collective memory and mythologizes this understanding of tradition and craft, which sustains and perpetuates craft's relationship with the past and heritage.[21]

However, in terms of commodification and product/object differentiation within the world of goods, craft as the embodiment of vernacular tradition enhances the potential for knitting as a souvenir. Tied to the tourist quest for authenticity, locally produced craft objects become cultural markers, regionally specific and bound with local traditions and practices. The souvenir in these cases is representative of a popular ideology and often iconography of the crafts,[22] whilst simultaneously offering the consumer a product connected with place, history and difference. The object becomes part of a regional narrative, a story of people and places, and therefore the object is representative of the authentic.[23]

> At the end of their Scottish vacation in 1979, Jenny and Pat Selfe – Jenny a graphic designer, and Pat, an accountant – looked in vain for a traditional Fair Isle sweater to take home as a souvenir. They returned to their Devon, England, home empty-handed because nothing they found was of the quality they expected.[24]

The disappointment experienced by the Selfes is not uncommon: their quest for a specific 'quality' item perceived to be inherent in traditional manufacture was not as anticipated. Indeed, the past and our conception of it is increasingly one dominated with a sense of a static timelessness, of memories as described by Simone de Beauvoir: the decaying

> … past is not a peaceful landscape lying there behind me, a country in which I can stroll wherever I please, and which will gradually show me all its secret hills and dales. As I was moving forward, so it was crumbling …[25]

The past appears as lost, a construct that can never be revived. The past, of course, is a construct built from memories, recollections, stories and artefacts, which remains potent in the present as not merely an indicator of how far we have travelled, but also as a testament to the strength of the lived present and of the desire to create meaning and narrative in everyday life.

The Romantic language applied to discussions of knitting highlights a sense of the otherworldly, the nostalgic and the traditional. This can be seen as a consequence of a cultural understanding of what knitting represents – a popular appreciation of knitting – but also the place in which knitting is situated within a fine arts hierarchy. Essentially, because knitting has a pre-industrial past and is largely associated with the handmade and the domestic, and because it is a learnable skill, its practice and objects are marginalized within an arts hierarchy that values cerebral, masculine and spontaneous creativity as demonstrated in fine art. In order for such a tradition to continue outside the realm of salvage and thrift crafts, knitting has become embedded with a language of loss and an idealistic and rural past. Therefore knitting combines two dialogues emanating from a discussion of heritage, authenticity and consensus, which requires a combination of 'real' historical artefacts, myths or other elements pertaining to longevity and a collective belief in that history and those objects/myths/legends.[26]

A sense of a timeless rurality is expressed in texts addressing folk knitting, in particular those referencing histories of knitting in the British Isles and Ireland – Shetland, Fair Isle, Aran and the Channel Islands. In *Irish Knitting: Patterns Inspired by Ireland*, Rohana Darlington expresses this sentiment in the introduction.

> I'd often been asked if I believed the romantic tales which maintained Bronze Age Phoenician sailors introduced intricate knitting techniques to the remote and windswept Irish Aran Isles. Inhabited since Neolithic times, the islands theoretically could have been visited by Mediterranean merchants skilled in textile arts, trading wine for copper from the Waterford coast and gold from the Wicklow mountains.[27]

Darlington's use of language is characterized by an idealized and mythical Ireland – a land of stories and legends that permeate a timeless place, with unchanging traditions. The emphasis on speculation again highlights such expectation, leading the reader into another time, place and sense of being. This sense of an inaccessible rurality, seemingly 'timeless' and to some extent undiscovered and therefore mysterious, exists in the literature surrounding knitting in the Scottish islands and the development of Fair Isle patterns. Sheila McGregor's seminal text, *The Complete Book of Fair Isle Knitting*, for example, outlines a cultural and historical background of the islands that evolves as a result of geography, distance and itinerant visitors.[28]

One could say that all cultures and cultural production can be seen as a response to the needs and desires of the population, of trade, import and export, and to changing responses to a world-view. However, notions of the rural and 'tradition', and romantic approaches to the landscape and indigenous peoples coincide with the emergence of knitting styles, techniques and patterns, and dominate the literature of knitting per se. Notions of the past are expressed nostalgically, with emphasis on creating a vista of landscape, primitive and often poor people, and traditional forms of creative practice currently threatened as a result of the onslaught of technological, social and cultural change. As Alice Starmore writes of the Shetland knitting industry in the 1970s following the discovery of North Sea oil:

> The effect of Shetland's oil boom on knitting was considerable. Knitters – or their husbands – could find well-paid employment in oil-related industries, and many gave up knitting commercially. Young people, like most kids today, with their high hopes and expectations, found that the financial rewards of knitting paled in comparison to the possibilities in the oilfields.[29]

Stanmore's assertion that the oil boom contributed to the decline of knitting in the Shetland Isles is not disputed; however, the tone of her comment in relation to the aspirations of younger members of the population indicates a notion that technology – and indeed time – has tainted these simple folk and turned them from their heritage. The notion of cultural decline and the potential loss of traditional forms of production that is evidenced in this kind of literature presupposes a sense of moral decay, which is in turn imprinted on traditional or heritage knitting styles.

The idyllic presentation of traditional forms of knitting as unchanging renders them static, unable to move on or indeed compete in the contemporary marketplace other than as 'heritage' or tourist objects. Similarly, the Romantic rhetoric surrounding modes of production, such as the term 'cottage industry', belies the hardship and difficulty of such forms of labour.[30]

One might suggest that the resurrection of interest in these techniques, motifs and styles emerges as a response to a desire to connect with one's ancestry as in features in North American knitting magazines that emphasize Scandinavian,[31] Germanic[32] and Eastern European[33] traditions, as well as a drive to maintain a connection with one's heritage in an increasingly homogenized world.[34]

The rural can also be understood as a connection with the land, which has associations with national identity, but also with a sense of place and time. Often, knitted design adopts the colours of the landscape, drawing reference from both the land itself and the indigenous flora and geology. This is particularly evident in knitwear that in winter adopts muted tones and hues and in summer reflects the scorched land or the abundance of nature in all its vibrancy.[35] Designers such Sarah Dallas are frequently inspired by the textures and colours of the landscape, and in this example the shingled coastline, fragmented, mutated and eroded over time, inspires and is juxtaposed against the newness of fashion. Dallas's knitwear evokes an untamed nature, engulfing the female form, aesthetically and symbolically reminiscent of the figure in the eighteenth-century sublime landscape. Nature here not only influences fashion,

Figure 12 Sarah Dallas, slate-inspired knitwear, featured in Sarah Dallas and Catherine Gratwicke, *Sarah Dallas Knitting*, Rowan, 2005. Photographer: Catherine Gratwicke. Image reproduced with permission from the designer and Rowan.

but overtakes and overpowers it, with knit growing almost organically on the wearer as if it were parasitic. Likewise, her designs for Rowan develop a natural palette of colours which, alongside promotional elements such as fashion-shoot styling, advertising and catalogues, make reference to the heritage and Romantic potential of the British countryside through evocative reference to the weather and a need to keep warm.

The sculptural knits of the American fibre artist George Brett explore the spatiality of the landscape and use vast reams of machine-knitted webs to negotiate and draw attention to the contours of the land, and the spectator's perception of inhabiting and moving amongst it. Like mass spiders' webs, Brett's sculptures attract the light and the morning dew, becoming part of the natural environment:

> The webs brought attention to two-dimensional space that had previously been taken for granted: the open space between two branches of a tree or between two buildings. The feeling is perhaps the primary emphasis of my work: the utilization of 'empty' space in such a way that it is not filled, nor does it remain empty ... I take space and fill it with a lattice of three-dimensional and two-dimensional objects. The shadows and reflections of the knitted panels create the two-dimensional images which delineate the negative areas of walls, floors, lakes and windows. This 'lattice work' further divides the space into smaller units ... The knitted panels create whole series of cross-reference points. They define the space as well as divide it.[36]

The use of knitted sculpture within the landscape as a means of negotiating and dividing the environment is a theme in the work of the British textile artist, Shane Waltener, who also creates knitted webs using a Shetland lace technique that directs the spectator physically and visually through knitted phrases such as 'over here' and 'out there'. The directional engagement in the landscape is created not just through the text, but through the ways in which the knitted forms dissect the vista and create a viewfinder that encourages a specific way of seeing.[37] Knitting, when presented as a web within the landscape, has a mythology,[38] yet the natural aesthetic of such sculpture creates a sense of the organic, as if the sculpture 'just grew there', and therefore suggests an integration into environment which makes the cultural (art) natural.

Whether the sculpture is situated within the landscape or constructed to represent the landscape, the conceptual and emotive response is the same: that the land is something that cannot be controlled and is ever-evolving, but is something that one can try to harness and manipulate, or capture in time. This understanding of the land evolves from a Romantic interpretation of nature and the rural or the pre-industrial past.

Figure 13 Shane Waltener, *A World Wide Web*, 2007. Shirring elastic, 25 sq. metres (269 sq. ft). A site-specific installation commissioned for 'Radical Lace and Subversive Knitting' at the Museum of Arts and Design, New York. Image reproduced with permission from the artist.

Reviving the Knitted Past

The revival of the past in terms of styles, activities and ideas, and the accompanying traditions (of which knitting is an element), frequently occur as a direct response to the contemporary world. At times of crisis, instability and anxiety, the past offers a sense of security otherwise absent.

> To articulate the past historically does not mean to recognize it 'the way it really was'. It means to seize hold of a memory as it flashes up at a moment of danger.[39]

From the 1970s onwards, there emerged a plethora of knitting texts and pattern books that investigated traditional knitting techniques and styles. Virtually all of these texts focused on what seemed to be a cultural imperative: knitting traditions were being lost as a result of the onslaught of capitalism and globalization and these texts were aiming to redress the balance by educating knitters about the history of vernacular practices, recreating the mythology of stitches and styles, and translating traditional patterns into wearable contemporary garments. These texts could be divided into two distinct, but related, areas

– texts that addressed Western knitting traditions and those that investigated non-Western traditions.

Texts that addressed non-Western traditions tended to take an anthropological stance,[40] imbrued with a primitivism and Romanticism that would not have appeared out of place in the nineteenth century. With a focus on 'ancient wisdom', and the spirituality of the land informing motif development and construction, space, place and time became central to an understanding of such knitting practices. From the indigenous peoples of Central and South America to Islamic and Moorish knitters, the Western appraisal of non-Western knitting reeked of colonialism and a revival of the 'noble savage'. Much of this literature reflected on the significance of 'folk art', a term that implies a genre of practices which exist outside a Western arts hierarchy and defy concepts of the avant-garde. It appeared that without the doctrines of an institutional understanding of fine art, these traditions were 'purer' or more authentic in their conception and practice, particularly, as traditions observed were often everyday practices:

> These people did not practise knitting as a parlour art, following printed directions as did genteel folk of the Victorian era. They mastered the craft to provide practical garments for daily living. This was folk knitting in its true form.[41]

The focus on the authentic seems of particular importance and the quote from Gibson-Roberts (above) is not unusual. Knitting under these conditions was representative of a sense of both the worldly and the unworldly, of the everyday and ordinary – but the everyday that is untainted, a place that exists outside the concerns of the industrial world. Effectively, one might construct this as a more 'natural' or 'pastoral' place, where design references come not from the trend-led world of fashion but from myth, tradition, spirit and the land itself. These forms of knitting are positioned as distinct from Western practices and are therefore understood as an extension of 'the Other': non-Western, non-industrialized and untainted or innocent and childlike. This approach is undoubtedly Western, but unlike earlier incarnations of this world-view, authors have no intention of 'civilizing Caliban', but the opposite: to preserve, memorize and take home a piece of this perceived 'purity' in the designs and techniques of these communities.

From a similarly colonial perspective, texts that addressed Western knitting traditions tended to focus on the European, in particular knitting traditions in seafaring communities – i.e. the Aran (cable), the Guernsey/Gansey and Jersey (dark wool fisherman's sweater), and patterned styles such as Shetland and Fair Isle. Each of these styles, and indeed geographic anchor, as outlined in the style/pattern's name, can be seen as both specific and generic. This means that these styles do have a regionally specific heritage and set of traditions that vary from place to place, yet they are also terms which are frequently bastardized and appropriated to refer to particular types of knitting that are visually similar to or derived from their namesakes, but are alien in history, myth, location and manufacture.

It is very difficult within Western societies to find 'authentic' communities suitable for anthropological study. We tend to live in communities without shared interests, habits, practices and activities, and with the few exceptions of religious or traditional communities such as the Amish in Lancaster County, USA,[42] or the Community of True Inspiration, Amana, Iowa,[43] opportunities for such studies are relatively small. Such communities often seem distanced from our own experience of the world and are often seen as being 'closed' or dogmatic. Therefore, studies that refer to Western knitting traditions look to a heritage which is romantic in two ways: firstly, they address working-class or (folk) practices which offer a heroicism that recounts a dialogue between poverty and everyday life, in which knitters use their skill to provide for their family against the odds, and secondly, like the approaches to non-Western knitting, motifs and practices have a communicative symbolism which evokes a visual language that transcends time and place – it predates mass literacy, demonstrating the generational transferral of tacit skills as opposed to formal institutional instruction.

A key aspect of a heritage knitting mythology is the notion of knitting as a sign of the familial. This extends to patterns as emblems of kinship, expressions of love through time spent knitting, and the creation of a genealogical narrative through garment construction and design. Traditional sweaters, particularly those made within fishing communities (Guernseys/Ganseys, Arans, Fair Isles and Jerseys), are said to act as means of identification should the wearer be lost at sea, with motifs communicating name, family and place of origin: a form of knitted identity tag.[44] Examples such as this outline the ways in which patterns and motifs could be read as person-specific, with each garment indicative of an unspoken language, developed through the visual and tactile manipulation of knitted yarn into a communicative garment. The pattern becomes text. The knitted text implies a form of communication that predates literacy and as such consigns the garments to a pre-industrial era of more rural and simple times.

Linking the Past to the Present

Whenever people emigrate from one country to another, they carry with them many of their cultural traditions. Sooner or later, at least some of these traditions become modified and established into the cultural whole of the new country ... Wherever Scottish people have established themselves, new tartan patterns have been designed to celebrate and commemorate events and places associated with the Scots ... In America since the mid-1970s, district tartans have been designed to symbolize some of the states, usually in connection with a commemorative event like the state's birthday. In some states the tartans have been presented to the State Legislature for approval, to make them 'official'.[45]

The creation of a knitted sweater in Ohio State tartan emphasizes the ways in which the traditional is recreated to suit the contemporary population. Each of the state tartans is specific: each encompasses symbols and colours of the region, but refers to the heritage and genealogy of the settlers. Traditional motifs, in these examples, are reappropriated and developed to create 'new' or revised histories which contribute to the stability of an otherwise émigré population.

Notions of genealogy and a desire to maintain a connection with a 'motherland' can be seen in more concentrated ethnic communities such as in Decorah, Iowa, where the majority of inhabitants hail primarily from Norway. Norwegian knitting traditions, patterns and styles have been cited as the continuation of local traditions, connecting immigrants with their own heritage whilst creating and establishing new ones. In Decorah, sweaters are constructed from imported wool or are purchased on visits to Scandinavia, adding a sense of authenticity to the garments, and the practice of 'sweater-watching'[46] (or admiring the style and patterns of sweaters) has become a contemporary local pastime. Such an occupation is not merely based on personal preference but on an acquired knowledge of Norwegian knitting, which implies a knowledge of the cultures of 'home'.

Although this approach is endearing, offering a rather sentimental appraisal of traditional knitting and its folklore, which aims to revitalize an interest in its practices in order to ensure its survival, it is equally problematic, contributing to and consigning such knitting to a 'timelessness' that stifles its development and continuation.

Britt-Marie Christoffersson, a Swedish knitwear designer working in the USA, references traditional knit techniques and motifs from her own heritage to design garments and patterns suitable for a contemporary audience of makers and consumers. Her aim is not to replicate originals, but to draw reference from them and to demonstrate how traditional craftsmanship can be utilized to meet current needs. She notes, for example, that traditional garments are stiff and lack the elasticity of their contemporary counterparts, and therefore are unsuitable for everyday wear.[47]

> My work is no attempt to meddle with the making of traditional garments. I do not intend to create a Delsbo or Jarvso sweater for the 1990s, but rather sweaters for everyday use, where tradition is only part of the garment's character.[48]

Christoffersson's intention to refer to original garments as an inspiration resource is not unusual within knitwear design, particularly that which is aimed at the home knitter. The fusion of the new with the old can be described as retro chic, a term devised in 1970s France to encompass the then popular taste for the revival of period styles.[49]

Tradition in these examples, it seems, is constructed to meet an understanding of what traditional knitting represents, rather than the realities and practicalities involved in its construction. This is the reproduction of tradition to meet the needs of the consumer, merely an aping of the 'original', which to anyone other than the connoisseur is acceptable and 'genuine'. However, it is possible to suggest that there is no one tradition, no one style that can be labelled as 'authentic', the genuine article, and this is the dilemma of history and all studies of the past – that facts, artefacts, documents and memories are all subject to reappraisal and no single reading is static or dominant. As Harold Pinter noted: 'The past is what you remember, imagine you remember, convince yourself you remember, or pretend to remember.'[50] The past is ever present because it is wanted, and that means that it is subject to manipulation, mainly because it must be distinct from, but link to, the here and now.

Classic Fashion and the Past as Cutting Edge

In terms of fashion and 'fashionable' styles, it seems paradoxical to suggest that garments can be described as 'classics'. Fashion is dynamic, changing and ever moving forward, whilst the term 'classic' implies a sense of the non-changing and stable, and as such the two terms appear diametrically opposed. It is true to say that clothing can be 'classic': a T-shirt or vest may be a perennial wardrobe staple and deemed a 'classic', but it is not fashionable. Fashion changes, 'classics' don't.

With this in mind, one might assume that design 'classics' are rather plain, devoid of the hallmarks of trends in terms of shape, colour, pattern and motif. This may make such items appear rather bland, constructed in natural fibres and neutral colours which seemingly transcend the frivolities of fashion. Such garments are rather stoic; yet they are also described as 'favourites' and are associated with the concept of 'style' which suggests a 'timelessness' never out of date. Garments included in this category tend to be understood as iconic, meaning that they have achieved a status which goes beyond the remits of fashion, displaying in the wearer an understanding of dress and display that is self-assured, confident and unbothered by current vogues – for example Chanel's little black dress, as worn by Audrey Hepburn, in which the design classic becomes a sign of iconic beauty through the garment and its association.

In term of knitwear, such an assertion is rather paradoxical; knitwear can be extremely avant-garde and embrace the nuances of fashion, whilst at the same time, much knitwear styling can be seen as derivative of the design 'classic'. This can be evidenced in three ways: firstly, through the use of natural fibres such as wool, cotton, linen and silk; secondly, the link to manufacturers with a long history; and finally, in terms of style, pattern and motifs that can be described as 'traditional' – a term which defies the historical process.

The use of natural fibres in knitwear significantly connects garments with heritage, the past and a sense of the timeless classic. In an era when the emphasis, for many garments, is on ease of washing and drying, 100 per cent natural fibres are increasingly rare. Such rarity, and the attention to garment care required, instils in the consumer a recollection of the time before spin-dryers, the luxury associated with dry-cleaning, and imparts a wholesomeness devoid of the taint of chemical and synthetic fibres and processes. Garment care, including seasonal wrapping to ward off insect infestation, suggests a preciousness only warranted, in these time-poor days, by extremely special objects. Such fibres are also associated with luxury, decadence and quality – there is nothing like the feel of cashmere against the skin, or the tactility of silk or linen knits, or the soft crispness of knitted cotton. Often the price of such garments reflects this sensibility, offering them as examples of 'the best', with everything else a hollow sham.

Manufacturers of knitted goods frequently trade on their heritage, which is perpetuated by their consumers who desire engagement with tradition. In these cases, an example of which is the Scottish knitwear company, Pringle,[51] the concept of tradition is not merely an association with longevity, but one of quality and distinction, as often these manufacturers have connections with royalty and celebrity. The consumer expects manufacture to a high level, high-quality materials and a rarity that transcends time. To own such an item is to mark oneself as connected, albeit tenuously, to such status. By association, manufacture and brand identity, such goods become understood as design classics. Similarly, manufacturers who have maintained a corporate identity based on heritage and tradition have an association with national and regional identity, which seems to transcend the contemporary.

Although fashion is constantly changing, and is never revived in a manner exacting the 'original', some styles do have a certain longevity that elevates them beyond the remits of 'fashion'. These garments recur as wardrobe staples and tend to fall into the category of 'ageless elegance', such as the twin-set, which can be worn at any age to express a notion of 'style'.

The twin-set, a matching jumper (often sleeveless) and cardigan, first entered wardrobes in the 1930s and has subsequently been described as a 'classic'. The combination of practicality and versatility (the garment can be worn in a variety of ways) means that the twin-set has never really gone out of style, yet it has never really stayed the same. One partial reason for the longevity of the garment and its elevation to a fashion or design 'classic' is its cultural capital as a sign of wealth and status, elements that traditionally transcend and bypass the fashion system. As Sandy Black recognizes:

> Middle-class values led to the adoption of the twin-set … as the classic, neat, understated and moderately sophisticated look. The country weekend dress of the British landed gentry was promoted as a role model for classic taste, and was ably supplied by the English and especially Scottish knitwear industries – a look which was, and still is, exported around the world.[52]

The cultural significance of the twin-set as an extension of aristocratic taste popularized the garment, imbruing it with the values of the group wearing it and, by implication, made it not merely an object of desire, but for the middle classes, an expression of an identification with the ideals and lifestyle of the ruling classes. The aristocratic connection symbolically aligns the twin-set with members of a social group who have an established and well-documented heritage, and are aware of their lineage and inherited social status, which acts as a sign of stability but also of longevity and wealth. By association, the twin-set becomes part of the iconography of a group Veblen would call 'the leisure class',[53] a social group deemed 'tasteful' primarily because members don't need to demonstrate their status through the consumption of goods, nor the world of fashion. The twin-set becomes a sign of luxury and status, an enduring emblem of timeless style.

The simplicity of the garment suggests a design that is both functional and devoid of fashion-inspired design details, whilst maintaining a plainness that can adapt to current trends. The design historian Catherine McDermott has charted the changes in the garment from its origins to the present day. She comments that the appeal of the twin-set is in its democracy, negotiating boundaries of age, class and time:

> In the 1950s, worn a size too small it was figure-hugging and sexy; worn by royalty it was accessorized with a single string of pearls; worn by middle-aged, middle-class women it was a casual but smart solution that said conservative but safe. Such an icon was ripe for exploitation in the punk era: Vivienne Westwood commissioned a range of twin-sets in bright colours emblazoned with her orb logo from the knitwear company John Smedley.[54]

The timelessness of the garment is maintained through its ability to change with the times. This process is a revitalizing of a wardrobe staple, and can be understood as part of the process of modernity. The constant attention to the zeitgeist as a trigger for revival offers the consumer something that is simultaneously familiar and new. The 'classic' therefore does not stand still, nor does it defy the historical process, but it changes, develops and is reworked to suit contemporary desires and tastes. The fluidity of the fashion 'classic' therefore can be both 'classic' and 'fashionable'.

Visions of the Past: Motifs, Patterns and the Iconography of History

As outlined, the establishment of knitting as an example of the resurrection of the past as a sign of authenticity in an increasingly inauthentic world, can be traced to three factors working simultaneously: (a) the meaning of craft, (b) a desire for difference, and (c) a fondness for nostalgia. The combination of each of these sentiments might suggest that knitting is merely part of a retrogressive move to recreate stability in contemporary society. The evidence, however, suggests the contrary; knitting embraces the new, particularly in fashion, and although motifs and patterns are presented as having a linear and unchanging history, they frequently change to suit the dynamics of style trends.

In this garment, the pattern designed by Kaffe Fassett and made by an amateur knitter, the traditional technique of diagonal patchwork knitting has been utilized to create an updated sweater. This type of decorative knitting, which resembles basketwork and is turned as one would to make a sock, has its origins in Scandinavia and is traditionally constructed in two vibrant colours: black and red. In Fassett's design, the traditional pattern engages a more muted and pastel palette, which also takes inspiration from other forms of Scandinavian knitting traditions through its inclusion of the cross motif patterning. The garment also has a more contemporary shape, employing a boat neck and a fitted, ribbed waist detail, which feminizes the garment. The sweater therefore refers to the past through technique and motif, but has been adapted to suit contemporary fashion by adjusting the shape and colouring.

By the 1980s, the past was being used as an inspirational dressing-up box for designers and consumers alike. Heritage had become an 'industry' and the term

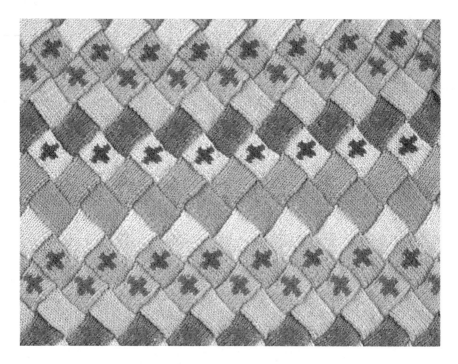

Figure 14 A Kaffe Fassett design and pattern, knitted by an amateur/home knitter, *c.* late 1970s–1980s. Fashion Museum, Bath. Image courtesy of Bath and North East Somerset Council.

had become a design buzzword. The style guru Peter York described this vogue for a retrospective gaze as indicative of British design at the time, which he believed to combine two opposing temporal positions, that of 'punk' and 'pageant'.[55] For York, 'punk' was representative of the new, the avant-garde and the forward-thinking, whilst 'pageant' exemplified a sense of the organic: design that appeared not to have been designed but had just 'grown' or evolved from a heritage, embracing the backward-looking. This temporal pull may appear paradoxical, but ultimately encapsulates a design confusion indicative of the period. The praxis at which the future and the past met was obviously the present, in which the avant-garde had to be made wearable and the past updated and re-presented in new ways in order to be called 'fashion'. The result of such compromise led to innovation that embraced both the old and the new simultaneously.

Innovation in aesthetics in knitwear design during the 1980s can be understood as a form of reappropriation, of borrowing from the past but combining it with elements of the high-fashion avant-garde. The past is a reference, a sign amongst many others, which is sourced as inspiration but developed rather than copied, or revived into a new form. Knitting frequently refers to its own history and can therefore be understood as self-reflective. This enables the formation of a history of knitting which is valorized and marked through examples of tradition. This history is referenced in revivals, returning to a quest for 'authenticity' which ultimately is self-defeating, as one can never return to the past, and one must therefore rely on attempts to reproduce it. Reproduction is, however, useful: it situates specific techniques and styles within history, which means that they avoid the historical process, suspending examples in stasis. Therefore certain styles appear 'timeless' and 'unchanging' and become representative of a stable past.

CASE STUDY. Winter Wonderland: The Snowflake Sweater and the Geographical and Cultural Journey of a Style

This study aims to look at the development of the 'snowflake' sweater in terms of style, heritage and its meaning in contemporary culture. Although there are many regional and national variations of the style and pattern, each employing different techniques, colours and yarn, this study assesses them collectively, focusing on the motif and its symbolism rather than on specific construction details. This study is not unusual in taking this stance or making stereotypical assumptions about motifs and designs; in popular iconography and language, the snowflake sweater encompasses all star, banded and two-colour knitwear, which is also generically described as 'Fair Isle'.

By investigating the ways in which these motifs and styles seemingly defy the historical process by rooting themselves within a series of historical narratives, the intention is to question the longevity of these patterns, their cultural

Figure 15 Traditional Fair Isle, hand-knitted wool, 1940s. Fashion Museum, Bath. Image courtesy of Bath and North East Somerset Council.

reappropriation and their significance within the contemporary West. This case study is therefore an example of material culture, of what Igor Kopytoff calls 'the cultural biography of things',[56] a method which he suggests can uncover social–object relations.

> Biographies of things can make salient what might otherwise remain obscure. For example, in situations of culture contact, they can show what anthropologists have so often stressed: that what is significant about the adoption of alien objects – of alien ideas – is not the fact that they are adopted, but the way they are culturally redefined and put to use.[57]

The study therefore assesses the ways in which the snowflake sweater can be understood as a design object and cultural artefact. Charting the geographical and stylistic origins of both pattern and garment, the study questions concepts of heritage

and authenticity seemingly inbuilt into the object, as well as investigating developments, translations and reappropriations of motifs over time. From this design perspective, the study addresses the cultural meaning and significance of the garment,
and how this has contributed to the enduring appeal of the snowflake sweater.

In terms of design, this pattern is essentially the marriage of banded styles
emerging from northern Europe (Scandinavia and the Scottish isles), involving the
use of two or more colours. Motifs in this study are described as a snowflake, but
are derivative of traditional forms of ornamentation combining the geometric for-
mations of the cross and the star.

In relation to design, patterning and motif-making is historically linked with the
culture from which it emerges. In ancient times, and certainly in times before mass
literacy, knitting historians have referred to the symbolism and mysticism that permeate patterning. James Norbury exemplifies this by stating:

> The concept of design is an integral part of the true philosophy of living and doing and
> being. It is rooted in the primitive mystery and magic that surrounded man in the dawn
> of time of life on this planet.[58]

As a starting point, phrases such as 'the dawn of time' seem rather unhelpful, as
they offer no specific date of origin, as a historian might require. Dating or
charting the origins of specific knitting patterns is, however, extremely difficult:
patterns were passed on either orally or tacitly, natural fibres deteriorate and decay
over time, and garments were literally 'worn out' and therefore physical evidence
is limited. Examples of early knitting histories do exist,[59] but one might question
the cultural significance of determining and defining the origins of a particular
pattern when phrases such as 'the dawn of time' add to the mystery and narrative
inherent in an understanding of knitting per se.

The snowflake is essentially a variation of a star motif. These motifs have a very
long history, both temporally and geographically. The star pattern is primarily
made from geometric forms – the octagon and the square. In terms of patterning,
geometric motifs are the simplest patterns to create as they are regular in shape and
can be easily translated into knitting patterns. They are also the oldest forms of
pattern, evident in all parts of the globe, with no one area dominant. As textile historian Sally Harding recognizes:

> The crisp points of diamonds and stars make them a clear-cutting element in textile
> design. To my mind, these two angular motifs are among the liveliest of the geometric
> forms ... Virtually every culture has brought out some different aspect of these themes.[60]

Diamonds, octagons, crosses and stars themselves all contribute to the development of the snowflake motif. As these designs predate mass literacy, their
symbolic content and value has been discussed as referencing the natural and

mythological environment of a given region. The development of the snowflake can therefore be understood as a response to the natural environment that the originators of the pattern engaged within on a daily basis. As a result, a 'true' snowflake pattern developed in nations where it regularly snows, particularly in Scandinavia and northern Europe.

However, such an obvious assumption does not necessarily indicate a clear origin of the snowflake motif. In discussing the eight-pointed star, Susanne Pagoldh notes:

> In knitted form it is regarded as typically Norwegian. Such stars were knitted and embroidered by the Arabs in Spain during the thirteenth century, and they are seen in the roof carvings of the Moorish Palace Alhambra. In Islamic art the eight-pointed star symbolized the four elements: earth, air, sun and water, and the qualities of heat, dryness, coolness and humidity. In Christian art, the eight-pointed star symbolized rebirth. The stars appeared as relief patterns on the expensive silk sweaters imported into Scandinavia during the seventeenth century and are still found on sweaters, mittens and socks knitted today.[61]

Pagoldh's brief history of the motif, which is also described as the 'star rose' or 'star of Bethlehem',[62] and the 'morning star' in Latvia,[63] questions the validity of the pattern as an indigenous northern European design, suggesting that it was adopted and adapted from imported goods to satisfy a domestic market.

The exact origins of the patterns are not known, nor is it possible to locate the ways in which early patterns circulated from on nation to another. It is, however, possible to identify regional variations on the pattern, which have subsequently become embedded within both national and cultural identity.

Colour stranding and a banded pattern combined with the use of geometric motifs is often referred to as 'Fair Isle', regardless of its geographic origins. In the UK, Fair Isle is a type of banded, coloured knitting originating in and associated with the Shetland Islands. There is no one specific pattern, but it is largely characterized by a series of 'OXO' motifs, no more than two colours in any one row, the use of diagonals and the creation of symmetry.[64] Traditional Fair Isle sweaters and cardigans are knitted in the round up to the armholes, then the knitting is transferred to two needles.[65]

The distinct, brightly coloured sweaters have remained popular and have become a sign of vernacular practices, even though the tradition is largely invented and the patterns a generic term for all two-coloured banded knitwear. Although the origins and heritage of the motifs are largely unknown and can only be assessed speculatively, there is evidence that outlines the regional, national and geographic development and disparity of such knitwear.

In Norway the most recognizable sweater pattern is the *luskofte* ('lice jacket'), originating in the early nineteenth century from the Setesdal region. The pattern can be identified by a speckled pattern reminiscent of embroidery, which works down the sweater from neck to a wide band of stars/snowflakes or flowers at the mid-section. The lower part of the garment is white. Traditionally, the pattern is knitted in two colours (*totradbindinga*) – black and white, with a black ground and white detailing.[66] The shoulders are marked, like Fair Isle, with an 'OXO' pattern.[67] Deviations from this pattern arise as an aspect of regional variation, for example the Fana sweater or cardigan, which is a two-coloured garment, wholly banded, with a Nordic star as a feature at each shoulder.

In Sweden, the patterning changes again, developing into a banded yoke in the Bohus sweater. Understood as a traditional garment, the history of the Bohus sweater is relatively recent, developed by Emma Jacobsson in the late 1930s to 1940s as a means of employment for the wives of unemployed stonecutters.[68] The motifs and patterns were not geographically specific, as there had been no indigenous textile production in the region, and as a result Jacobsson borrowed from more general Swedish folk traditions.[69] Similarly, the Icelandic Lopi,[70] a yoked sweater with a pattern resembling icicles radiating down the garment, also only gained recognition and popularity during this period.[71]

The Scandinavian patterns are distinct from Shetland Fair Isle, as is the use of colour. In terms of pattern mythology, the distinct dark/light colour contrast is said to represent the disparity between day and night, and the designs are said to be a commentary on the shape and climate of the landscape. The sense of a specific place created around these garments is a significant element in the establishment of artefacts as signs of national identity. The renewed interest in – and popularity of – these traditional designs during the Second World War is not incidental: the revival of traditional knitwear during this period acted as a sign of defiance and patriotism.

Although there is artefact evidence of two-colour banded knitting from Ancient Egypt, and examples throughout history to date, the regional tradition of this type of knitting in the Shetland Isles is largely a construct, with a much shorter history. And rather than an activity that people just 'did' as part of the vernacular, the tradition of Fair Isle knitting emerges as a response to mechanization. As Michael Pearson acknowledges:

When the Hawick frame knitters took over plain hosiery from the hand-knitters, the latter responded by producing lace shawls. The large-scale mechanization of these lace patterns, based in Nottingham, provoked the reintroduction throughout the whole of the Shetlands of two-colour knitting which, until then, had been exclusive to the tiny island of Fair Isle. When this in turn became mechanized in the early twentieth century, the hand-knitters responded in the only way now left to them, which was to sell their garments as ethnic, original and knitted by the islanders themselves. This sales practice continues to the present day.[72]

Pearson's emphasis highlights the way in which tradition has been constructed to suit contemporary needs and markets. Tradition here has been invented out of necessity, developing from a very local and minor practice into a seemingly major regional indigenous industry in order to maintain employment for the islands' inhabitants. The development of Fair Isle knitting in the Shetlands can be seen as the establishment of an early form of regionally branded goods to satisfy a 'heritage' market.

The mythology of the islands, interwoven with knitting traditions, had been firmly established by the nineteenth century in the writings of Robert Louis Stevenson[73] and the Shetlander Miss Eliza Edmondston,[74] whose Romantic sensibilities speculatively commented on the correlation of local mythology, the landscape and indigenous knitting traditions, which proved popular with their Victorian audience. These tales of the rugged, sublime landscape, invasion by the Spanish Armada (unsubstantiated), and a hardy rural population, created a myth of simple and traditional folk engaged in vernacular and pre-industrial creative practices. The creation of a 'history' that spoke directly to an industrialized population on the mainland fed directly into the audience's desire for escapism through a nostalgia for a rural past.

Although there was an interest in the social history of the islands and their folk practices, there was less interest in the patterns and garments themselves.[75] Although the industry sustained itself by making warm clothing suitable for outdoor pursuits, it wasn't until the 1920s, when leisure became increasingly available to the mass population and, following a publicity campaign coordinated by the Shetland Wool Board in 1921, when the Prince of Wales (the future King Edward VIII) wore one at a golf match at St Andrews, that the popularity of Fair Isle knits really boomed. The royal patronage revived the flagging Shetland knitwear industry, and the Fair Isle sweater became a fashion item for society members and home knitters alike. Interestingly, it is this constructed heritage – the myths, landscapes, stories and peoples – that informs a contemporary understanding of the snowflake sweater, with histories recreated to appeal to a contemporary consumer market.

There are two sociocultural factors evident in these two approaches to the resurrection or reinvention of 'traditional' knitting. Firstly, revivals of patterns, styles and garments arise as a result of commercial interests fuelled by the market; the industry is revived as a means of sustaining regional employment and revenue. And, secondly, consumers respond to the cultural and nationalistic meaning of the garment, re-popularizing it. In both cases, tradition has been invented or manipulated to suit the needs of the consumer/population at a given time.

> Traditional styles were, of course, in demand, but they were usually adapted to meet the
> requirements regarding shape, style, colour and, in particular, amateur knitting tech-
> niques. The bending of the rules of Fair Isle and Aran has given rise to misconceptions
> about their origins. One popular mistake is to think that the knitting of Fair Isle is iden-
> tified by two-colour patterns, usually a tree of life and star, concentrated around the

yoke. But this image is, at best, a tasteful adaptation determined by commercial considerations and it bears little relation to the original tradition.[76]

The relationship between a mythology responding to landscape, as well as vernacular traditions and materials (such as yarns and fibres derived from indigenous animals), instils in the snowflake sweater an iconographic sense of place and nationhood. As previously indicated, 'heritage' is ostensibly the invention of tradition, maintained and sustained through the creation and recreation of myths, narratives, memories and artefacts. Identity in relation to nations is created and maintained in the same way, as a means of building a continuity of that nation through objects, language, literature, institutions and through the teaching of history and the preservation and presentation of artefacts and ceremonies, all of which contribute to an understanding of a linear continuum.

This continuity is not natural, and traditions and histories are invented continually to ensure a distinct collective identity that distinguishes one nation from another, and from interior fragmentary identities (class, gender, ethnicity) which might destabilize its dominance.

The implications of an invented tradition are exemplified in Liz Gemmell's reworking of Fair Isle for an Australian audience, which refers to folk traditions of the southern hemisphere. Two-colour banded knitting is developed to incorporate Aboriginal art techniques and motifs, and indigenous flora and fauna such as the kangaroo feature in the patterns.[77] She states: 'Mini figures run along the bottom bands of this bold jumper. The dots represent raindrops, and the yoke is decorated with Aboriginal patterns.'[78]

In Gemmell's designs and patterns, more recent signs of nation are adopted and adapted, including the Sydney Opera House, which indicate the triumphs of a contemporary nation's heritage, demonstrating the progression of peoples and a 'traditional' style. Contemporary motifs have also been developed for a 'new' Fair Isle by designers such as Patty Knox, who refers to forms as diverse as aeroplanes and flowerpots.[79]

The reinvention of traditional items has been central to fashion design since the 1980s. One might assume that this is merely a response to the development of identifiable consumer lifestyles, or a postmodern yearning for an alternative to the present, but fashion by nature is distanced from the mundane and is itself very much part of the otherworldly – we wear clothes, but fashion is dynamic. Fashion's interest in the past is not merely retrogressive, but more of a form of self-referentiality and means of passing social comment. As the dress historian Caroline Evans recognizes, critics of the 'abuses' of history in fashion have argued that

> history was plundered to make a postmodern carnival, and the incessant return to the past was itself a kind of deathly recycling of history which emptied it out of meaning, rendering it bankrupt, good only for costume drama and fantasy.[80]

Figure 16 Author's father wearing a Fair Isle sweater knitted by his mother, 1964.

Indeed, designer Edina Ronay built her reputation on reworking Fair Isle patterns from the 1930s and 1940s into 'antique'-inspired collections:

> Showing these sweaters at a fashion trade fair in 1978 was so successful that a new business was born in those few important days. The old clothes were left behind, and the Fair Isle she now designs have lost their rustic roots to become the delicate patterning for clothes knitted in silks and luxury fibres that coordinate with her beautifully cut classic separates.[81]

Perhaps there were examples of self-referentiality as dressing-up costume, but in knitwear and particularly the snowflake sweater, both motifs and garments were utilized as signs of national identity, of the ravages of globalization and as signs of class and personal identity in an increasingly homogenized world. For example, in Vivienne Westwood's 'Britain Must Go Pagan' collections from 1989, Fair Isle patterns became embedded with a sign of the contemporary through changing the binary 'OXO' patterns to those associated with computer gaming, promoting the concept that tradition can be saved through reinvention. She returned to the Fair Isle pattern in 2001 with a body-hugging cardigan, buttoned diagonally across the bust, to create a style evocative of Miss Marple meeting Marilyn Monroe. In Westwood's reappropriation of history, styles are parodied as a means of challenging their cultural meaning, morphing them into something strange and innovative. Famed for her reinterpretation of Britishness, Westwood has used the iconography of national identity to challenge notions of class in an attempt to redress the meaning of couture in everyday life.

The construction technique and materials, alongside the pattern, firmly make the snowflake sweater a winter garment. As such, the sweater has become part of the iconography of Christmas, a sentimental garment for a holiday which has also been subject to reinvention and market manipulation as a result of 'the carol philosophy'[82] – a response to Dickens's *A Christmas Carol*. The significance of Dickens's novel and the formulation of a 'traditional' Christmas is largely an emotional construct in which family harmony and morality encapsulate the meaning of the season. This is largely an impossible ideal, but nonetheless permeates concepts of Christmas globally, regardless of the religious persuasion of a society. The sweater is significant because it embodies the values of Christmas; it is an object of nostalgia emanating from a rural tradition, and it depicts snow. In his study of the Swedish Christmas, for example, Orvar Lofgren notes that even in the 1920s people had a general belief that the perfect Christmas was rural and in the past.[83] The association of an ideal and the past doesn't hinder the desire to recreate the ideals of Christmas in the present; indeed, decorations, greetings cards, food, magazine articles and television programmes centre on the creation of a 'traditional' Christmas, and part of this emphasis is on following tradition and making things for yourself and your family.[84] Crafts are seen as one way to bond the family, particularly excited children, who are encouraged to make cards and gifts and to stir the pudding as a means of instilling family values and harmony.[85] Likewise, the Christmas sweater is redolent of home-made gifts of Christmases long gone, and as it is rather jolly and somewhat embarrassing,[86] expresses the spirit of the season. One can assume therefore that there is a distance between the ideal and the real experience of Christmas, and the wearing of a snowflake sweater is at least a nod in the direction of the ideal.

The motifs and designs are obviously reminiscent of traditional patterns and garments and therefore embrace the notion of authenticity and escapism as outlined. However, the designs are not just a symbol of a nostalgic yearning, which one might conclude is rather retrogressive and impotent, nor are they signs of seasonal distinction, i.e. associated with winter or signs of Christianity, part of an iconography of Christmas. They also symbolize something far more active and contemporary – the significance of sport and leisure.

From the late 1960s onwards, the traditional snowflake sweater was transformed and emerged as an indicator of a leisured lifestyle, of wealth and status, and of active sports participation, particularly as a sign of skiing, the sport of choice for the newly affluent middle classes. Sleek synthetics that hugged the body and bore the snowflake motif were highly fashionable and increasingly practical for the serious skier. Traditional chunky and warm wool knits were the garment of choice for the après-ski set, popularized in lifestyle magazines and advertising for warming alcoholic beverages, as well as in racy films such as *Girl on a Motorcycle*,[87] in which the sexually adventurous young characters engage in both ski and après-ski activities, imbruing them with sexual potential. As skiing originated in Norway, and ski resorts started to develop throughout mountainous regions of northern Europe, it was appropriate to adopt traditional regional garments as a sign of a personal connection with a specific place and lifestyle that exemplified travel and wealth. The connection between the garment and sporting activity further popularized it as a sign of the 'great' outdoors and of healthy living. The juxtaposition of healthy pursuit and excessive consumption of 'unhealthy' and luxury products such as rich food and alcohol as promoted through a 'ski' lifestyle may appear somewhat paradoxical, yet it mirrors, and offers a return to, the lifestyles of the landed gentry in the eighteenth and nineteenth centuries, understood as the prestigious expression of leisure and pleasure.

The notion of the snowflake sweater as a biographical object enables a discussion of the object as both simultaneously symbolic and transitional, part of a process of historical and traditional reinvention, and it can therefore be viewed as a site of discourse. The sweater and its patterning evolves from the positioning of a series of geometric shapes that are associated with narratives of peoples and places which predate mass literacy, and therefore are understood as representative of a visual language, referencing stories and myths emanating from the land and the landscape. Equally, the use of indigenous fibres in the production of the garments clearly situates them amidst a specific geography. One might assume, therefore, that these objects are regionally specific, and somewhat unchanging, and as they also are subject to Romantic appraisal as 'folk' artefacts, they become part of an iconography of the past.

As a heritage object, the snowflake sweater becomes a sign of pre-industrial tradition, of national identity and a souvenir. In this respect the garment is tinged with a nostalgia for times and practices which remain in the past, nearly lost and in need of revival. Indeed, their continuation is reliant on the mythological past to maintain them in the present.

The centrality of landscape and the vernacular to the garment, in addition to its hand production, site the sweater as a leisure object. As outlined, the notion of landscape as a social construct acts as a site of leisure, whilst the woolly construct of a sweater is not seen as a formal item of attire. This means that it is a garment to be worn outdoors, a garment associated with leisure, and as such connotes a distinction from the world of work.

Traditions and heritage, are, like the objects themselves, not static, changing and mutating to meet the needs of the society from which they emerge; likewise, as patterns change to meet the ideals and desires of the contemporary consumer, so does the meaning or significance of the garment. As a fashion item, patterns change in accordance with style trends and a quest for something 'new', whilst as a souvenir, patterns and fabrics attempt to adhere to the 'authentic'. The sweater

Figure 17 A hand-knitted, traditional-style Fair Isle pullover, worn Bath, UK, 2008. Photo: Jo Turney.

therefore becomes a paradoxical object, taking meaning from its context and use. Even when the object is understood as a sign of national identity, or as a heritage item, the garment is subject to transformation and reinvention, positioned as an expression of the ideology of a nation at a given time.

The snowflake sweater has a constantly evolving history, emerging from a variety of geographical regions. In an era of postmodernity, the sign (or motif in this case) becomes subject to interpretation and reinterpretation, and as we witness the 'shrinkage of the world', local signs become gobalized, and cultures and traditions merely a storage box from which to borrow and draw inspiration.

Conclusion

The history of knitting has become a sign of heritage. Developed from Romantic sensibilities, constructs of the rural and the untainted vernacular practices of 'simple' people, existing in more simple times, knitting often is situated within stasis. This standpoint dominates many knitting texts and patterns, and although such perspectives contribute to a history of practices and objects, they also tend to approach knitting as retrogressive, backward-looking and consciously self-referential.

Examples in this chapter have aimed to demonstrate that such conceptions can be challenged and the past can be used as a springboard for innovation, development and fashion.

Heritage is now an industry of which knitting is frequently a part, creating a sense of the authentic within the inauthentic, whilst providing much-needed employment for home workers. Unfortunately, too often patterns and styles are reproduced, copied and mass-manufactured, emphasizing the questionable value of 'authenticity' in the contemporary world. The past has been pillaged and the authentic or original reduced to a sign that can be reproduced, copied and imitated. Nonetheless, traditions, styles, patterns and motifs continue to be reinvented, reused and sustained, not merely as a sign of the tourist industry or even sentiment, but as signs of progress and fashion.

Figure 18 Knitted Christmas novelties, Christmas craft market, Wokingham, UK, 1999. Photo: Jo Turney.

−3−

Twisted Yarns: Postmodern Knitting

This chapter investigates the ways in which knit, since 1970, has been transformed as a consequence of both a condition of postmodernity and as a result of post-modern theory. Postmodernism is difficult to pin down primarily because it exists, affects or is a condition of many things simultaneously. Regardless of this difficulty, it is important to establish a working definition in order to demonstrate the impact of discourses and stylistics, emanating from studies of the postmodern, on contemporary knitting. Firstly, postmodernism is a movement in the visual and material arts, and therefore can be seen as embracing, communicating and displaying certain conceptual and aesthetic qualities. Yet these qualities are neither fixed nor specific, relying largely on the viewer, spectator or audience to acknowledge and interpret the object or image before them. Therefore the cultural knowledge the viewer brings to the work in terms of its interpretation is as important, if not more so, than the person who created it. In its most prolific manifestation, postmodernism within the arts is a layering of existing cultural referents that when combined present a new way of approaching an idea, theme or subject.

Secondly, the potential to layer cultural referents or signs has become increasingly possible as the media, throughout the twentieth century, has become far more pervasive. Television in the UK, for example, is no longer restricted to four channels and viewers are now able to watch hundreds of channels for every moment of every day. Images and ideas are circulated quickly, in bite-sized chunks, enabling channel-hopping, with adverts often indistinguishable from programmes. Viewers are able to formulate their own understanding of the world through this form of cutting and pasting, and it is this aspect of culture and its appropriation that enables a condition of postmodernity. So, postmodernism is an artistic movement, but one which is heavily reliant on a technology-based society.

Thirdly, technology has not merely enabled the circulation of ideas and images, but has facilitated communication on a global scale and with these developments has established a global economy based on the circulation of knowledge (ideas or services instead of products) and the development of global brands such as Disney, McDonald's, Gap etc. Such widespread domination by a few companies has created a state commonly described as 'the shrinkage of the world', implying both an increased ease of communication and a standardization of products. This form of standardization challenges the notion of geographical and cultural difference, with logos and brand identities promoted through advertising cutting across language barriers. For example, one doesn't need to speak English to know that the golden arches 'M' of McDonald's has an association not merely with standardized burgers, but also with the American Dream. Postmodernity emerges as a condition of prolific global domination by large corporations and the resultant circulation of capital as traditional, national and regional products and differences are replaced with easily recognizable and homogeneous signs, goods and services.

Finally, postmodernism emerges at a specific historical moment, and although academics argue as to when this was, it is largely seen as a post-Second World War phenomenon, and a response to the failure of the Left to make any significant political headway and the election of right wing governments in the USA and Europe. Fundamentally, this represents a cultural shift in which there appears to be no alternative to capitalism, which is largely socially accepted and demonstrated by a swing towards a world-wide conservatism, particularly following the students' riots and political demonstrations in 1968 and the media circulation of images from Stalinist death camps.

Postmodernism is indicative of time, a particular time in history and the speed with which messages are communicated. It also emphasizes a particular economic situation in which capitalism is accepted (there is no viable alternative), enabling the powerful spread of multinational corporations globally. It also promotes the fragmentation or layering of information within daily life, privileging individual interpretation, which creates a sense of cultural capital that is manipulated and reproduced by artists, designers, filmmakers and so on.

As indicated, postmodernism is notoriously complex and theorists offer differing hypotheses regarding the ways in which it is manifest and its key components. Within visual and material culture, postmodernism aims to turn the world upside down and inside out; express and juxtapose ugliness with beauty, vitality with decay, seriousness with humour; and question and reference concepts of time, space, dimension, form, and generally accepted norms or ultimate truths. Essentially, nothing is as one expects and everything and everyone is reduced to a series of signs, reference points and symbols, which are open to interpretation; what is said is less important than how it is said, or, the medium becomes the message. This chapter cannot aim to pin down or provide an extensive critique of postmodernism, aiming merely to focus on specific elements of theory and knitted practice that can be described as postmodern. These include discussions of bricolage, intertextuality, pastiche, irony and kitsch, and themes arising from a reassessment of the medium, such as questions surrounding private/public, hand/machine, interdisciplinarity and performativity.

Modernism and Postmodernism: New Approaches and New 'Truths'

Terms such as postmodernism are notoriously difficult to define or indeed understand, largely because the word 'modern' is sandwiched between a complex prefix ('post') and suffix ('ism'). Confusion arises initially because to suggest that something is 'post' modern is to imply that it extends beyond our own time, is more than the here and now, which seems impossible outside the realms of sci-fi. Yet 'post' could imply 'after', and when combined with 'ism', the term simply means 'after modernism' – a philosophical and aesthetic movement that emerged and dominated the European avant-garde in the early twentieth century. Therefore, historically, postmodernism can be seen as a post-Second World War phenomenon or state. Indeed, this is the starting point for this chapter: to outline the differences between modernism and postmodernism and to demonstrate the ways in which postmodern theory and aesthetics have influenced aspects of contemporary knit and challenged the perceptions of the medium.

Modernism, as a creative and cultural movement, emerged largely as a response to social change in the early twentieth century. Ultimately this can be seen as the culmination and fusion of art and life, in which changing ideas, attitudes, forms and needs were redressed holistically. Design, for example, became a means of addressing and solving social problems, whilst simultaneously adhering to a philosophy that aimed to demonstrate 'truth' in objects. So, modernist design demonstrated truth in materials, emphasized function, and employed and showed new industrial techniques, creating objects that were 'honest' as their inherent properties and use value were untainted by the masking of decoration or ornament. The emphasis on use, stripped-away forms and industrial technique demonstrated an ultimate truth within objects, which left consumers or users, in theory at least, the time and space to contemplate the spiritually uplifting and perform daily tasks efficiently, without the distraction of the frivolous, decorative and useless.

If the primary aim of modernism was to seek and demonstrate ultimate truth through form, function, materials and so on, postmodernism expresses the opposite: the potential for a multiplicity of potential truths and possibilities. If modernism is linear, a progressive point which leads to the formulation of an ultimate 'truth' or grand narrative, postmodernism is fragmentary, expressing layers of meanings, which explore and challenge the expected. Modernism is deterministic; it has a set conclusion. Postmodernism has no such structure, embodying a wealth of possibility, none of which is privileged over any other.

In *Housecosy*, by the Australian artist Bronwen Sandland, the domesticity of knitting becomes manifest whilst simultaneously questioning the validity and relevance of the masculine and modernist 'white cube'. In this work, Sandland shrouds or encases a formal flat-roofed modernist house in knitted squares, making 'cosy' the rational building, turning house to home. The modernist house, a site and sign of the fusion and rationality of art and life and icon of functionalism, devoid of decoration, here is redressed. The ideals of functional and rational living are replaced with the actual functions of the home; the hidden private interior becomes public and the masculine architectural form is feminized, parodying the notion of the modernist white cube whilst celebrating the failure and impossibility of modernism. The modernist house becomes a sign of home 'making', and the modernist dream of the home being 'a machine for living in' is superseded by the realities of everyday life, economies and creative practices.

> This was an intelligent commentary on the tension in the Bauhaus ethos itself between the handcrafted and the industrially produced, a tension which remains largely unresolved. Handmade, when not done by an unpaid, usually female workforce, in the spirit of 'knit for peace' campaigns, is prohibitively expensive: an obstacle neither William Morris et al., the Omega Workshop, the Wiener Werkstätte nor the Bauhaus could overcome. It paradoxically inhabits the world of the poor and the rich, product of both necessity and luxury.[1]

In this example, class is declassified, value upturned and rituals such as tea-drinking and warming the pot with a tea cosy become exaggerated, larger than life – made spectacular, monumental and visible. Art meets craft meets design, male and female cultural forms merge, labour replaces contemplation, and form and function are violated and celebrated in equal measure. The modernist doctrine that offered design solutions to combat the problems of contemporary living, as demonstrated by Sandland, are no longer viable, and the theories and 'truths' presented have become merely signs and motifs, ideas and ideals, ripe for challenge.

Postmodernism offers a multiplicity of meanings which can be extremely liberating, an idea which has been developed throughout the post-structuralist writing of Roland Barthes, most notably in *The Death of the Author*,[2] in which he questions the authority of the author in the reading of any given text. Barthes concludes that the author alone does not give meaning to a text, but offers merely one reading of it, which is as valid as any other. There is not one ultimate meaning, but many variations. The implication of such an assertion is that 'truth' is not absolute, merely one of multiple 'truths' which exist simultaneously at any given time.

Although theorists argue about the validity of a link between Barthes's writing and postmodern thought, a connection can be made in relation to the authority of grand narratives or ultimate truths within the contemporary world. The French theorist Jean-Francois Lyotard outlined that the contemporary world was incredible and therefore nothing could be believed.[3] From this standpoint, nothing or everything was wholly credible and therefore grand narratives (ultimate truths) should be rejected or dissolved. So, ultimate truths such as the position of the monarchy, religion, family and so on could no longer be relied on; everything could and should be questioned and challenged. Lyotard's hypothesis emphasizes a move away from institutional thought, placing pressure on the individual to make personal judgements outside those of traditional authorities. This does not mean that nothing is 'true': it merely queries the potential for an unquestionable truth.

Postmodernism, therefore, can be identified to a certain extent (remembering that nothing is absolute) as embracing the death of grand narratives, enabling the circulation of free-floating truths, meanings and ideas. Such a condition offers the potential for interdisciplinarity, intertextuality, the blurring of once stable boundaries and the continual challenging of perception, belief and expectation.

In this respect, the media plays a significant role in the circulation of images, news and ideology, and as a consequence is an important feature of a postmodern society and a mainstay of postmodern culture. Indeed, the media has replaced traditional forms of power, with culture and society merging. One might suggest that society no longer produces culture, but culture determines and forms societies. This has been described by the French theorist Jean Baudrillard as 'the cinematization of society',[4] in which everyday life is played as if it were a series of narratives or scenes from a movie, and culture is the expression of the ordinary. From this perspective, we might assume that postmodernism not only challenges the 'truth', but also 'reality', obliterating the distinction between reality and fantasy.

Postmodernism offers new and disparate ways of seeing and interpreting the visual and material world. As nothing is ultimately 'true', history becomes a dressing-up box to be pillaged by artists and designers, texts become a point from which to critique other texts, and signs float freely in order to be appropriated and reappropriated, creating layers or tissues of meaning for readers to interpret.

Postmodern Knitting

On the surface, knitting is ostensibly an ordinary activity associated with the domestic sphere and on the surface has little connection with postmodernity or the postmodern. Yet, because knitting is so firmly established within popular culture through its iconology and iconography, it is an ideal genre to exploit, manipulate and challenge.

Postmodernism emphasizes the merging of the sign (object) and signified (meaning) and by association privileges the image over everything else. The sign is free-floating: open to interpretation, reinterpretation and negotiation by spectators and over time. Nothing is solid and meaning is fluid and negotiable. It also assumes that the consumer/viewer or spectator is intelligent, an accomplished semiotician, who can read or interpret signs and their meanings easily. This means that postmodernism in visual form draws reference from a variety of existing visual sources, collecting and collating them to create a 'new' visual whole, which remains open to interpretation, which has been described as bricolage.

Critical debate rages as to the meaning and intent of bricolage and that of the bricoleur (the person responsible for bricolage),[5] with investigations in cultural studies assuming the role of the bricoleur as one who transforms the meaning or significance of things through reappropriation,[6] such as a punk rocker putting a safety pin through his nose, whilst Michel de Certeau argues that it is the expression of making in everyday life,[7] as in the display of possessions in a domestic setting. Bricolage is ultimately an exercise in intertextuality: images, signs, forms, ideas are largely self-referential, drawing from a wealth of history of images and cultural references. Intertextuality is a self-conscious interplay of motifs, signs and metaphors, which refer back to the discipline or object (self-referentality), distorting the expected in new ways:

> It can mean anything that's sort of old but sort of new, a little bit ironic, or kind of self-conscious – like movies that steal bits from old movies, or photographs of the photographer.[8]

Figure 19 Sue Bradley, op art coat, *Sense of Sight*, produced for a performance at the opening of the exhibition 'Sense and Sensuality', organized by BlindArt at the Bankside Gallery, London, May 2006. Photo: Sue Bradley.

Intertextuality is exemplified in this piece of wearable art by Sue Bradley. Initially one may see the paradox of the term 'wearable art': the merging of the practical with the useless. In the garment, Bradley makes use of a variety of historical reference points, from constructivist motif to the kinetic styling of 1960s op art. In terms of colour one is confronted by a modernist palette, whilst in terms of style the garment draws influence from the Romantic frock coat and Edwardian fashion.

The garment displays evidence of aesthetic intertextuality through the intricate patterning, use of techniques and motifs, and its form. Likewise, the garment, produced for a charitable organization, Blind Art, makes obvious the predominance of sight as a means of assessing knitted objects. Yet the garment, regardless of its 'eye' motifs, is highly tactile, utilizing felted knitting as a medium to express other forms of sensory perception.

A constant, yet seemingly abstract, cycle of intertextuality, of bricolage and the mixture of signs, metaphors and media create a confusion and, indeed, a compression of space/time dynamics. In a postmodern world, which is dominated by the media and communication technologies, individuals have access to times and places from the comfort of their armchairs: one can effectively travel in time and space. From television recreations of history, to historical battle re-enactments, to talking to friends overseas by telephone or web cam, watching events thousands of miles away via the Internet and witnessing world events as they unfold on the daily news, everyone is able to involve themselves to some extent in different times and places. This form of simulation is a hyper-reality in which the image or idea has replaced the 'lived' experience and 'reality' has been replaced by a plethora of recreations or imitations.

History, once a grand narrative, has become merely a source of positions and styles to be raided and reappropriated. This is most evident in fashion, where styles are revived, mutated and juxtaposed as part of a nostalgic exercise in time travel, in a quest to create new forms and meanings. Fashion designers such as Vivienne Westwood, John Galliano and Jean-Paul Gaultier refer to the history of knitting, redeveloping it with references to historical styles and themes, the results of which express contemporary twists on styles and history. For example, Gaultier's knitted overdress (Autumn/Winter 1998–9) is reminiscent of Edwardian costume, recreating a corseted bodice formulated from a variety of stitch techniques, including traditionally lumpy cables, which create a body-hugging garment that vertically flows into a lace knit and appliqué structure at the hem. Similarly, his Aran sweater dress (Autumn/Winter 1985–6) transforms a traditional garment into a highly gendered and sexual item with the inclusion of cable-knitted breasts complete with nipples.[9] These are not merely examples of revival; to reproduce items as they had been originally would be the creation of costume and not fashion. For Gaultier, history, in terms of style and technique, becomes a source of inspiration which is subsequently manipulated and transformed into dynamic forms that challenge the stasis of the term 'tradition'. Similarly, the boundaries of what constitutes a knitted garment and its expected styling is equally challenged and distorted.

Discourses arising from postmodern theory question the role of the commodity in society. For Frederick Jameson, for example, the postmodern commodity, unlike its modernist counterpart, bears no trace of human labour, and the concept of work involved in the production process has been both concealed and lost,[10] making the value of things reliant on what they represent or communicate, rather than the labour invested in their construction. Substance, or in this instance, production, is completely superseded by surface, or hollow sign exchange through consumption. To remove the maker and means of production is to dehumanize the object; it removes the animate from the inanimate and removes the connection between makers and things.[11]

Craft objects, or objects made by hand such as knitting, are inherently connected to the maker. Each object is unique because it cannot be exactly replicated although it is repeatable; it bears witness to the imperfection of the maker's hand, carries DNA, and therefore each object is testimony to this imperfection.

Within crafts criticism, the imperfection of the maker's touch has been central to discourses that separate craft from the fine (and mechanical) arts. Indeed, it might be suggested that the predominance of the maker's hand inherent in craftwork has negated its significance from academic discourse and discussions arising from consumerism, which have tended to privilege the plastic arts as demonstrated by Baudrillard. Yet in a society so swamped with mass-manufactured goods, the handmade offers a reprise, an alternative and access to a world where technology takes the form of simple tools, and objects are understood as 'safe' and nostalgic.[12] Similarly, handmade objects are imbrued with touch and therefore offer a sense of the 'authentic' in an inauthentic world: they offer a connection to the maker through the skill and learning apparent in their construction and they demonstrate time spent in a way in which other objects cannot.[13] The handmade therefore exhibits the antithesis of Baudrillard and Jameson's definition of the postmodern commodity – it exerts and communicates labour and human relationships as well as exhibiting an element of 'truth'.

In saying this though, the handmade object is not merely an alternative to the postmodern commodity as it can – and frequently does – demonstrate aspects of postmodernism, which challenges the perception of the craft object as a stable entity. For example, hand knitting is perceived to be very homely, warm and comforting, but this is challenged in the work of Freddie Robins, whose *Knitted Homes of Crime* installation, a series of knitted houses which appear to be reminiscent of oversized yet familiar tea cosies, represent and replicate houses where murders have taken place and where each crime was perpetrated by a woman. The series challenges the dual notions of knitting and femininity in a particularly disturbing way, implying that home is not always where the heart is and that there is something sinister beyond the soft and cosy exterior.

The distortion of an accepted perception is an obvious expression of the lack of truth in a postmodern world. Similarly, perceptions of classifications and disciplines also become more fluid, extending and expanding boundaries and creating an arena for the interdisciplinary to flourish. Traditional disciplinary boundaries that delineate art, craft, design and fashion are now less stable, with disciplines crossing, fusing and borrowing from one another. It is commonplace to see hand knitting in catwalk collections, art installations, graphic design imagery and so on, with motifs, techniques and metaphors entwined in order to question the validity of expectation, hierarchy and accepted 'truths'. The ceramicist Annette Bugansky knits traditional and experimental patterns which are cast in porcelain, becoming covers for her ceramic vessels.[14] The ceramics, all of which are muted tones of white, add a surface that has depth and is tactile, whilst the porcelain appears visually translucent. For Bugansky, the coolness of the porcelain merges with the warmth of the knitted impression, which challenges the perception of sight as a

Figure 20 Annette Bugansky, selection of 'knitted' ceramics, 2007. Image reproduced with permission from the artist.

primary sense, emphasizing the tactility inherent in both textiles and ceramics. The concept of materials is redressed, and knitting takes a solid and impenetrable form through the media of ceramics.

Likewise, the adaptability of disciplines, and in particular the ways in which they can coincide in a single piece, is exemplified in German artist Rosemarie Trockel's 'knitted paintings', which emerge from a variety of techniques incorporating fine art, design and craft. Patterns are generated on a computer and then produced on a knitting machine. Drawing inspiration from easily recognizable motifs such as the Playboy Bunny, the Woolmark logo and the hammer and sickle, which are abstracted through repetition and patterning, Trockel creates pieces that challenge concepts of femininity and women's work, whilst also creating a discourse on technologies, contesting perceptions of old and new, hand and machine.[15] Here, knitting becomes both medium and message, interrogating boundaries of classification and discipline.

Regardless of such dynamic transitions, knitting is still very much understood as an expression of the traditions of the past, frequently used as a medium to metaphorically comment on the homely, women's work, the harmless, and warmth and softness. Paradoxically, these seemingly negative connotations have launched knitting into the limelight, simultaneously challenging knitting as humble and mute. For example, in fine art that uses knitting as a medium, the exhibited object/installation frequently refers back to the meanings and connotations of knitting itself. The medium is effectively driving the communication of the message. It is self-referential. Nonetheless, the referencing of knitting as a safe medium and discipline does not challenge the discipline itself, and this has been addressed by artists, designers and craftspeople investigating the relationship between old and new techniques and methods of production, which aim to challenge and extend the boundaries of practice and objects.

One way of doing this is by creating a dialogue between the handmade and the industrially produced. The interrelationship between two seemingly disparate practices firmly places knitting at the forefront of technological innovation, creating objects potentially suitable for mass manufacture as well as small-scale production. For example, Kelly Jenkins's 'knitted' tubular steel radiator *Overlooked* (2004) explores the potential in making visible activities and objects that are marginalized or 'overlooked'. By combining industrial knitting and the radiator, Jenkins creates a functional sculptural piece which draws attention to the beauty inherent in the mundane.[16] Equally, by fusing industrial design with an activity presumed to be domestic hand work, Jenkins challenges perceptions of male/female disciplines whilst challenging the perception and remits of knitting. In her work, knitting is functional, industrial, large scale, not made from wool or traditional yarn; it is not soft, and is not solely the domain of the domestic interior. Jenkins's work exemplifies an aspect of postmodern intertextuality and bricolage in which perceptions are challenged and metaphors become mixed. Jenkins

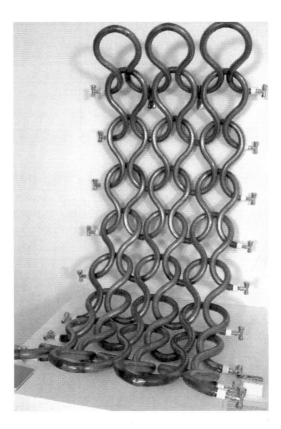

Figure 21 Kelly Jenkins, *Overlooked*, London, 2004. Photo: Dominin Tschudin. Image reproduced with permission from the artist.

extends the potential and perception of materials utilized in knitting practice, whilst other artists and designers use knitting as a form of decoration and inspiration for their work in non-yarn-based disciplines.

Technology, materials and production have been central to the innovative knitted work of Dave Cole. His performative and sculptural objects incorporate a series of metaphors that confront the perception of knitting as both noun and verb. The relationship between knitting, value, love and time extolled by artists such as Janet Morton are inverted, as Cole expresses the futility of misplaced effort. For Cole, knitting is no longer a sign of familial love and bonding; he juxtaposes toxic and disconcerting fibres (silica, Kevlar, lead) with homely objects traditionally constructed in soft and homely yarns (teddy bears, blankets, hats and scarves).[17] Here the useful becomes obviously useless, the practical becomes impractical, caring becomes harmful, and the futility of making becomes all too evident. He also challenges the predominance of hand work in the knitting process, employing industrial techniques and methods of construction, as in *Knitting Machine* (2005), which utilized two excavators, directed by Cole to knit with two 7.6m (25ft) aluminium poles and over a mile of red, white and blue acrylic felt[18] to make an enormous performative rendition of the American flag. In Dave Cole's work, knitting becomes a sign of senselessness in a senseless world, the mixture of metaphors par excellence, and an expression of the inversion of perception.

Like Cole, Arno Verhoeven utilizes new technologies and forms, but intends to convey the implicit properties of knit to unexpected objects such as furniture, stating:

> From an experimental perspective, I am interested in making use of the knitted form and technique in making solid objects that possibly contain the same symbolic and emotional value that standard knit objects carry. How would one create a knitted chair? Table? Ceramic bowl? Or even architecture? In my work, I am less interested in the form of the final object. I am more concerned with the symbolic and emotional content of the object, and how these contents are transferred and exchanged between peoples using the objects in question. To that end, can I transfer the emotional and symbolic content of the knitted garment into other objects simply by knitting them as well? My goal is to go beyond the application of knitted textile over a substructure, but to truly knit these objects themselves, making use of the traditional stitch techniques and patterns found in all commonly knitted forms.[19]

Figure 22 Arno Verhoeven, *Ceramic Shawl*, 2008. Materials: Bekaert Bekinox VN, stainless-steel thread, porcelain. Photo: Pirjo Haikola.

For Verhoeven, knit offers new structural possibilities, whilst directly referring to the inherent qualities and cultural meanings of knit. In these projects the sentimental, emotional and homely elements of the handmade and domestic are applied to industrial processes and techniques in a way that fuses the 'personal' of craft with the 'impersonal' of design.

The influence of technology and a plurality of meanings emerging from a climate in which 'truth' is a fluid and transient term means that knitting has become subject to reappraisal both within the traditional confines of its constituents as well as becoming an aspect of other disciplines. Knitting has emerged from the confines of the domestic sphere and moved into the public arena of galleries and museums; similarly, hand knitting has become a means of expressing the tactile within the anonymity of machine production. Metaphors have been mixed, materials developed and extended, and a self-conscious knowingness has been employed to create a self-referential intertextuality. Postmodernism has created an environment in which knitting can be anything or nothing and its potential is multifarious.

Sizing the Field: Knitting, Irony and the Postmodern Carnivalesque

A key feature of postmodernism is humour, and with the dissolution of grand narratives, everything and everyone is fair game. Developing from the irreverence of the world-turned-upside-down of the carnivalesque, postmodern humour is characterized by wit, irony, kitsch and pastiche, all of which are reliant on the audience's abilities as accomplished semioticians and as intelligent consumers of images, texts and signs. Jason Rutter says of postmodern comedy:

> Postmodern comedy encourages its audience not to seek a specific meaning within the performance but to look at it afresh, find new ways of seeing, and explore links between the comedy and other items. Further postmodern comedy enjoys a 'mixing up' of different stories, styles and techniques, a quotation of different sources and the integration of the real within the fictional.[20]

Rutter's explanation refers to performed comedy, but one can equally apply it to aspects of visual culture; texts, ideas, beliefs are used as sources of quotation, points of reference, layered and mixed, one upon another, to encourage new ways of approaching images and objects. Therefore humour arises as a response to the presumed, expected or anticipated; it challenges and distorts what the audience believes they 'know'. It is also disrespectful, rejecting traditional niceties and etiquette in order to make a challenging and witty statement.

Postmodern approaches to knitting address concepts of scale. This is largely a response to concepts of the 'real' world, the place of knitting within it as a 'mute' object/practice and the potential for its manipulation, but also as the articulation of the fluidity of spatiality, the distortion of perception and of the expected. In this respect, the stable and familiar is questioned, as if it were a trick of the eye, and the expected is transformed into not merely the unexpected, but presented as a series of discourses in which no one perception is dominant.

In her recent book, *Knitted Icons: Twenty-Five Celebrity Doll Patterns*, Carol Meldrum presents patterns of cultural icons of the twentieth century in knitted form. From Che Guevara and Chairman Mao to the Beatles and Madonna, Meldrum produces knitted replicas of familiar figures: iconic, with a wealth of associated imagery and cultural references that in this context become signs of irreverence and kitsch.[21] The reproduction of an iconic political figure such as Chairman Mao, or of the distant glamour and beauty of Audrey Hepburn, at a small scale and in the everyday medium of knit, could be understood as a means of bringing those on pedestals 'down to earth', whilst simultaneously and conversely reinforcing their iconic status by deeming them worthy of reconstruction.

This emphasis on irreverence, particularly in respect of size and scale and disproportionate forms of representation, refers to Mikhail Bakhtin's concept of the carnivalesque, a form of folk culture evident in the Middle Ages, which combines the shocking with elements of ridicule and humour.[22] In the carnivalesque, the world becomes distorted, turned upside down; the large becomes small and vice versa. It indicates a form of satire in which the accepted order can be lampooned or brought down to size, and the lowly elevated. Equally, it visualizes the grotesque, challenging norms of perception, disquieting the viewer and the social order. Emphasizing the body (a physical body and a body of knowledge or expectation), the carnivalesque therefore celebrates all that is low whilst making humorous political comment. In the postmodern world, humour also derives from the conception and realization of opposition, or irony. So the useful becomes useless, the male becomes female, the big becomes small, the serious becomes amusing; this can be seen as a continuation of the carnivalesque. In Lauren Porter's *Knitted Ferrari* (a detailed to-scale model knitted in red wool squares), feminine, low or unpaid hand knitting is ironically represented as masculine, potent, and a sign of leisure and luxury. Here, the industrially crafted is replaced with the handcrafted, and speed replaced with time. Ironic detail is further enhanced through the immobility of the knitted object, inverting the notion of a red sports car as a 'penis extension', rendering it impotent. Similarly, the knitted Ferrari is a pastiche: it looks like the 'real' thing, it is the same size and the same colour, but it is not the genuine article. It requires a second look; the mighty is brought down to size, machinery becomes handmade, 'engineering' is reproduced by amateurs, and as such valorization is questioned, power removed and balance restored in an inverse and ironic manner.

Likewise, the current vogue for knitted food, popularized by Rachael Matthews,[23] is an example of the social commentary at the heart of the humorous surface. Knitted doughnuts, burgers, fries and milkshakes are not fattening, they

Figure 23 Lauren Porter, *Knitted Ferrari*, Bath School of Art and Design degree show, 2006. Photo: Jo Turney.

Figure 24 Knitted burger, maker unknown, 2007. Photo: Jo Turney.

merely replicate their demonized counterparts. They cannot be eaten and are ultimately useless, and it is this uselessness, the treat-less treat, that makes them
amusing. Serious social concerns surrounding the overconsumption of junk food
by children in the West, as well as the global domination of branded fast-food
retailers and the concomitant creation of a monoculture is also evidenced in
knitted 'edibles', which whilst questioning the problem of McDonald's, Burger
King and the like simultaneously reinforces the brand and products within the
minds of consumers, particularly as knitted food is promoted on eBay as suitable
a plaything for children. One can, it seems, have one's cake and 'eat' it.

Although the postmodern carnivalesque creates a chaotic state in which irony
and pastiche question the status quo, it also references the body, making public that
which would be hidden, exaggerating form in terms of size and scale. Just as the
medieval carnivalesque celebrated life, death and the baseness of bodily functions,
the postmodern carnivalesque focuses on the body as a surface, a site of inscription, and also as a non-stable entity – abject, penetrative, weak and in a state of
flux.

In Sonia Rykiel's Autumn/Winter 2007–8 collection, vast, chunky knitted coats
dominated the catwalk, with knit swathed and draped around the body, distorting
what lay beneath. Garments were finished with huge knitted pussy-bows, presenting models as gifts waiting to be unwrapped. The animate has been made inanimate and the body commodified through a woolly casing which begs possession;
it is concealed yet anticipating and inviting the surprise of the reveal, which only
another can do. 'Take this off', suggest the garments, further eroticizing the body,
as in the promise of striptease, whilst simultaneously demonstrating 'Tie me up' –
the exemplification of sexual domination and submissiveness. In a postmodern
world, where surface is everything, the concept of clothing as merely an attractive
wrapping is not without significance. In Rykiel's garments, we can never be sure
of what lies beneath them, what the unwrapped may reveal. The surprise may be
horrific or disappointing. Yet the covering is seductive, the bows inviting, the knit
so draped and vast that one might get lost in the act of unwrapping.[24] These actions
appear without consequence as desire for and possession of the object engage the
participant in acts of acquisition and commodity fetishism.

Rykiel's collection expresses the significance placed on clothing in the contemporary world to conceal the frailties of the flesh, to create a 'false' impression of
the body beneath. In this example a perception is monumentalized; an insecurity
is verbalized and lampooned. However, in the work of Janet Morton, hidden or
mute objects are made visible. Inspired by the trans-Canada highway, which is
marked by jumbo iconic structures that are more of a landmark than a sculpture,
Morton embarked on a series of works that referred to the combined themes
of monumentality and Canadian folk art Morton's investigation commenced
with an appraisal of what was perceived to be monumental in Canadian culture.
Centralizing on the significance of the proletariat, a work ethic and issues

Figure 25 Sonia Rykiel, Paris Fashion Week, Autumn/Winter 2007. Photo: Michelle Leung, WireImage, 75872330 (RM) Getty Images.

surrounding labour, she explored methods for expressing such ethereal concepts in physical form. Wanting the work to contrast with the monumentality of public sculpture, she returned to non-institutional understandings of art that fused both love and work, settling on knitting. She made one huge work-sock, which reflected a cultural appreciation of a work ethic, whilst representing a familiar and familial item of a labourer's clothing.

The metaphors inherent in the construction process (mundane, women, domestic) lingered with Morton, and the huge knitted sock attempted to recreate these humble activities in epic proportions, making the ordinary and hidden visible and heroic. Equally, the knitting of such an item questions the value of time spent in labour, questioning the adage that 'Time is money', for traditionally such garments would have been produced as a thrifty, domestic necessity, and therefore in

Figure 26 Janet Morton, *Memorial*, 1992. Installed at Queen's Park, Toronto, Canada, 1992. Reproduced with permission from the artist.

the sock, time is ultimately without financial reward. To challenge popular perception in relation to value being solely about financial worth, Morton aimed to demonstrate what she calls 'the insanity of contemporary systems of valorization',[25] monumentalizing an ordinary object through both scale and perception and elevating it to the status of 'art'. Art demands contemplation; it challenges and stimulates the spectator cerebrally. Yet here Morton has reproduced the familiar, the non-challenging, and as such ironically poses the question 'What is art?'

One sock is ultimately useless, and one of such magnitude defies function and as such could be classified as art merely by its uselessness. Similarly, the idea of knitting as a useful occupation married to an item that is ineffective in relation to actual function questions the usefulness of art per se. This concept was further expressed in the sock's display: positioned draped over monumental pieces of

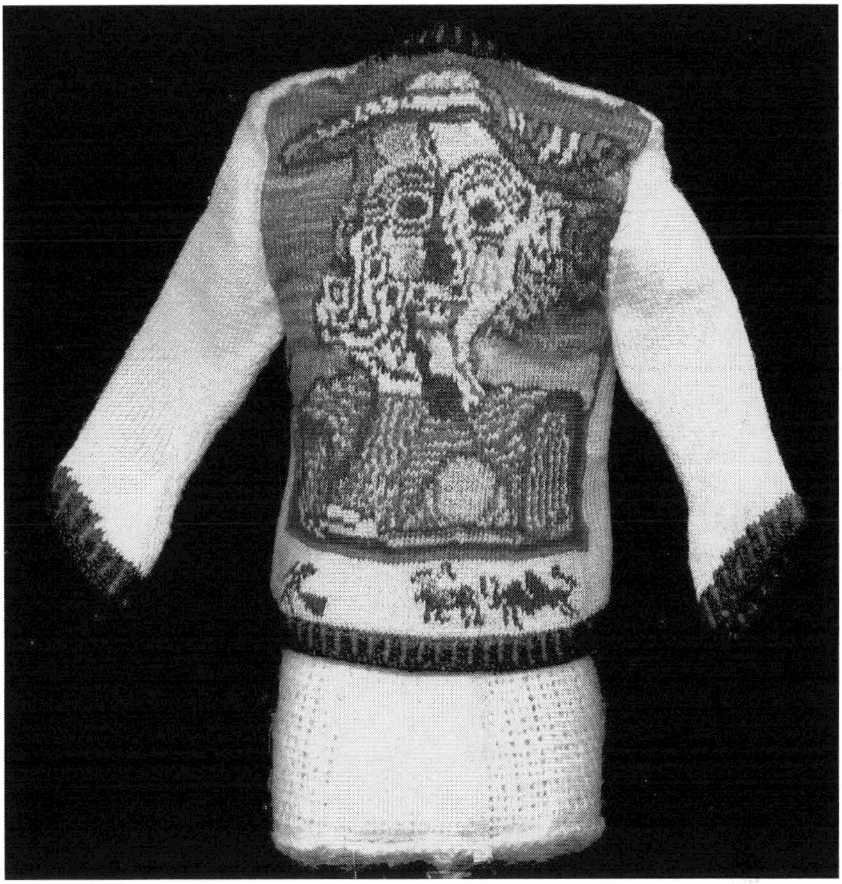

Figure 27 Althea Crome (Merback), *Picasso Sweater*, 2007, Bloomington, Indiana, USA. Reproduced with permission of the artist.

public sculpture, including a statue of Queen Victoria, which linked the work of the people with colonial rule and the power of institutions. The sock therefore becomes a sign of the fusion of high and low culture, the questioning sociocultural values and ways of seeing, and the turning upside down of perceptions.[26]

If the huge or the gigantic exudes the potential for the silent to gain a voice and the overlooked to be made visible and monumentalized, its converse, the miniature, can be seen as a means of deflating the elevated, of 'bringing down to size', and of controlling the otherwise uncontrollable.

The miniature has associations with childhood, but also with the role of fantasy in the imagination. Gaston Bachelard, for example, suggests that everything appears smaller in the imagination, and as such offers a means of condensing and encapsulating the 'bigger' picture.[27] Similarly, Susan Stewart describes the miniature as a means of containment that avoids contamination,[28] which suggests that the shrinkage of things keeps them close and out of harm's way, as in Althea Merback's (now Althea Crome) knitted miniature clothing, i.e. the Bugknits collection, a range capable of clothing a caterpillar. Each garment is functioning: it can be fastened with buttons, and even has a label sewn into it.[29] The tiny, yet perfect, scale of Merback's garments make the spectator into Gulliver, giant and protective, focusing on the intricacies of the design and technique. Here the world is controlled, yet wondered at. We are compelled to witness the wanderings of the imagination and recreate it in microcosm.

The fusion of big and small, and the homely and depraved, is demonstrated in this Bill Gibb knitted ensemble, which consists of skin-hugging patchwork leggings and an oversized, sprawling jumper, which barely touches the torso it covers. In this example, the concerns of fashion are addressed as the juxtaposition of

Figure 28 Bill Gibb, knitted patchwork ensemble, early 1980s. Fashion Museum, Bath. Photo: Brenda Norrish, FashImage. Courtesy of Bath and North East Somerset Council.

clothing's potential to both reveal and conceal the body. The tight leggings contour the lower part of the body, whilst the oversized sweater creates a sense of distortion in the torso. Distorting and drawing attention to the body's form through a garment constructed of knitted squares is reminiscent of a fragmented and damaged body that has been reconstructed. With the skill of the surgeon's knife, the broken or sick body can be penetrated, investigated, and the inside accessed, made whole; on completion, the flesh is sewn together, closing the boundary between the inside and outside.

> When the biology of the body breaks down, the skin has to be cut so as to give access to the inside, later it has to be sewn like fabric. The inside has the same importance as the outer shell.[30]

The use of patchwork references the carnivalesque and the grotesque, turning conceptions of clothing as a sleek, impenetrable second skin into the representation of the segmented, fractured and fetishized body: a series of locations and joins with erotic potential. Patchwork here is also reminiscent of armour and the hard body, the formation of a barrier that is solid and impervious, concealing the fleshiness beneath.

> If patchwork could be regarded as a felicitous metaphor for the operations of fashion and its combination of games, dress in general, through its literal manipulation of materials, may be seen to dramatize the interplay of smooth and striated spaces, of movement, change and flux, on the one hand, and system, pattern and stasis on the other.[31]

Within the carnivalesque, the body is a metaphor for heaven and earth, of high and low, of life and death, with the torso upwards indicative of the heavenly, and below this the earthiness or baseness of death, bodily functions and so on. In the Bill Gibb ensemble, the eye is drawn both simultaneously up and down, to witness a body that is sewn together, made disparate yet whole, through a series of joins, selvedges and stitching. The ensemble therefore can be seen to encapsulate the moral and immoral, the revealed and concealed body, its skin and its ruptures. It creates an ambiguity, the correlation of the social and interior self. As Elizabeth Wilson comments:

> If the body with its open orifices is itself dangerously ambiguous, then dress, which is an extension of the body yet not quite part of it, not only links that body to the social world, but also more clearly separates the two. Dress is the frontier between the self and the not-self.[32]

The perception of size and scale within postmodern iconography becomes a praxis at which wider social and cultural issues can be redressed and discussed.

The gigantic can offer a means of celebrating or of monumentalizing issues, techniques and objects which otherwise would be marginalized or mute; the miniature offers the potential to contain and control that which is otherwise overwhelming. Postmodern humour derives from repetitive juxtaposition and inversion: the copy, the fake and the opposition. References to the carnivalesque and the grotesque further heighten the potential for sociocultural subversion in which accepted norms are subject to investigation and things are either 'blown out of all proportion', or 'brought down to size'.

Knitting and Anarchy: DIY Culture and Punk Knits

When the Sex Pistols screeched 'No future' in 1976, it was not merely a hollow battle cry towards anarchy, but a comment on the socio-economic condition of UK youths in the mid-1970s. Unemployment was at a record high, and young people with few or no qualifications had limited employment prospects. The future was indeed bleak, and an alternative to the glaring prospect of a life on the dole was social change. For punks, this was complete anarchy, a complete overhaul of the social order, and although impossible, the sentiment manifested itself – as it had done so ably in earlier youth cultures – through dress, attitude and social approach.

The creation of a punk aesthetic is largely attributable to Vivienne Westwood and Malcolm McLaren. Influenced by 1950s design and youth cultures, Westwood started to knit mohair jumpers in the early 1970s,[33] which became a major part of her Autumn/Winter 1977–78 collection[34] and a mainstay in the wardrobes of punk rockers.[35] The properties and cultural attributes of knit became central to Westwood's conception of punk, offering the potential for manipulation, deconstruction and the challenging of social boundaries. In particular, the loosely constructed string jumper, knitted on very large needles, embraced the chaotic ethos of punk, and overturned concepts about knitwear in terms of structure, neatness and warmth. It also referred to working-class garments such as the string vest,[36] and offered consumers access to the DIY ethos of punk with the opportunity to make a simple garment, inexpensively, regardless of skill level. Indeed, the string jumper started a minor trend for knitting amongst 1970s youth, demonstrating new forms of the dissemination of fashion outside the fashion system.

The combination of attitude and dress established a style with surprising longevity, which was to be hijacked and reappropriated by the myriad of youth cultures that superseded punk and proved inspirational for future designers. In an interview in 2006, Malcolm McLaren stated that punk 'makes ugliness beautiful',[37] and this sentiment predominates the legacy of original punk.

In Alexander McQueen's distressed knitted garments from his Autumn/Winter 2001–02 collection,[38] he playfully mixed metaphors and reappropriated signs and motifs which encapsulated a play on words, techniques and imagery. Emerging from the dual themes of the sinister and the gothic, McQueen's knitted garments evoked the inner turmoil of the mind through the perception and expectation of the themes and techniques. For example, knitted dresses were unravelled and dishevelled, juxtaposing the manifestation of the gothic mind with the inherent properties of knit (it can be unravelled), whilst Romantic motifs such as the skull and crossbones evoked eighteenth-century piracy, pillaging and notions of the outsider. This was fashion as decay, the imperfect and the troubled: the antithesis of beauty, perfection and glamour, emphasizing the converse of an understanding of the world of fashion per se.[39] For McQueen, garments became an expression of the past in the present, of the internal and the external, mixing metaphors to create an intertextual bricolage that is both conceptually challenging and anarchic.

The concept of punk knitting essentially embraces a challenge to the norm, a questioning of the accepted and a desire to upturn the expected or anticipated. These ideas can be understood when knitting is both a noun and a verb, or object and activity. As previously outlined, knitted objects and garments can challenge the perception of what constitutes such items, but practice can equally be challenged.

As an activity, knitting is frequently understood as an activity that involves one person. This definition is developed within a popular mythology as a practice undertaken in private within the confines of the home, assuming it to be a solitary and exclusive pastime. In recent years knitting has become more visible, more inclusive and performative. For example, a series of stories about wool and knitting, entitled 'Hat', set to music and performed by the BBC Radio 3 presenter Ian McMillan, encourage audience participation – which enhances and contributes to the piece.[40] The noise and rhythm of an audience of knitters creates a variation in each performance whilst challenging the notion of knitting as solitary and isolating. These performances, including an appearance at 'Craft Rocks' at the V&A, capture a moment in time and the experience of being there, and although performances continue, it can never be exactly replicated.

Equally performative, inclusive and anarchic, the recent deconstructive sculptural work of Celia Pym questions knitting as a progressive activity. In a recent performance held in her London studio, Pym hung a series of vast machine-knitted lengths of fabric from the ceiling, inviting guests to unravel them. Initially timid, guests tentatively started to undo the knitted pieces. Gaining in confidence, participants became more adventurous, and possibly spurred on by the engagement in obvious and wilful destruction, secured lengths of yarn to the nearby lift, and watched the pieces deconstruct as the lift went up and down. Within a matter of minutes, knitting created through hours of work was reduced to piles of yarn spooled on the floor, bearing the imprint or memory of its making. Knitting became unknitted, construction became deconstructed and the progressive journey of knitting was transformed by its anarchic converse.[41]

Challenges to acceptability and location dominate the performative work of the Houston-based group, Knitta, who reclaim public spaces with knitted graffiti.

Figure 29 Celia Pym, *Caroline Unravels*, London, May 2007. Photo: Celia Pym. Image reproduced with permission from the artist.

Drawing references from male-dominated hip-hop culture and their practice of 'reclaiming the streets' through graffiti, the 'anonymous' artists, who give themselves witty, knit-based pseudonyms in a similar manner to rap stars (i.e. SonOfaStitch, P-Knitty and so on) 'tag' streets, buildings and private property with hand-knitted cosies or wrappers (rappers), which demonstrate plays on words indicative of a postmodern double-coding. The group's activities are largely undertaken during the hours of darkness, using knitted cosies complete with buttons for ease and speed of attachment to objects, suggesting a guerrilla approach to knitting. Bridges, fire hydrants, car aerials, lamp-posts, street signs and the Great Wall of China have been targeted by Knitta, the results of which have been recorded photographically and circulated via the web and MySpace video, aping the underground activities of graffiti artists. The secretive and subversive (and illegal) act of leaving one's mark, albeit in an impermanent and humorous manner, imbrues knitting with an edginess and urban quality that challenges both medium and message. The group states: 'We go beyond simply wanting attention. We prove that disobedience can be beautiful and that knitting can be outlaw',[42] creating a scenario in which the masculine urban space is vandalized, transformed and reappropriated by a feminine touch or tag, which eventually, over time, becomes part of the urban landscape.

Guerrilla knitting embraces two aspects of spatial dynamics in which knitting becomes a public activity, either through participation or evidence of a public outside the remits and influences of traditional art institutions. In both cases, knitting embodies the spontaneous, the unexpected, and offers a touch of chaos or anarchy in a rather regimented world.

Deriving from the aforementioned guerrilla tactics, knitting has been seen in recent years as a form of subversion and socio-political commentary through craftivism and DIY culture. DIY culture draws directly from a punk aesthetic and attitude as it aims to transform the ordinary into the original and extraordinary by reusing and 'repurposing' or customizing existing clothing, thrift shop finds and everyday waste materials into wearable and unique garments. Websites such as Knitty.com and magazines such as *Readymade* offer advice and ideas to crafters who want to make their own clothes as an alternative to the mass-produced goods offered in the High Street. Reusing yarn or redeveloping sweaters adds a personal touch and can be quite a simple process, and as vintage fashion becomes part of wardrobe mainstays, the opportunity to reappropriate discarded items becomes more appealing to the populace.

CASE STUDY. Celebrity Knitting

> Knitting is back in fashion, with Julia Roberts and Cameron Diaz, whiling away hours on their film sets knitting jumpers and scarves. Without anyone to show you it can be difficult to learn, but a short course will help budding fashion designers produce their own original creation.[43]

The above quote is indicative of the threefold concerns arising from the relationship between knitting and postmodernity: celebrity, fashion design and originality. Each of these aspects contributes to a sense of difference, of distinction and of the otherworldly, which can be created within everyday life. Through knitting, as the quote suggests, anyone, with some help, can emulate the lifestyles of the rich and famous. Anyone can be a fashion designer, and anyone can make something distinct and out of the ordinary. This case study investigates why these factors are subject to such desirability, stimulating a popular knitting revival as well as outlining the ways in which they can be understood as indicative of a postmodern society.

The case study is concerned with the concept and significance of celebrity and why it is predominant within contemporary culture. It addresses the influence of celebrity on setting trends in knitwear and knitting revivals, whilst uncovering how and why 'named' knitwear designers have become predominant in the home knitting market throughout the period of study.

A postmodern society has been described by Jean Baudrillard as 'cinematized'. This essentially means that our reality is mediated and presented like its cinema equivalent: we construct our own life narratives, experiences and lifestyles through the consumption of media images and expectations as well as through consumer goods, which the media equally promote as 'life enhancing' in one way or another. Effectively we are all players or performers, directors, writers and producers in our own life script, and consequently we judge and compare our successes and those of others by their cinematic counterparts. We therefore live life through the media, but also seek to recreate it to some extent. Indeed, it has been reported that Londoners are captured 300 times per day on CCTV cameras, and therefore society is becoming increasingly literally cinematized, as ordinary people are captured on film as they go about their daily lives.

As communities become dissipated, and the community spirit inherent in traditional neighbourhoods is in decline, people are keen to establish friendship/gossip relationships with those perceived as social equals or betters.[44] These are 'ready-made friends', constructed and perpetuated by the media and offer the potential to have 'distant' yet intimate relationships; celebrities 'tell all' in gossip magazines, allowing readers access to their innermost thoughts, homes and lifestyles, which encourage a sense of 'knowing'.

This construction of celebrity gossip acts as a means of making and maintaining relationships within social spheres, not just giving people something to talk about, but also establishing a group of fantasy friends who can freely be discussed without fear of recourse.[45] Equally, because celebrity lifestyle details are reported in magazines, on television and the Internet, readers/viewers are able to follow and engage in the minutiae of their day-to-day lives in a way which is increasingly difficult with 'real' people. Readers are encouraged to feel as if they 'know' celebrities, because their reported successes and failures, diets and style are shared with the public, and through consumer choice, their lifestyles can be emulated and recreated.[46] The celebrity therefore is objectified, and to a certain extent fetishized, reduced to a series of constructed pieces that are reconstructed and extended as the media bricolage increases.

Postmodernism has been said to have eroded grand narratives, ultimate truths, which has left society without a system of unquestionable belief that potentially guides and directs life. Without an organized system of 'truths', social role models have changed, and traditional models such as family, religion, monarchy and class have been replaced with a more fluid series of social idols, who encompass a group that can be loosely called 'celebrity'. Such a position is ambiguous, as Chris Rojek suggests in his definition of the term: a combination of public fame and swift fall, highlighting the precarious position such a title conveys.[47] Celebrity, therefore, is about time and not longevity – the process of modernity and the role of the market in its quest for newness and the 'next best thing'. Celebrity is therefore a commodity, bought and sold, disappearing and replaced as time moves on.

As a commodity, celebrity is a constructed sociocultural ideal; the person presented publicly is a representation rather than the actual or 'authentic' private self, and as such is really a two-dimensional image rather than an animate individual. This is not to say that celebrities are without frailties, and these too are presented publicly as a means of expressing a 'human' connection with the spectator. So, when stories about celebrities' drug habits, romantic failures and so on are reported, they effectively draw the celebrities closer to their public – they are less distant, forgivable, like the reader, but with more money, glamour, better clothes, bodies and so on. This is the paradox of celebrity: celebrities are distant from the public whilst also being just like them, blurring the boundaries between fantasy and reality. Those imbued with the title are constructed, elevated and promoted by the media and consumed by an audience hungry for 'ideal' beings whose lifestyles are a site of emulation or celebrification.[48]

Figure 30 Elvis tea cosy, maker unknown, 2007. Photo: Jo Turney.

The significance of the celebrity in relation to knitting may not be initially apparent; what do a domestic hobby and a glamorous lifestyle worthy of celebration and emulation have in common? Initially, one can start with product placement. The lending of a celebrity name to a brand or item can increase its desirability and therefore its popularity; add the magic of celebrity to a product and it becomes imbrued with the aura of that celebrity. In the 1970s, knitting patterns often featured well-known television personalities – such as Leonard Rossiter, Jimmy Saville, the cast of *Are You Being Served* – but these tended to be as an aspect of the actors' charity work, with advertisements and patterns acting as a means of fundraising rather than as a sign of glamour. Indeed, these early forms of celebrity knitting endorsement matched comedians, comedy actors and/or 'homely' stars with what tended to be novelty knits, heightening the amusing elements of the patterns and, indeed, knitting. In these instances, knitting remains homely, very much part of the real world, distanced from the realms of celebrity and fantasy.

In Richard Dyer's seminal book, *Stars*, he notes that celebrities should be interpreted as semiotic texts to be read,[49] encouraging the reader to establish narratives around a given persona, which juxtapose and blur distinctions between the real and the cinematic person.[50] From such a standpoint the ways in which a celebrity is presented and represented creates a mediated sense of self, emphasized by behaviour, demeanour and dress. For example, in the 1970s, the disc jockey-turned-children's television presenter Noel Edmonds became synonymous with the novelty sweater, wearing brightly coloured and patterned knits that demonstrated his sense of fun through clothing appropriate for his young audience. Edmonds, a Radio 1 DJ, hosted *Multi-Coloured Swap Shop* (1976–82), transforming himself from a trendy man about town into a kindly but prankster uncle through his sweater-wearing. This comfortable clothing presented Edmonds with a homeliness and aura of safety, which also enabled him to pursue televisual mischief as demonstrated on his Saturday evening programme *The Late, Late Breakfast Show*.

Edmonds became an icon of British television during the late 1970s and 1980s, and became so associated with jumpers that his style was emulated by fathers and older men, nationally.[51] The relaxed novelty jumper became an indicator of cosiness, and a perennial favourite with television personalities in Britain during this period. In particular, breakfast television presenters such as Frank Bough and the astrologer, Russell Grant, were keen novelty sweater-wearers, emphasizing their 'at home-ness' with the daily viewing public. Such garments became a sign of not merely casualness, but of a laid-back or fun personality, and presenters were portrayed as 'friends' rather than the voice of the daily news. Drawing from the sartorial tastes of earlier television favourites such as Val Doonican, the novelty jumper became a sign of the non-threatening and of light entertainment. Similarly, US television stars such as Bill Cosby became infamous for his jazzy sweaters as embodied by his character Dr Huxtable on *The Cosby Show*.

To return to Dyer's hypothesis that stars are to be read as texts, it is possible to suggest that by deliberately wearing clothing as an indicator of one's sense of humour and fun-loving sensibilities, such signs might well be read conversely, as a need to proclaim oneself as amusing, rather than actually displaying those characteristics in person. The novelty of the novelty sweater wore off and to a certain extent backfired, rendering the wearer rather awkward and out of place, trying too hard to promote himself as 'fun'. Similarly, the relationship between the novelty sweater and its 'as seen on TV' persona quickly became associated with the anodyne and boring, removed from the remits of good taste and fashion, and as such symbolized an out-of-step and out-of-time mediocrity.

In the 1980s, however, this approach developed, with celebrities featuring in knitting patterns as an extension and expression of their on-screen characters, as well as being a means of promoting yarns and specific lifestyles. For example, the soap opera *Eastenders* produced a knitting pattern book in order for the home replication of garments potentially worn by Walford's major characters – Angie and Sharon Watts, Dot Cotton, Simon Wicks, etc., who were pictured in their fictional Albert Square environment. In examples such as this, fiction and reality became fused; the public personas of on-screen characters and the opportunity to dress like soap opera characters merged. Interestingly, as *Eastenders* was, and remains, a television drama about 'ordinary' Londoners who seemed to buy the majority of their clothing from the local market or 'up West' for special occasions, it was never really about setting fashion trends, so the production of a pattern book inspired by the everyday character's clothing had little to do with escapism or glamour, but was more to do with personal identification with a specific character. At this time, *Eastenders* was broadcast on BBC1 three times a week, with two half-hour episodes and an hour-long omnibus edition. Audience figures were large, the show was extremely popular, and the characters entered the homes of the British public possibly more frequently than anyone else. They were like 'family' (which also was the focus of the show). Knitting an *Eastenders* jumper could, therefore, be seen as knitting for a sibling or other relative.

During this time knitwear was the height of fashion, with both hand and machine knits featuring heavily in designer collections. Indeed, knit was at its most exciting during this period as styles, shapes, colours and patterns were developed to suit new consumer tastes. By the mid-1980s, knitwear designers were household names, publishing books of knitting patterns and selling kits to make up at home.[52] Indeed, the trend to knit 'designer' patterns at home was a response to new trends in leisure, which focused on home-centred activities.

In his study of British leisure in the 1980s, Ken Roberts identified four key leisure trends which had developed as a response to sociocultural and economic conditions of the period: home-centeredness, out-of-home recreation, connoisseur leisure and the threat of the mob.[53] Primarily, the move towards leisure spent at home resulted from a dissipation of local communities and the predominance of a nuclear rather than extended family. This seeming isolation within the home distanced its inhabitants from their environment, which became more attractive through a rise in connoisseur leisure, a factor defined through engagement in specialist and/or luxury activities such as the consumption of fine foods and wines. Finally, the fear of the mob can be described as a social anxiety revolving around large group activities that may incur violence, crime or involve others 'who are not like us'. In relation to the rise of home knitting and specifically the construction of designer-branded patterns, Roberts's analysis is demonstrative of home-centredness, connoisseur leisure and fear of the mob, in which knitting activity is largely practised within the confines of one's home, involving a specific knowledge of fashion and fashion design, and a quest for the 'unique' which sets us apart from the mob. Such a hypothesis promotes a sense of individualism and isolation, which deliberately attempts to distance the self from others whilst emulating concepts of a leisure society defined in the previous century.

Knitting therefore becomes a sign of difference, of standing out from – rather than being part of – the crowd. It acknowledges wider cultural concerns such as fashion, and as such creates a sense of intelligence or knowing within the consumer and practitioner. This distance can be described as an escape from the mundane: a challenge, through both skill and knowledge, to make (or knit) a personal statement which is special. Leisure marks lifestyles; it is an indicator of personal wealth (as leisure must be paid for) and of aspirations. To knit a designer sweater connotes personal investment in that designer or brand, as well as the ideology or 'personality' such a designer or brand affords. The ordinary (knitting) becomes extraordinary.

Conversely, since 2004, celebrities have been actively engaged in knitting as a pastime. In particular, knitting has become a favourite hobby of glamorous female celebrities such as Madonna, Sarah Jessica Parker, Julia Roberts and Cameron Diaz. The ambiguity arising from the engagement of celebrities in such ordinary and domestic pastimes can be understood as an aspect of postmodernism and postfeminism, in which 'have it all' women are able to do what they want and perhaps equally want to culturally 'downshift'[54] or to calm the pace of life.[55] One might also suggest that this is a celebrity lifestyle choice, which can be imitated by anyone, and as such makes the celebrity appear more down to earth or 'normal'.

Within celebrity culture, the expression of the celebrity self as a 'normal' person is a significant factor in celebrities' popularity and emulation. Celebrities have to be like their public, but distanced from them; they have to be able to identify with them and want to imitate certain aspects of their character and lifestyle. This is a process of identification and objectification. But ultimately, the public, their public, wants to see them engaging in activities that they too engage in. For example, the most popular features of celebrity lifestyle magazines are the candid photographs of female celebrities baring their cellulite, without make-up, popping to the corner shop in their slippers and so on, as are 'human interest' or 'tell all'

Figure 31 Model knitting, Olympus Fashion Week, spring 2005, day four. Photo: Scott Wintrow, Getty Images Entertainment, 51290517 (RM) Getty Images.

exposés. This is not merely a sign of *schadenfreude*, although there may be some elements of this, but more of a performance of the everyday, heightening identification, empathy and the animate qualities of the celebrity. It reaffirms that celebrities are 'just like us', and that they too have to eat, run out of milk, and suffer. This performance of the everyday by those whom are seemingly distanced from it has been described as a quest for a new form of authenticity.[56] The creation (because it is staged) of this perceived authenticity offers the viewer/reader an insight into the 'private' (albeit captured on camera) life of the celebrity, creating an intimacy between the viewer and the viewed. This relationship is voyeuristic: the off-guard photograph, usually unflattering and ordinary, removes the trappings of glamour from the celebrity and captures her in a vulnerable, almost naked, position. The viewer has seen something that perhaps she shouldn't have; she has glimpsed beyond the red carpet and therefore believes she has witnessed something secret.[57]

This rather paradoxical and fluid relationship between the ordinary and the extraordinary, endemic in contemporary celebrity culture, is the crux of Wendy Parkins's appraisal of the recent trend for knitting as a celebrity hobby.[58] Parkins concludes that knitting, for the celebrity, offers a connection with the ordinary, whilst simultaneously offering an escape from busy lives into another slower mythological construct.[59] Knitting, in recent years, has become linked to a slower or more traditional way of life,[60] and although this might be described as a return to some construct of domesticity, the act of knitting is distinct from other forms of consumption. Knitting takes time: making something is a considered and lengthy process, as is learning to knit beyond plain and purl stitches. Therefore, knitting something is distinct from buying something; knitting is an investment not merely of cash, but of time.

In a society that is cash-rich and time-poor, it seems like madness to knit something, particularly when it is possible to buy good-quality knitted goods. What knitting offers is 'time out', an alternative to mass consumerism and a means of slowing down the pace of life and absorbing oneself in a tactile occupation, connecting the self with the object under construction.

This contradictory shift from one unreality to another is a facet of postmodernism in which the ordinary and the extraordinary become blurred, and glamour and lifestyle become available to all regardless of budget. Everyone can be like media icons, and they too can be 'normal', and the distance between the sign and the signified merges.[61]

The relationship between celebrity and knitting can be seen as a paradox in which the extraordinary meets the ordinary and vice versa. Here, culture and society become indistinguishable and the everyday becomes an opportunity for escape. The desire for celebrity lifestyles and the opportunity to emulate their pastimes has certainly been instrumental in the re-exploration of knitting by the young. One might also suggest that the insistence of the media in promoting knitting and glamour through the focus on glamorous stars who knit, rather than headlining the unglamorous, is also responsible. If one knits like Cameron Diaz, does one become associated with her; does the magic rub off?

Hand knitting and the role of the celebrity or 'named' person in creating leisure lifestyles during the period firmly moved knitting into the world of trends, fashion and consumerism. Patterns were now imbued with a sense of dynamism previously unseen, and access to learning to knit no longer seemed to require the dull following of specific patterns. Anyone and everyone could knit, design their own patterns, be a 'fashion' designer, and stand out from the crowd. Of course, such an assumption is problematic; knitting, specifically garments that can actually be worn, is an extremely difficult and skilled endeavour, and although manufacturers promote kits in which you can 'make a sweater in a day', there is no evidence to prove that this is either possible or desirable. One might suggest that this exemplifies the deskilling of knitting, the professionalizing of the amateur and, by association, the demystifying of design, which heralds the death of the designer, an extension of Roland Barthes's *The Death of the Author*.[62] Making has become commodified, and designers branded and reduced to signs.

Conclusion

Postmodernism can be seen as the expression of the fragmentary; the free floating of signs and a multiplicity of meanings circulating simultaneously, which are open to continuous negotiation. When nothing is 'true', everything can be. Time and space become compressed; beliefs and traditions are subject to renegotiation, and objects, people, places are reduced to recognizable signs. The constructed becomes reconstructed and deconstructed, and meanings become fluid and transitory.

A concentration on inverting perceptions makes disciplines such as knitting, which appear to have a stable sociocultural meaning, fair game for interpretation and reconsideration. Knitting is no longer solely the domain of the elderly or infirm, nor the remit of domesticity and femininity. Knitting need not be woolly, undertaken by hand, or even made or knitted. It need not be traditional or old-fashioned, nor exist in the 'real' world as a physical entity, as with virtual knitting. Yet frequently these characteristics, these sociocultural norms, come to the fore as a starting point, a position to challenge or subvert; but the cyclical, non-narrative formation of postmodernism and its reliance on the surface ultimately re-establish these perceptions. What we are offered is a potential for change: knitting as valued, edgy, different and new in relation to construction and form. Yet what we are left with, after a temporary lapse, is a cultural stasis, a self-referentiality, a state in which nothing has really changed.

—4—

Unravelling the Surface: Unhomely Knitting

In this chapter, knitting is investigated as an extension of the psyche, as a bridge between the physical and the psychological, or as an example of the distance or barrier between the inside and the outside, a marked boundary.

Much of this book has addressed the ways in which knitting can be understood as 'homely', as a comforting series of objects and activities emit a sense of calm, safety and security. Yet this is not the only way in which knitting can be understood or indeed exploited. Knitting may not, for example, be enjoyed, the tactile qualities of knitted garments may be disliked or reviled, or knitting may conjure memories of unpleasantness or even horrific life experiences. This is a rather general starting point for this chapter, but nonetheless it is important to address the ways in which seemingly innocuous items and activities can investigate and instigate darker emotional responses, as well as address issues surrounding the body, flesh and its functions.

This chapter aims to analyse knitting from a psychoanalytical perspective and draws from the work of Freud, Lacan and Kristeva as a means of discussing knitting as an extension of the body and mind.

Psychoanalysis and Knitting: What Lies Beneath?

Psychoanalysis essentially deals with the ways in which the unconscious mind informs and mediates social and conscious behaviour. This means, in Freudian psychoanalysis, that bodily actions are mediated by the mind and ultimately the body is both present and absent; it is physical and exists in the real world, but simultaneously exists outside the physical world as it is constructed through thought, memory, imagination and so on. Psychoanalysis, therefore, is an attempt to make whole, or to piece together and understand, the fragments of experience, dreams and neuroses, much like a jigsaw.

For Freud, the human psyche consists of three conflicting but interrelated components that contribute to the patterns of behaviour of a given individual. These are the id, ego, and super-ego, all of which are formed and developed throughout childhood. In simple terms, these areas can be seen as primal urges that predate socialization (the id), the socialized and 'real' – but flawed – self (the ego), and the perfect self, or social conscience represented by a role model (the super-ego). Each of these components expresses conflicting desires, and the dominance of one or others determines actions, anxieties and behaviours in individuals. For Freud, each component develops at a different transitional life phase and the progression from one to another may well be difficult and fraught with ruptures, events that may hinder the child's development to 'normal' adulthood.

In analyses of the psychology of clothes, authors comment on the ways in which clothes express not just a sense of self, as in identity formation, but the ways in which culture and society dictate sartorial norms, which enable individuals to be accepted or indeed rejected from the group.[1] Similarly, once an individual is aware of the prescribed dress codes, which can also be seen as codes of behaviour, they are able to accept or reject them – to fit in or stand out. One might suggest that this is the purpose of fashion as an aspect of the avant-garde: to question and challenge existing conventions of dress and to move boundaries.

Historically, this has been understood as the diametrically opposed sites of modesty and display, of covering up or undressing, which equally respond to the Zeitgeist. So, at times of economic decline, society covers up, and the converse can be seen in times of economic prosperity. A rather crude demonstration of this can be understood through hemline histories that chart the rise and fall of skirt lengths over time. In a discussion of the economic climate and its cultural expression in the UK in the 1970s, Christopher Booker noted that:

> Two unfailing barometers of cultural optimism in our century have been the height of buildings and the height of girls' hemlines. In times of high excitement, like the Twenties and the Sixties, when people looked forward to the future with hope, the sky-scrapers and the skirts went up. At times when men became fearful of the future, or began to look back nostalgically to the past, as in the early Thirties and the Seventies, they stopped building towers and the skirts came down again … Never, in either case, was the reaction so complete as it had been in the Seventies.[2]

Although there is evidence to suggest that issues of modesty and display are inter-woven with the mood of the times, for writers approaching clothing from a psycho-logical or psychoanalytical stance, modesty and display are expressions of the psyche and of the traumatized self. For example, writing in the 1930s, the psychologist J. C. Flugel,[3] who had witnessed the change in the political landscape of contemporary Europe, argued that increased modesty in dress, particularly over-formalizing sarto-rial codes such as stiff suits, shirts and ties, were indicators of a rigid personality, which at best could be explained as an overwhelming compulsion to follow the rules and maintain control (anally retentive), and at worst, as a sign of Fascism.[4]

Arguments surrounding the significance of modesty and display in dress are also highly gendered and as such revolve around the notion of revealing or con-cealing sexualized flesh.[5]

The problems of female flesh can be understood psychoanalytically and culturally in two ways: firstly, as a sign of a decline in morality, and secondly, as an indicator of uncontrollable sexual appetites. Either way, the display of flesh is seen as
threatening to the status quo, as the expression of unfettered desire and a rejection
of social norms. For example, this is particularly significant in relation to the creation of the fashionable body, as flesh and its manipulation and concealment has
dominated notions of perceived beauty historically.[6] Women have been, and continue to be seduced by the cult of thinness, in which a refusal to eat is equated with
both discipline of the body and control of the mind. To be fleshy therefore is to
display a wantonness, a lack of control, or a natural state that rejects the rigors of
fashion.[7]

The relationship between mind and body derives from Cartesian thought and,
using knitting as an example, can be demonstrated by the proximity of yarn to
flesh, a skin-like covering, potentially offering and demonstrating protection,
modesty and display, eliciting sensory perception, touch and pleasure, as well as
unpleasant responses such as disgust, horror and discomfort. Psychoanalysis acts
as a tool that assists in an uncovering of what lies beneath the surface; such a critique encourages a discourse arising from cultural symbols and norms, as well as
discussing the relationship between the internal and external self. This chapter
intends to investigate knitting as an extension of the psyche – dreams and night-
mares, holding together and unravelling.

Inside/Outside: Knitting and the Body

Knitting and the knitted object are indicative of revealing and concealing, and the
creation of a deliberate juxtaposition of the inside/outside, front/back, plain/purl.
Knitting is the creation of a surface through the looping and entwining of a single
thread. With each knitted loop, the fabric is formed and a deliberate hole made, an
imperfection that contributes to the creation of a potentially 'perfect' whole.

All textiles have an inside and an outside; conventionally it is the most beautiful
or perfect side that is worn on the outside as an aspect of display, whilst the inside
or the converse side exhibits the techniques of manufacture and is usually hidden,
i.e. unprinted surfaces, hemming, embroidery knots, and in the case of knitting,
evidence of changing colours, finishing and so on. In this respect, a clear correlation between textile interiors and exteriors and the conscious and unconscious self
is evidenced – the public display of the 'perfect' self and the concealed, chaotic
and imperfect interior. Yet clothes are not impervious to destruction – they fray,
unravel, or expose their identity when removed, revealing that which had been concealed: the imperfect converse of the perfect surface. Such an assertion implies
that the self is presented as a façade, a dressed-up image of what an individual
wants to project at any given time, a hollow sham of the real and shameful self.

Clothing therefore masks aspects of our physical or psychological self that we choose to hide.

All fabric has a close proximity to the skin: textiles are worn, sat on, walked on, and as such are constantly subject to sensory and bodily interaction. Textiles are protective: they keep wearers warm and dry, they cover things and keep them clean and, to a certain extent, eliminate the possibility for contamination. Effectively, textiles have a physical protective purpose: Equally, textiles as clothing act as a social protection: they cover bodies and therefore modesty, preventing the potential shame of nakedness.

Conversely and paradoxically, textiles are not completely protective. They are full of deliberate holes, part of the construction process and, much like skin, which is covered in pores, they enable certain levels of contamination and penetration. Clothing can be pierced, torn or eroded, making the wearer vulnerable to outside threats such as thorns, knives, acid and so on. Similarly, clothing can and does conceal nakedness, but it can equally reveal and proclaim the body beneath. Clothing therefore is an entity that is simultaneously protective and vulnerable, revealing and concealing, suggesting both modesty and display.

In Clare Qualmann's sculptural cosy, *Knitted Cover for Three Kids* (2003), the concept of knitting as a protection from the world outside is particularly evident. Qualmann stated:

> This piece was inspired by a spate of news about child-safety debates over whether children should be allowed to walk to school alone or to play outside. I thought that if you put them in one of these they'd be safely protected from the world, and very warm.[8]

The notion of binding babies and children is not a new one; from traditional forms of swaddling to wrapping children up tight as protection against the elements, the notion of security through textiles is manifest. For Qualmann, the rather humorous visual reference to the cosy is both poignant and ambiguous; the cosy is a symbol of home, of stability and refuge, and by completely covering her children she is enveloping them in the mythology of home and its comforts. Alternatively, the impossibility and futility of such an object is obvious: movement and growth is restricted, vision impaired and the world outside completely hidden. The message is simple: one can try to wrap one's children and protect them, but to do this would stifle their development and experience of the world.

Similarly, the textile artist Françoise Dupré's *Brooder* (1999) emerged as a result of investigating and manipulating babies' and children's socks. Stating that the heel of the sock was reminiscent of a nest, and of the mythical imagery of the stork carrying newborn babies in a papoose, she noted:

> The egg is a very obvious choice, but one that I at first rejected, but chose at the end because it is a simple and clear metaphor for life, food and motherhood. The fresh

heavy egg, often too big for a nest, stretches the fabric around the hook. There is an element of fragility and danger in the installation. The room filled with eggs is a brooder (a heated house for chicks), a factory farm. A brooder is also a person who broods, and the installation aims to raise questions about fertility.[9]

For Dupré and Qualmann, knitting provides a protective surface, a barrier between the inside and outside, or in Dupré's case, life and death – if the knitted papoose gives way, unravels or loosens from its hook, the egg will fall and break. Both examples draw attention to the precariousness of parenthood and the impossibility of achieving and maintaining the complete safety of one's charges (and indeed, the self) in a precarious and unstable world. It is possible to extend this metaphor to the knitting itself: it looks like it can protect, but because it is made not merely from loops of yarn but also from holes, it is inherently vulnerable.

Vulnerability is the expression and acknowledgement of the imperfect. We might see this in Lacanian terms as a sign of 'lack'. Like Freud, Lacan based his theories on the relationship between childhood development and future adult behaviour, but his focus is the third stage of development, the mirror stage (*stade du miroir*). At this stage, the child recognizes his/her reflection and is confronted by a seemingly whole self. From this point of recognition, the child sees himself/herself as imperfect, flawed and separate, a sign of lack, whilst the mirror image is intact, whole and perfect, an image or state that can only be imagined. For Lacan, this stage is the recognition of an internal and external self and is fundamental to the ways in which individuals view themselves and behave throughout their life.[10] This stage might be understood as the beginning of an awareness of the self and the development of subjectivity.

For both Freud and Lacan, the baby starts its life as an entity driven by need; it has no separate identity as its survival is reliant on its mother, i.e. food, warmth, comfort etc. These needs are satisfied by an object such as a breast, blanket or clothing and so on, but the baby has no concept of the object as separate from itself or as part of another being (mother), so therefore everything it needs is essentially an extension or part of itself. For Lacan, in this stage, the baby exists in the realm of the real. This is not a physical place or space, but a world that exists in the mind, a perfect world which is devoid of loss and lack. The child develops through a process of identity formation that involves a distancing or breaking away from the mother. Such a move instigates a fragmentation, a rupture – a move from the world of dependence towards one of independence and into the world of culture and signification. This rupture establishes a sense of loss and the realization that its world will never be the same again. This loss is understood as a break from unity, where the baby and everything it needs is satisfied in an arena that predates (for the baby at least) language and signification.

From this point onwards, the child is constantly seeking to restore this loss. This loss may be fulfilled, temporarily at least, through objects and their possession (a form of sublimation), so comfort might be gained from sucking a blanket, stroking a pet, or from buying a product that offers something seemingly lacking, such as love, friendship, style, status and so on.

For Jacques Lacan, the biological body disappears. He sees the body as only existing in the symbolic or imaginary. The crux of this train of thought is that language (the spoken or written word) 'murders the object', and once things/objects are named, new meanings and expectations are placed on them, thus challenging their original meaning. So if the body is murdered by language, the way in which the body is understood is through representation. Lacan is not saying that bodies don't exist, merely implying that bodies are culturally meaningful and meaning comes from understanding cultural norms, practices etc., so the comparing and contrasting of individual bodies with those of others becomes an act of social comparison. Therefore bodies are meaningful when they are represented – shown as examples of good, bad and so on – otherwise they disappear or have no meaning.

From childhood onwards, personal and fantastic narratives are constructed; the child may imagine meeting her favourite celebrity, daydream, and inhabit a world in which she is top dog – beautiful, successful and generally less in a state of lack. Individuals are constantly looking to make themselves whole and resolve the fragmentation that is returned to as a memory of the mirror stage. In Lacanian terms, bodies are the threshold – the boundary between the real and the desired self, the actual and the imaginary, the interior and exterior.

Frequently, textiles act as substitutes for the body, marking transitions from one life phase to another. In later life these practices are based on ritual and cultural/social expectation (christening gown, wedding dress, shroud and so on), but there is evidence that suggests that the tactility (of textiles) in relation to human development precedes the development of language.

The body and textiles are therefore borders marking the distance between the interior and exterior, the social and the individual, which are, of course, subject to change over time and space. The fluidity of the boundaries created by textiles and the body itself are, in Lacanian thought, merely illusory surfaces that attempt to protect or appear to make whole that which never can be. This will always be the case, as all surfaces are vulnerable: all can be penetrated, and ultimately are fragmented.

Each surface (textile or body) has margins, boundaries at which fragmentation is more apparent, and this is marked for Lacan by gaps or the rim or cut. The cut has erotic potential; it is literal inasmuch as is connotes sexualized areas of the body such as the vulva, tip of the penis, anus, eyes, ears, mouth or pores in the skin. Yet it is more than a physical entity, as the cut is representative of discontinuity and therefore exerts no sense of continuity or meaning.[11] To be whole would mean that all of these gaps, rims and cuts would need to be filled, which in real terms would lead ultimately to death – one could not breathe, eat, excrete, etc. Yet individuals realize, as a response to their earlier confrontation with 'lack', that they must attempt to do so; to join, conceal or cover the fragments, or to make meaning where there is none. For Lacan, it is this process that is most significant, for this is desire, the bridge between fracture and potential completion.

In its most basic sense, desire is seen as a continual and unfulfilled process by which the individual is constantly engaged in a forceful process of recognition and substitution. The individual recognizes his or her lack, represented by a rim, cut or rupture and is driven to conceal or fill it; but this is futile, so the individual transfers what is lacking on to an *objet petit a*, an object of desire, which will temporarily fulfil his/her quest for wholeness. This is merely an illusory stopgap; such an action will never make the individual whole, desires will never be fulfilled and consequently the quest is never-ending. This concept is very much part of a consumerist society in which advertising promotes 'magic' products that offer the promise of more friends, lovers, success, beauty, money and other things missing from the life of the consumer, which will make him or her complete.

Therefore, surfaces (textiles and the body) are ruptured by holes, cuts or rims, which denote vulnerability and a sense of lack, which becomes a transgressive site of the formation and driving force of desire. Rims can be penetrated and therefore they are sites of the erotic, but this also emphasizes their frailty and their ability to submit to the will of outside entities and influences.

In Freddie Robins's *Craft Kills*, a knitted shell, representative of an absent body, hangs like an aggressive Saint Sebastian, pierced by knitting needles, emblazoned with the words 'Craft Kills'. The explicit text proclaims or pleads to the viewer as the lifeless knitted (absent) body confronts from a powerless and hollow posture. This work presents the viewer with a paradox: knitting and craftwork in general is frequently understood to have restorative properties, yet Robins presents it as the death of the maker. Knitting here is not homely or comforting, but aggressive and painful, strange and horrific. Like Saint Sebastian, Robins presents the audience with a vision, highly recognizable in Western culture, of suffering for one's art and ultimately dying for one's beliefs. In Robins's installation the body has disappeared; the creator of the work is absent, leaving the result of her labour: hollow, but largely intact, punctured with the tools of its construction.

Craft Kills is a commentary on work, art and craft, and as such questions the visibility of the maker (a name, physical entity) and the body of work, and the interrelationship between the two as a craft or art piece. In craft, unlike art, makers are largely anonymous, and technique, materials, skill and so on are fundamental to an understanding of the work, whereas they are much less so in art. This is a battle of hand and mind. Here, method 'kills' concept; the physical attacks and obliterates the cerebral and the psyche. Craft kills art.

The absent body in Robins's work is disquieting; there is something missing – something that has vanished, possibly as a result of the puncturing. In other knitted work, particularly in fashion, as in this ensemble (see Figure 34) for Body Map, the body is present, seemingly larger than the garment itself, and the holes allow

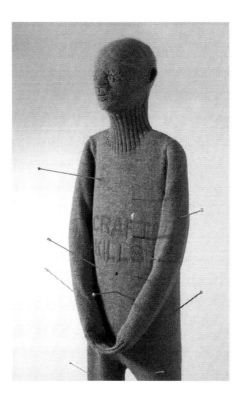

Figure 32 Freddie Robins, *Craft Kills*, machine-knitted wool, knitting needles, 2002. Photo: Douglas Atfield. Image reproduced with permission from the artist.

the flesh not only to be revealed, but to protrude. The knitting here is like a second skin, stretched over the human form to such an extent that the fabric cannot contain what lies beneath. The inside becomes the outside and the uncovered flesh part of the design detail. In this example, the knitting becomes ambiguous: it is both revealing and concealing, exhibiting aspects of modesty and display simultaneously.

Knitting, like skin, has a boundary; it has a beginning and an end, and is likely, unless knitted in the round, to have seams (unlike skin) that hold it together. Yet, like skin, knitting is constructed from – and is punctuated by – holes. This makes the work vulnerable and imperfect and, by association, a metaphor for the body.

Knitting and the Unheimlich

'The uncanny' (from *unheimlich*, which translates as 'unhomely') is a concept which has emerged from Freudian psychoanalysis and focuses on the notion of the unfamiliar in action, place and objects, and the fearful yet exciting responses

Figure 33 Body Map, Dress of the Year, 1984. Fashion Museum, Bath. Image courtesy of Bath and North East Somerset Council.

elucidated from them. The uncanny exists as diametrically opposed to the homely, a phrase and experience of the familiar and comforting and therefore the unhomely or uncanny is that which is uncomfortable, disquieting and frightening. For Schelling,[12] the uncanny is everything that should be hidden but has come to light. This implies that the manifestation of the uncanny is the return of the repressed, in which the horrors that have been hidden (or forgotten) deep within the psyche return to haunt or confront an individual unexpectedly in everyday life.

The confrontation with the uncanny or the engagement with an uncanny experience is essentially a process of unpredictable and disquieting recognition, an inexplicable strangeness within the mundane. We might, for example, see something moving in our salad, yet nothing is there, but we are reminded that it was a bug and of its potential threat as a form of contamination, and we can no longer eat; we may hear a noise, be sure that it is an intruder and become aware of our

Figure 34 Donna Wilson, *Cannibdoll*, 2005. Image reproduced with permission from the artist.

mortality, and so on – unfamiliar and unnerving events in what would be otherwise a normal and inconsequential routine. This is the confrontation of the unfamiliar within the familiar, and its consequences have a profound psychological impact.

Knitting, of course, is a familiar practice, the outcome of which is everywhere within everyday life, and it is so mundane, domestic and familiar that it can be described as 'homely'. Yet it is precisely these qualities which inform the work of artists such as Donna Wilson, whose knitted toys express a familiarity through their genre, materials and techniques, but become horrifying examples of hidden fears and desires through their subject matter. For example, in Wilson's *Cannibdoll*, a monstrously angry doll 'eats' its baby, questioning the notion of motherhood as a nurturing role and bringing to light the fears of parenthood in general – could I kill the life that I have given? Such a concern reflects the Medea syndrome, in which infanticide, incest and other horrific behaviours are enacted through a conscious choice, which is indicative of the calculating 'evil' inherent in women, as opposed to the 'accidental' or unassuming behaviours of the male counterpart, as in the Oedipal complex.[13] For Freud, motherhood was a means through which women could attempt wholeness or a release from the self, as in orgasm, or in Lacanian terms, fill the lack. In Wilson's work, that gap, cut or lack is obviously filled, as the baby is situated in the mouth of the 'mother'.

Wilson also questions notions of femininity for both woman and child, suggesting that women's work can be subversive and represent inner turmoil. In relation to the mythology of Medea, we might also see Wilson demonstrating the mother's sacrifice, to surrender or destroy the thing she loves most in order to be accepted as a woman.[14] Here, it is possible to suggest that to be accepted as a woman, knitting has to be political; traditional roles and pastimes have to be sacrificed, and questions regarding contemporary society must be raised.

Similarly, the work of Maria Porges, in particular *Bomboozle* (2003), a collection of knitted bombs, is reminiscent of baby toys; although in comforting pastel colours, it is horrifyingly redolent of the violence of childhood and the contemporary fear of the threat of the suicide bomber. Such 'toys' are disquieting; they look like playthings but they are horrific and offer an alternative discourse to notions of childhood, and inter-generational, gender and inter-social relationships. They confront notions of 'the Other' through a media and iconography that is familiar and homely.

Both Porges's and Wilson's work also make a statement about knitting in general, which is an expression of the uncanny. They communicate that knitting is not homely or unthreatening, and although it may be familiar and domestic, one should never take it for granted and make assumptions pertaining to its homeliness, nor indeed the domesticity and passivity of women.

The social anthropologist, Daniel Miller, adopts a psychological rather than a structuralist methodology, i.e. nothing precedes language[15] and turns to psychology, in particular educational and child psychology,[16] to investigate the 'symbolic' interactive relationship between people and their things.[17] The significance of the role of play in child development highlights an active sensory and imitative interaction between the child and the object world that precedes the spoken word. This suggests that very young children are able to 'understand' the world and resolve personal conflicts through a sensory relationship with objects. Indeed, the resolution of 'real life' conflicts through 'play scenarios' has long been a marketing ploy for the selling of children's toys, especially in the case of fashion or action dolls, such as Action Man and Barbie, in which the clothing, packaging and accessories are seen to determine specific child/object play scenarios.[18]

The return to studies of childhood and the 'unconscious' activities of the very young with the object world, found in psychoanalysis, have resonance with textiles and have been exploited by crafts critics in recent years. In particular, Freudian analysis,[19] and the interpretation of the object as fetish, have been developed in favour of the tactility of practices and objects. The properties of cloth, central to these debates, seem to defy visual contemplation. For example, the weaver Peter Collingwood noted that his own work suffered as a result of not being 'touched'.[20] The textile object as fetishistic is further developed when linked to the sensuous[21] and the skin (in terms of proximity to, and material similarity to, i.e. age, decay and decomposition).[22]

The psychology of people and their things as outlined is frequently understood as 'inauthentic'. The object (thing or possession) becomes a substitute for an 'authentic' or interpersonal relationship, as in the examples of toys, blankets and so on. In terms of culture, the 'inauthentic' implies a non-genuine existence, or that which does not comply with existing hierarchical categories based on style, taste, class and so on. Miller disputes this analysis by suggesting that the relationships that people have with their things, as well as the objects themselves, are unmistakably disparate and eclectic, and it is this non-conformity or 'inauthenticity' that characterizes most people's lives.[23] In terms of material culture, Miller's use of psychoanalysis establishes a pre-linguistic relationship between people and objects, demonstrating the significance of ordinary objects in everyday life, using the example of child psychologist D. W. Winnicott's 'smelly blanket'.[24]

Winnicott's theory of 'transitional objects' could be applied to 'transitional object practices' such as learned actions, and tool and appliance use (children's cutlery to 'adult' cutlery, knitting clothes 'like Mum wears' for fashion dolls) that demonstrate progression to levels of ability and responsibility. These transitional stages can be seen as indicative of familial education or emulation – a series of learned practices determined by the habits and social norms within the learning environment. The anthropologist Pierre Bourdieu, whose theory of Habitus acknowledges the inseparable bond of the material, cultural and social world, developed this process of behavioural acquisition through the interaction between person and object(s).[25]

Bourdieu's study is class- or group-based. By studying households in terms of decoration, use of tools (such as cutlery) and the formation of habits, Bourdieu saw Habitus as the process by which individuals learned to interact with the material world. This included the value(s) groups (families) placed on specific objects, as well as the use (etiquette) of objects in everyday life (aspiration and manners). The ways in which learning was directed, he discovered, was determined by the social class of the group (family); therefore, individuals from particular social backgrounds displayed particular behavioural characteristics seen as typical for that social group. This similarly applied to regional differences. This may suggest that regardless of any attempt by individuals to dissociate themselves from the social class of their birth, they may well be betrayed by their accent and manners. Indeed, Bourdieu acknowledged the awkwardness or 'disgust' experienced by individuals in social situations where they felt 'out of place'.[26] In turn, this sense of not being 'comfortable' or 'at home' can be understood in relation to 'the uncanny' (*unheimlich*), an acknowledged awkwardness in which the familiar becomes strange and distorted.[27]

Knitting and Fetish

In Freudian psychoanalysis, objects are often understood as inauthentic substitutes for authentic body parts and as such are described as fetish objects. Freud's theory of castration is highly important here – the lost penis or the potentially lost penis is replaced with something else, something that reminds the owner of his own sexual potency and power. Often these objects are phallic – the fast and stream-lined car, stiletto heel and so on. But not all fetish objects are phallic. In terms of form, they also are likely to contain reference to orifices, as in Freud's three stages of psychosexual development (oral, anal, genital), which are seen as metaphors for body substitutes.

Freud's approach considers the moment when a child becomes aware of sexual difference. For Freud himself, this occurred whilst playing under his mother's skirts, when he noticed that she didn't have a penis. He sees her as lacking and an awareness of difference is established. In order to move on into adulthood and not be castrated (punished with femininity), the child must remove or suspend his rela-tionship with his mother. A fetish can be seen as one response to separation: fear or anxiety about powerlessness or castration.

Part of the nature of fetish is the relationship between power and powerlessness (phallic power and submission) – masculinity and femininity, suppression and repression, concealment and coveting. Power is exerted in terms of control (pos-session, masculinity, the phallus), whereas the thrill emerges as a response to hidden knowledge, secrecy and the coveting of the potential lack – the substitute penis.

So the possession of a fetish object is seen as an appendage – an extra body part. This disproportionate focus on a thing, as greater than the rest of the body, exem-plifies the power of a fetish. Therefore fetish is about presence and absence; an acknowledgement of flaws and the attempts made to fulfil a perceived potential.

In relation to knitting, the display of fetishistic qualities is apparent. Depending on the yarn used in its construction, a knitted object can reflect and represent ele-ments of shame, as in a haptic resemblance to pubic hair, or desire, through knitted clothing that constricts the body. An example of this is demonstrated in the work of the Swedish hair-weaver, Nina Sparr, whose knitted undergarment *Swedish Country Style* displays discourse surrounding psychoanalytic appraisals of the body and the proximity of textiles to it. In the piece, Sparr has knitted a pair of knickers from human hair, which are displayed as a lifeless tribute to the tradi-tional Swedish craft of hair-knitting and hair-weaving, a means of using the waste product from haircuts.[28] The garment expresses the bodily; it is of the body and for the body, but mimics and references Freudian notions of women's shame. It replicates pubic hair, but also references popular phraseology – the 'hair shirt' is a traditional garment made from goat's hair and worn to cover the genitals, instilling the garment and the piece with a notion of penance, which further draws attention to the social role of women.

Nakedness or the revealing of the concealed body, as with the display of under-wear as in Sparr's knickers, has been described as a loss of being, a loss of the social self, and as a consequence creates a state of emotional discomfort. Mario Perniola states:

> Clothing gives human beings their anthropological, social and religious identity, in a word – their being. From this perspective, nudity is a negative state, a privation, loss, dispossession ... being unclothed meant finding oneself in a degraded and shamed position, typical of prisoners, slaves or prostitutes, of those who are demented and cursed.[29]

This description of a lack of clothing, and its associated sense of the dissolution of a social self, emphasizes the role that clothing plays in masking the body and the presentation of a whole self. Yet, although clothing acts as a psychic shroud, the ambiguity it presents is equally prevalent in a desire to display, to reveal, to express or free that which is hidden. This disparity can be assessed as the distance between the individual and social self, the making real of the fantasy.

The concept of fetish in knitting is not merely the domain of the fine arts and crafts. In a recent popular knitting pattern book, *Domiknitrix: Whip Your Knitting into Shape*, the author, Jennifer Stafford, presents learning to knit as requiring harsh discipline.[30] With sub-headings that include 'Make it hurt so good', 'Dominate your style', and 'Knitting in the missionary position', the novice knitter is guided through knitting as a discipline, which requires discipline. Similarly, Nikol Lohr's *Naughty Needles: Sexy, Saucy Knits for the Bedroom and Beyond* offers risqué, adult-oriented patterns such as 'Kinder-Whore', a schoolgirl costume, and knitted blindfold with handcuffs and whip.[31] Blog sites on the Internet discuss the fetishistic potential of knitted objects, including examples of knitted masks and pony hoods,[32] handcuffs and chastity belts,[33] events that offer participation in knitted burlesque,[34] and patterns for knitted breasts[35] and penises.[36]

Knitting is also an activity executed by hand and therefore involves repetitive touch and the engagement of sensory perception. At knitting events and perform-ances, participants are often encouraged to engage with the knitting process by immersing their whole body, dancing and gyrating amongst pools and spools of yarn.[37] Here, knitting is at its most fetishistic; the sensory and bodily engagement with yarn offers a freedom or escape from the norm into a hedonistic world where the body merges with fibre, much like the merging of two bodies.

Knitting as an activity is penetrative; stitches are formed through the penetration of a needle, the tight looping of yarn around it and its withdrawal. The equation of knitting with the sexual act is a theme that permeates the current knitting revival: knitting is both fun and sexy, it is humorous and not particularly threatening; one can see the irony in knitting as a form of pornography. This is certainly the crux of Kelly Jenkins's knitted wall hangings, which embrace a genre of textile art that can be classified as porno-knit.

This new emphasis on knitting as sexually deviant and sexually empowering may well be a consequence of the new feminism, and indeed the ensuing rise of a raunch culture in which women are increasingly reclaiming feminine pastimes whilst expressing their desires in a way which, historically, had been the remit of men.

Knitting and Horror: Abject Knitting

Whilst Lacan is focused on the rim, the ruptures that signify frailty through potential penetration, the feminist psychoanalyst Julia Kristeva reclaims the vulnerability of the rim with an analysis of the abject. This might be described as the symbiotic relationship between introspection and projection, the externalizing of the interior of the body, and the internalizing of the exterior world.[38] For Kristeva, the abject is the expulsion of that which disturbs or threatens, that which is unimaginable or unspeakable. The abject is not an object, real or imagined; its only defining characteristic is that it is not 'I'.[39] The abject is a pre-linguistic state which initially occurs as a response to the rupture of childbirth, the expulsion of baby from the womb, and develops as a form, in its most basic sense, as self preservation. In these terms we see the abject as a separation of that which is beyond words – horrific and repulsive – from the self; so bodily excretions, noxious smells, fears and the like are reviled and projected from the body in order to distance and 'clean' the self from the ultimate form of the abject, death and the cadaver.[40] The abject is the acknowledgement of a boundary between life and death, between cleanliness and the improper or unclean, and it is constantly undergoing a process of repulsion and expulsion. The body is the physical site of this boundary, a margin that marks the division between the external and internal, but which is proactive in creating a barrier from prospective defilement. The abject is therefore something that is both of us and not us; it is a state that exists beyond comprehension, outside the remits of language and meaning, yet it is a state which is perpetually with us, and ultimately draws us away from death.

In the vein of much feminist art that addresses issues of the internal/external female body and its horrors, Lindsay Obermeyer uses knitting to communicate the expression of the womb as a site of renewal and continuity. In her recent work, which is reminiscent of feminist art practitioners such as Kiki Smith and Carolee Schleeman, Obermeyer uses the form of a hanging sweater to metaphorically

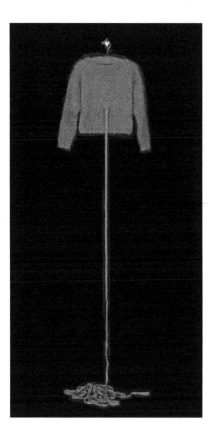

Figure 35 Lindsay Obermeyer, *Bloodline*, 2006; hand knitting, machine knitting, mohair yarn, rayon yarn, padded hanger, coathook. Photo: Larry Sanders. Image reproduced with permission from the artist.

articulate the female body as a site of discourse which address relationships between mother and child, and the relationship between the interior and exterior self. In *Blood Line* (2006), a disembodied bright red jumper hangs on a coat hanger whilst its central knitted spool bleeds into a pool on the floor; what was once a conduit for life hangs lifeless, useless. The jumper, a garment worn on the outside of the body as a form of protection, becomes a metaphor for the body, an empty shell and, by association, a symbol of the internal, the hidden and the abject.

Blood Line demonstrates the abject as a means of cleansing, of rejecting unwanted bodily substances (and in this case, the umbilical cord) and highlighting the power women in particular have to expel that which is potentially harmful or toxic, thus guarding against penetration and vulnerability.

There is something undoubtedly repulsive about the potential to actually wear the garment, something potentially shameful and too revealing. The viewer is drawn to and shocked by the blatant symbolism, but also by the means and method of construction. The garment and blood 'line' are knitted, a homely practice associated with the niceties of motherhood and child-bearing; it is a clean practice, yet here it becomes messy and defiled, the private becomes public, and the homely unhomely. Nonetheless, *Blood Line* evokes a sense of renewal, of the potential for the creation of life, and as in much feminist work, the reproductive cycle and menstruation in particular becomes a site for celebration and rebirth.

If feminist creative practice communicates a sense of life through the language of the abject and the horrific, other work focuses on death, completing the cycle. In the work of the French artist Annette Messager, *The Boarders* (1971–2), a series of dead taxidermic sparrows are arranged in groups, seemingly 'sleeping' in knitted 'jumpers'. Reminiscent of newborn babies in a maternity ward, the sparrows appear as delightful playthings, yet they are obviously dead and untouchable, unclean and vile – the maternity ward becomes the morgue. Their shrouding in knitted jumpers normalizes what is a horrific tableau in which the dead may wake from their sleep as the viewer watches – we are repelled but equally fascinated by that which is displayed. The title of the piece is significant; these are 'boarders' at rest, sleeping as if in a communal dormitory, yet the birds are representative of the border between life and death, between the speakable and the unimaginable, the cosseted and the rejected. For Kristeva, the cadaver is the ultimate expression of the abject: it is the definitive horror. She writes:

> The corpse, seen without God and outside of science, is the utmost of abjection. It is death infecting life. Abject. It is something rejected from which one does not part, from which one does not protect oneself as from an object. Imaginary uncanniness and real threat, it beckons to us and ends up engulfing us.[41]

In Messager's work, the dead are presented as if they were alive; the wearing of clothes adds signification to that which defies language or meaning. Here, the knitting adds 'life', referring to the familiar and the comforting through a semiotic appraisal of materials and presentation. The horror and repulsion emerges at the realization that one is confronting death – as in Kristeva's 'cadaver' – whilst not accepting it, dressing it in the vestments of birth.

One might also suggest that the activity of knitting is the expression of the process of abjection. In contemporary knitting literature, attention is drawn to the ways in which knitting is either 'compulsive' or 'addictive'. Although such statements have no basis in medical research or diagnosis, the use of this language consigns the practice of knitting to a world outside the realms of the socially acceptable. Knitters, apparently, need to knit, and once they have started they seemingly cannot stop. Knitters keep stashes of yarns, kits and patterns, which they hide and store for future use; they contribute to Internet knitting blogs, attend knitting groups and knit cafés, and are essentially consumed by what is merely a 'hobby'. Texts proclaim that knitters are wholly consumed by knitting, and magazines provide evidence to confirm this. But the discussion of knitting 'addiction' is not presented as an anti-social form of behaviour, something to be ashamed of, rather as something to be expected when one takes knitting seriously.

Knitting is rhythmic, involving the repetition of bodily and tactile actions in the formation of stitches. It can induce states of calm, release tension and anxiety, and act as a means of catharsis. The rocking motion and repetition of knitting provokes a state of introversion, of oblivion or escape, and through such activity the body disappears and the psyche regresses to a state of nothingness where, as Kristeva might intimate, 'meaning collapses'. Knitting and the compulsion to knit, therefore, might embrace the abject in two ways: firstly, through the attraction towards the formless, the incomprehensible (the state of knitting), and secondly through the outpouring of the internal (the knitted object). One might suggest that the compulsion to knit is a response to inner turmoil, to release or vomit feelings of that which is unspeakable and threatens to harm through a creative outlet. This might be considered a state of madness,[42] the result of which is knitted objects. There is seemingly no treatment or cure for this knitting 'madness', 'addiction' or 'compulsion', nor is one sought; these behaviours are celebrated and accepted as central to the reasons for knitting, a process of catharsis, and therefore the anti-social and unclean becomes accepted and socialized.

CASE STUDY. As Seen on CCTV: Anti-Social Knitting and the Horror of the 'Hoodie'

The aim of this study is to assess what has become, in recent years, a media furore and by association a moral panic, stemming from a seemingly innocuous piece of clothing – the hoodie. The hoodie is a leisurewear garment: a sweatshirt with a hood – a knitted piece of mass-manufactured clothing just like a T-shirt. It is ordinary; most people have one in their wardrobe. It is a practical garment, keeping the wearer warm with the added benefit of warming the head as well as the body. The garment is inoffensive, democratic even, readily available to everyone regardless of income, age, class, gender or educational background.

In 2005, the Bluewater Shopping Centre in Kent banned the wearing of hooded garments (specifically hoodies) on their premises. Why was this? Why were hoodies so much of an issue? Indeed, Bluewater continued to sell them, so what made such a simple piece of clothing evoke such a drastic response? It seemed that once the sweatshirt was worn with the hood over the head, the garment took on transformative properties, changing from casualwear to something much more problematic, and indeed threatening to the status quo.

Bluewater management stated that 'hoodies' were 'intimidating', a statement approved by the deputy prime minister, John Prescott, who outlined a personal experience:

> I went to a motorway café about a year ago and some kid said something to me. I said 'What did you say?' and he came back with ten people with hoods, you know, these fellas with hoods on. What struck me about it is not only did they come back with this kind of uniform, as it is, but they came with a kind of movie camera to take a film of any such incident. I found that very alarming. I think the fact you go around with these hats and these covers ... I rather welcome what they have done at Bluewater.[43]

Prescott, it appears, although he mentions it several times in his recollection, was less bothered by the hooded garments per se than he was the number of individuals approaching him and the potential for any 'incident' being captured on camera. This is unsurprising, as he has a bit of a reputation for responding with violence in the heat of the moment, and any video footage would further damage his public standing. Nonetheless, statements such as Prescott's firmly situate 'hoodies' as intimidating and frightening, linking them with wider social fears associated with youth culture.

Youth culture, since its cultural inception in the early 1950s, has always been shrouded with an air of disbelief and misunderstanding – deliberately so, separating youth from everyone else. Clothing has been central to this form of separation: a visual indicator of difference, a sign of rebelliousness. The hoodie perhaps is merely another garment in a long line that includes jeans, T-shirts and leather jackets.

> It is not made of chain mail, of Batman's off-cuts, or of the very fabric of evil itself. Indeed, nowadays, you're lucky to get one that's 100 per cent cotton. And yet, the hooded top can strike fear into the heart of even the most courageous among us. A lone figure behind us on the walk home – hood up, head down – and we quicken our steps. Someone solitary and hooded at the back of the bus, and we opt for a seat near the front. A group of hooded teenagers on the street, and we're tensing our shoulders, clenching our fists (round handbag strap or house-keys-cum- weapon), training our ears for verbal abuse in order to emphatically ignore it. Just as leather trench coats are associated with goths, Matrix fans and ageing lotharios, so the hoodie has become a signifier of disgruntled, malevolent youth, scowling and indolent. The hoodie is the uniform of the troublemaker: its wearer may as well be emblazoned with a scarlet letter.[44]

The deliberate distancing of youth clothing from that of the mainstream is significant not merely in its style, but its gestural potential and its performativity. The clothing one wears is significant, but the ways in which clothes are worn are more so. The hoodie itself is not a threatening garment, but when worn with an attitude of disaffected youth, the hoodie becomes a sign of difference. The relationship between clothing, youth and gesture is not new; all youth clothing, particularly that which is associated with violent groups who potentially threaten the status quo, embodies a sense of threat, which is heightened and perpetuated through media portrayal and commentary. For example, a young man in a leather jacket is transformed into a leg-

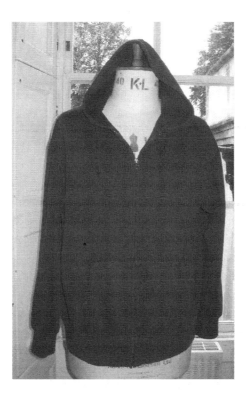

Figure 36 Just an innocuous piece of mass-produced knitwear? Hoodie on a stand, 2008. Photo: Jo Turney.

endary screen rebel like James Dean or Marlon Brando when the collar is turned up and he adopts a nonchalant swagger. This form of gesture transforms both garment and individual, questioning the established moral order.

The fashion historian Aileen Ribeiro notes that morality aims to establish and maintain a group understanding of what is right and wrong; clothing is a social signifier that acts as a means of belonging or, indeed, isolation or alienation from the group.[45] Clothing in itself is neither 'moral' nor 'immoral', but subject to social mediation that the art historian Quentin Bell describes as a 'sartorial consciousness'[46] cultivated by social norms and responses to changing sociocultural circumstances. The development of a sartorial consciousness highlights the social impact of clothing, and more notably fashion, as both an aspect of the avant-garde and everyday life, emphasizing a contradictory praxis that potentially challenges the norm. This distinction between culture and society is immediately recognizable as an implication of the modernist avant-garde – the quest to challenge and overthrow existing boundaries of acceptability, or an understanding of the importance of conformity. In the case of the hoodie, there seems to be no real fashion-led impetus to the wearing of the garment; it is not avant-garde, and appears to be unchallenging primarily because it's so ordinary. It can be therefore suggested that unlike garments that are deliberately worn as a statement of the rejection of the dominant ideology, hoodies became, merely by association, a symbol of youth, specifically disaffected youth, with no regard for the law – a threat to the law-abiding majority. Of course, the media furore surrounding the intimidating presence of such garments gave them a new 'street credibility', popularizing them further with a section of society seemingly isolated for wearing them in the first place. The hoodie and its wearers, it seemed, became a self-fulfilling prophecy. As India Knight suggests in an article in *The Sunday Times*:

> Everybody is scared of hoodies: other teenagers, men, women – and dogs probably. That's why hoodies sell. No teenager is so well adjusted that he can't do without a bit of anti-social backup from his clothing.[47]

The hoodie therefore appears to represent a clear distinction between wearers and the moral majority; it became a sign of attitude and conformity to social stereotypes surrounding the problems of youth, but more importantly a signifier of moral decline, ASBO culture and a general social downward turn. So knitting had become anti-social.

The anti-hoodie faction claim to champion the law: by wearing a hood, one can conceal oneself from the glare of CCTV cameras and therefore potentially commit more crimes without the consequence of identification. A report in the tabloid newspaper, the *Daily Mirror*, noted:

> Hooded tops and baseball caps have been adopted by cowardly yobs up and down the land to hide their faces from CCTV cameras while they commit crime or terrorize victims unable to identify them.[48]

One might comment that the increased usage of CCTV cameras in towns and cities in itself is a problem, as it could be seen as a means of social control, infringing civil liberties, rather than a method of maintaining public safety, as addressed by design groups such as Vexed Generation, who have specifically produced garments for an anti-surveillance range. Similarly, the sub-text underwriting the banning of hoodies, i.e. social control, etc., has been hijacked by the left-wing media. Writing in the *Socialist Review*, Andrew Stone notes:

> The government sees hoodies and caps as an affront to its surveillance culture. We're all meant to be constantly available for monitoring on the ever-present CCTV cameras. To want privacy, anonymity, is inherently suspicious, perhaps criminal. Hence the need to 'stop and search' anyone wearing such clothes which, handily for the fashion police, are often worn by young black men. To be stuck on a street corner is equally unacceptable. They should be out doing something 'useful', preferably consuming in a privatized space where they can be observed and regulated.[49]

The hood as a sign of mistrust and suspicion, even horror, is not a new one. All of the great fictitious and mythical figures associated with evil or fear wear hoods, which indicates that the covering of the face or head hides the wearer's true identity, personality and intent. This has been recognized by reports into the 'horror' of hoodies.

> The big daddy of them all, the Grim Reaper, comes cloaked and hooded, as do the Four Horsemen of the Apocalypse, various minions of Satan, and harbingers of evil from all creeds, religions, mythologies, science-fiction universes and fantastical worlds of dungeons and dragons. 'Hooded figures' appear in crime reports, horror films, nightmares … For thousands of years, we have been bombarded with images of menacing hooded figures. Crabby youths wrapped in cotton/polyester-mix tops are just the latest entry in the catalogue of devils; they can't hold a candle to the Ku Klux Klan.[50]

So hoodies are merely part of a mythology of folk devils; they are nothing new. Yet the creation of what has become a moral panic surrounding the wearing of hooded garments has entered the political arena in an unprecedented way. With the prime minister and the Labour government supporting Bluewater's edict to ban hoodies and other head coverings from its premises, and the leader of the Opposition, David Cameron, attempting to reach out to disaffected youth by suggesting that we 'Hug a Hoodie', youth issues have never been so central to political debate. At the epicentre of this debate are issues relating to poverty and crime, from which it appears most anti-social behaviour derives. This presupposes that public safety and social control are at the heart of this discussion and, one would imagine, places a great deal of responsibility on a rather small and powerless group – the young. However, in McLean's article, the mention of the Klu Klux Klan is not without significance; issues of race and racism appear as a sub-text to all of the discussions surrounding hoodie-wearing.

The hoodie has its origins in black American street culture; it is an urban garment appropriated from sportswear into hip-hop culture and favoured by young black men. It speaks of the assertion of power by those who have none and encourages a sense of gang mentality and belonging. Indeed, David Cameron has also been highly vocal in expressing what he sees as a correlation between hip-hop and gangsta rap and increased knife crime in the UK.

All of the reports in the broadsheet newspapers have drawn attention to the underlying racism in the anti-hoodie lobby; youths do wear hoodies, but those who favour them most are young black men, and by association, the issue is not just with youth, but one section of it. Similarly, such an argument merely scratches the surface and ignores more complex social issues, pointedly highlighting a tendency towards racism and a fear of difference within what is celebrated as a multicultural society.

Such fear of difference can be aligned with the hoodie's similarity to the ski mask – which has become, since the 1970s, the literal face of the contemporary terrorist. The ski mask covers the whole face, with cut-out eyeholes, rendering the wearer seemingly invisible. Such a garment is emotively significant because it signifies terror on actual and metaphorical levels. Firstly, the presence of such imagery in the media and its association with actual acts of terrorism firmly places the ski mask in the public consciousness as a sign of political dissidence and fear; and secondly, the masking of the terrorist contributes to a sense of unease, in which that which is 'invisible' and potentially horrific could be lurking anywhere. In contemporary society, where the threat of terrorism pervades the social climate, such forms of dress become potent symbols of a collective fear, not merely of terror itself, but a difference of race, religion, politics and so on, as indicated in recent media reports surrounding the wearing of the hijab by Muslim women.

The mask has a long history and significance within dress and display. The mask is ambiguous: it conceals the wearer, yet it offers the exciting potential of revealing the secrets that lurk beneath. The mask then acts as a fracturing device: it hides like a shroud, it camouflages and conceals, rendering the wearer oblivious to the concerns of vanity, social norms and behaviours, which consequently is viewed suspiciously by non-mask-wearers. One might assume that this form of dress as anonymity is mysterious to the extent that we are always awaiting the moment of 'reveal' – the removal of the mask – which will in some way restore harmony.[51]

The ski mask, however, is worn as an item of deliberate concealment; there is no potential 'reveal', which heightens its potency as a garment of threat. The mask conceals the face, but not the body; the body is present, but the face disappears. And this is the site of terror: the physical presence is amongst us, but we don't know from whom we could be under attack. This is evident in the work of the artist Andy Diaz Hope, whose performative pieces *Everybody is Somebody's Terrorist* demonstrate a seemingly normally dressed individual walking amongst a crowd wearing a knitted, flesh-coloured ski mask. The political intent of his work highlights the anonymity of contemporary terrorism, whilst highlighting a general culture of fear and anxiety.

Hoodies, unlike ski masks, are not merely garments that cover the head and render the wearer 'faceless'. They are also notoriously baggy, concealing the body of the wearer to the extent that he or she becomes gender-neutral. Essentially the garment conceals, but it also conceals to such an extent that it disembodies. The hoodie can be described as demonstrating a surface of the abject, a breaking free from the boundaries of the body into a state of amorphousness. The body becomes ambiguous: it is neither man nor beast, inside or outside; it is veiled in a shapeless mass like a monster emerging from the quagmire. This can be seen as a move from the symbolic world of form, language and meaning into a realm of confusion, distortion and shapelessness – a realm beyond comprehension.

Such an analysis is appropriate for the discussion of youth clothing. The abject represents a move from the awareness of the womb into a state of differentiation,

Figure 37 Andy Diaz Hope, *Everybody is Somebody's Terrorist*, 2003. Photo: Laurel Roth. This is a performance piece, entitled *Financial District Infiltration*, in which the artist was photographed emerging from the Montgomery Street BART (Bay Area Rapid Transit) station in San Francisco. Image reproduced with permission from the artist.

which parallels the ambiguous and transitional stage between childhood and adulthood; the lack of form implies a stage of transition, a praxis, in which one will either emerge into the symbolic realm or return to the quagmire from which one originated. Similarly, a state of abjection can be marked as a foray into nothingness, a means of displaying no form of identity whilst simultaneously creating a primal one-ness, as demonstrated in the creation of an unstable unity of perceived disaffection in hoodie-wearing. Indeed, hoodies, when the hood is worn, offer a form of comfort: the hood shields the wearer from the gaze of not necessarily the CCTV cameras, but the world outside. The wearer literally distances himself from his surroundings by covering the head and avoiding any form of social engagement. This can be seen as a form of hiding, of fading into the background, unable or unwilling to form a solid identity, which is far more psychological than it is anti-social. Nonetheless, such a desire to disappear is disquieting, as Peter Schjeldahl notes in 'The Empty Body':

> Fashion is, we suppose … 'nothing in itself'. It needs a body in it to tell us something and then is constrained only to signify about that body …[52]

The hoodie allows the body to disappear. It allows the wearer to move away from a form that is at the same time natural and bodily, and repellent, whilst creating attraction in the same measure. Kristeva acknowledges:

> Unflaggingly, like an inescapable boomerang, a vortex of summons and repulsion places the one haunted by it literally beside himself.[53]

Although, for Kristeva, the abject is the inability to objectify the object, the similarities between the potential for hoodies to be perceived as abject can be illustrated through this concurrent juxtaposition of attract/repel; hoodies hide the wearer, conceal and disembody the body, moving it from shape to shapelessness, whilst at the same time drawing attention to its alien mass.

One could say similar things about other 'outsider' knitwear. For example, the black polo-neck jumper has become a mainstay in the wardrobes of intellectuals and fine art lecturers who consider themselves on the margins of society. The history of black in fashion is one that coincides with the emergence of European Romanticism and the cult of the outsider. It is a colour that defies fashion and its rules, and as such is seen to transcend the frivolities of a quest for the new. Consequently, black has been categorized as a 'classic' in fashion terms, perhaps best demonstrated by the perennial 'little black dress', which in itself was initially a form of oppositional clothing, devised by Coco Chanel in the 1950s as a reaction against Christian Dior's 'New Look'.

In menswear, black was the colour of revolutionaries, emerging as a style choice for those with Romantic sensibilities in the second half of the eighteenth century. The adoption of black under these circumstances created not merely an air of aggression, but one of masculinity and oppositional belief as well as dress. It was the colour of anti-conformism and the anti-Establishment, and by association became a sign of social distance, of marginal thought and deed. As the Romantic tradition developed throughout the nineteenth century, black became associated with intense emotional feeling, the cult of the individual and the outsider. Literature drew on such men, centralizing them as fictional heroes – passionate and untameable loners consumed by inner turmoil. Such men had little compassion or social responsibility, preferring or guided by higher concerns such as experience and the meaning of existence.[54] By the late nineteenth century, black had become the colour of mourning (in the West), associated with loss and the distance between life and death, furthering the signification of colour with transcendence, the outsider or 'the Other', and otherworldliness.

With such a cultural heritage, it is unsurprising that black became part of the iconography of existentialism and the uniform of post-war intellectuals. Indeed, by the 1950s, black had become associated with 'black' humour and nihilistic philosophy exemplified by the writing of Jean-Paul Sartre.[55]

One garment encapsulates this form of thinking more than any other – the black polo-neck jumper. The garment is significant because when worn (and unlike the hoodie, which disembodies, or the ski mask, which obscures the head) it decapitates, visually removing the head from the body. The body disappears, but the head remains, often giving the impression of floating freely, unaided and unsupported. In Samuel Beckett's dramatic monologue 'Not I' (1972), the character appears as a mouth, floating seemingly in space, talking in confused sentences, which becomes a discourse arising from four of her life events. Within the performance, the audience becomes aware of the movement of the mouth, of the relationship between articulation, gesture and free-flowing thought, and the distance between articulation and action. Here, the mouth is a vehicle for the unconscious: a tool for the expression of the hidden and confused. The dialogue is circular, repetitive and from this premise and use of language, meaning is created from the meaningless. The body, shrouded and obliterated, has disappeared; the character is reduced to a single unsupported organ from which utterances are open to interpretation through the experience of the audience.

The polo-neck jumper enables the wearer to present his or her face, but not body. Unlike the use of white, particularly as a background in fashion photography, which enables clothing to stand out and shine, black offers the opposite – it conceals, hides and obliterates. For an intellectual to wear a black polo-neck jumper is a statement of defiance: it says the wearer is more than a body, more than a physical shell, and that his mind and soul is of paramount importance. Without a body, there is no canvas for cultural inscription, no empty space to carry brand names and logos, no vehicle on which to express the language of fashion, or other signs of social and cultural conformity. There are no signs to be read, no clues to identity through sartorial choice. Yet, of course, the garment's obvious refusal to communicate enables it to do so, to express a clear message of the self as an outsider, of anti-conformity and a sensibility purporting to a higher purpose. Indeed, many photographs of Andy Warhol show the artist wearing such a garment, which focuses the viewer's attention towards his shock of white hair, which situates Warhol as the intellectual artist and artwork himself (subject and object) in the consciousness of the public. This is a technique used in the portraiture of the Old Masters, as Juliet Ash notes:

> Later, in old age, clothes have almost disappeared in Rembrandt's self-portraits, and instead the focus is on the expression on his face, on the poignant (lonely) presence of himself and his feelings.[56]

The removal of the significance of clothing as a means of expressing identity is obliterated by a desire to focus on inner turmoil, on the self rather than society and its wider concerns. Such an assertion distances the subject/wearer from the world, transporting him into an inner realm, supposedly enabling the communication of the psyche and soul.

The current media furore surrounding the wearing of hoodies is essentially nothing new, and emerges as a response to the reappropriated meaning of the garment – as a sign of opposition. In the wake of such bad press, hooded garments really need a change of image, particularly as they are not solely the domain of the young or the criminally minded. The Australian leisurewear company, Bonds, have addressed this by launching a range of brightly coloured hoodies, with an accompanying advertising campaign that highlights the positive potential of hoodie-wearing. In the adverts, young and vivacious models wearing hoodies with hoods up embark on a quest for romance; the culmination of this quest is an *E.T.*-like embrace, in which the male and female create a private world in which they can only see and concentrate on each other – a kind of 'funnel of love'. Ultimately, hoods create a private space within a very public sphere; they create intimacy in a world of surveillance and social propriety. Hoods, therefore, are the embodiment of a 'private space' for contemporary urban nomads.

Hoodies elicit a gaze that is simultaneously inward and outward. Essentially, a confrontation with a hoodie is a confrontation with a society that is inherently

Figure 38 Kevlar hooded tops are produced for school uniforms in the UK as knife crime increases. 2007. Photo: Matt Cardy, Getty Images News, 7390395 (RM) Getty Images.

racist, conservative and unforgiving, afraid of difference or 'the Other'. It is also a confrontation with innermost fears, the horrors that lurk deep within the psyche. So a look into the dark recesses of a hooded head is the addressing of issues in both microcosm and macrocosm, staring into the face of both collective and personal fears. The hoodie acts, therefore, as a social shroud; it conceals the elements of social and personal prejudice previously hidden.

Similarly, the shapelessness of the hoodie conceals an unformed identity and appears to exist outside the realms of comprehension; like the wearer, identity has no form and appears alien, both hidden and visible, repellent and interesting, simultaneously. As Jennifer Craik acknowledges: 'The "life" of the body is played out through the technical arrangement of clothes, adornment and gesture',[57] and if the body seemingly disappears, the onlooker is confused and fascinated.

Clothing alone cannot be immoral or horrific, but it can, and frequently does, encapsulate a mood of the times. By scapegoating a piece of knitted clothing and marking it as an indicator of the anti-social, it highlights the garment as 'edgy', imbruing it with an 'attitude' of youth and rebellion. It can therefore be seen as the perfect fashion object: rock and roll, grungy, challenging and on the edge. Indeed, these very factors became the buzzwords of journalists writing on the style trends for Autumn/Winter 2006–7, declaring the season's penchant for the revivalist parka (Prada, Belstaff, D&G) as 'ASBO chic', genuinely derivative of street style, and that:

> hoodies are everywhere – or at least they will be as soon as the temperature drops and the High Street unleashes its cheaper copies on to the fashion-hungry public.[58]

Such reports express the rather tongue-in-cheek irony that has befallen the hoodie; couture versions of the garments appear to be worn with an attitude that is not just the prerogative of the young, but also of fashionistas (a kind of haughty 'Whatever!'), which will eventually be sold back to the youths who set the trends in the first place. Suddenly the anti-Establishment has become part of the Establishment and the horror of the hoodie merely a passing style trend. So are hoodies now 'goodies'? Possibly, but only until next season ...

Conclusion

Psychoanalysis enables an investigation of knitting which uncovers its relationship with and to the interior and exterior self. In its most prolific guise, knitting engages with the body through clothing, and in garment form expresses a great deal about the wearer and his or her social persona. It might also express, either consciously or unconsciously, the interior or the psychological self.

Knitted garments have the potential to reveal and conceal the physical and psychological self, as they are constructed from the duality of stitch and hole, which

Figure 39 Male in hoodie, Bath UK, 2008. Photo: Jo Turney.

can be seen as representative of the human condition, the combination of strength and frailty, easily unravelled and precarious. From this perspective, knitting can be assessed as vulnerable, creating a surface that is merely an illusory attempt to make the self whole, or as a site of abjection, in which the horrific is expelled from the body.

Knitting and knitted objects have a long, symbolic association with the home, domesticity and femininity, and as a consequence, have been viewed as a stable construct – unchallenging, almost defying the historical process. Psychoanalysis enables the reappraisal of this concept, engaging knitting in a discourse that is both bodily and psychological. As the chapter has demonstrated, knitting is not necessarily comforting, domestic or homely; it can instil and stimulate fear, horror and the unknown. Similarly, it can exert an awareness of the meaningless, the incomprehensible, the erotic and the insane. Knitting, therefore, can be understood as a boundary or margin at which the interior and exterior merge; a precarious site, which is easily unravelled.

–5–

In the Loop? Knitting Narratives, Biographies and Identities

Textile objects and practices have long associations with stories and narratives. This is indicated through textile words used in everyday language – for example webs are 'woven' and truths 'embroidered', communities are described as 'tight-knit', reinforcing the relationship between practice and stories or 'fictions' as well as referring to the significance of these practices within the construction of life narratives. The aim of this chapter is to discuss knitting as a form of narrative, drawing from the ways in which practice enables the construction of personal and social identities through narrative. Themes for discussion include concepts of home and the familial, as well as the sociability of knitting as exemplified in group activities, and as a communication of these narratives through website and blog discussion. As Patrizia Calefato comments:

> A textile is a text, one of the texts of which our clothing imagery is made: just as the metaphorical weave gives life to a text – in the common sense of the word, whether written or oral – so the weave of a textile is what gives it a plot, a narrative, which exist thanks to the contact of the textile on the body.[1]

Narratives are characterized as a formulaic structure, comprising of a beginning, middle and end, and under these constraints can be seen as temporal structures. Similarly, knitting projects can be characterized in the same way: they are started, worked and completed within a specific time frame. One can also suggest, from an anthropological standpoint, that knitted objects also exist in time and within commodity exchange structures and are therefore subject to their own biography.[2] The chapter investigates knitting as a temporal narrative, a means of marking time, and therefore understands knitting as a continuum, representative of both the life of the knitter and the ensuing life of the knitted object.

Developing from a history of knitting as a means of therapy and occupation for the infirm,[3] the contemplative and meditative potential of knitting has been explored by writers and knitters in recent years. The potential for knitting to enhance a sense of the spiritual self, and to act as a means of self-healing and catharsis, will also be addressed. The chapter centralizes on the practice and experience of knitting, and therefore refers to the testimony of knitters, the majority of whom are amateurs or hobbyists.

The case study returns to a more literal understanding of the term 'narrative', and investigates new forms of fiction in which knitting is central to the plot. The study examines two genres of popular fiction, the murder mystery and chick lit, questioning the meaning of knitting to the contemporary – and largely female – readership.

The chapter concentrates on the ways in which knitting can be understood as a narrative, both literally and metaphorically, enhancing and contributing to a sense of the self and personal life narratives.

Knitting Narratives: Language and Storytelling

> Without wishing to load this two-sticks-and-some-yarn activity with inappropriate symbolism, there is something about it that necessarily sparks memories of care and attachment, no doubt based on the fact that most people are taught as a child, by a probably female someone of enough involvement and patience to have been important. Everyone who can knit, in other words, has a knitting narrative.[4]

The history of textiles is interwoven with narratives and stories. Whilst textiles were made, stories were told, and as objects constructed, so were tales, each seamlessly interconnected. The natural rhythms of textile construction – the clicking of needles – mirror the lilt, repetitions and gesture of storytelling, each offering the articulation and expression of the body and mind in harmony. As traditionally the making of textiles was a domestic activity, one might assume that storytelling was a means of entertainment and occupation for children whilst mothers worked, and although often the stories told were moralistic and offered social education, they could also be bawdy, horrific, and suitable for a much wider audience.[5] The stories told emanate from a folk culture and as such can be seen to embody a rich heritage of oral and craft traditions.

Analyses of the significance of the relationship between oral and craft traditions have often been eclipsed by a Romanticism for a nostalgic past, yet studies have uncovered a clear link between storytelling, work and life narrative, which include a strong sense of identity-building, political comment and critique of the everyday, regardless of whether the content of these stories can be considered 'factual'.[6] The content and purpose of craft narratives or stories are distinct from other forms of narrative, as they embody or reflect the inherent practice of craft per se. In these narratives, like the act of making, stories are performed, gestures articulated and repeated rhythmically, and themes, characters and tales knitted (woven or embroidered) to an ultimate conclusion. Like the spoken (rather than written) story, craftwork produced by hand cannot be repeated exactly; variations occur as a result of the inherent imperfection (or 'human' quality) of the maker, and as such, performances, processes and objects are variable, distinct and diverse. Craft, like narrative, cannot be understood as static, as in the making of each piece and with each telling of a story, time challenges and transforms, offers reflection and reappraisal, potentially adding to and enhancing both. From this perspective it is possible to see the ways in which events, issues, and aspects of daily life are built into craftwork and as such the process of making becomes as significant as the made object, marking time and representing life narratives.

In Celia Pym's work, narrative and the consumption and evidencing of time are central. In a knitting and travel project, Pym knitted her way around Japan, creating a long ream of knitting which measured both time and place. Her remit was simple: knit every day and move to the next destination when each ball of wool had been knitted; the knitting became a sign of time spent in one location, with memories of peoples and places entwined in the construction. She said of the work:

Figure 40 Celia Pym, *Blue Knitting*, 2001–2.

Well, I would try to get a ball of wool, knit it and move on; so the idea was that time spent in a place was determined by how long it took me to knit. And sometimes I did want to stay longer, so I would slow down a bit, but I would also go and look for wool somewhere else and switch hotels and say well, I've moved somewhere different. There was a little bit of flexibility, but on the whole it was a matter of the knitting determining time and the journey. And really, I noticed it most when I'd hit a slow patch where I'd maybe been on the road for a long time or where I'd done a very long journey – I'd been on the train, and I'd feel tired so I'd be inclined to knit less, so it was like the knitting provided me with a little bit of a rest. Because I'd knit less, I'd take it slower, or if I didn't like somewhere I'd knit furiously so I could get myself out of there.[7]

The yarn used in the construction had to be blue and fifty stitches in width:

I wanted to settle on one colour to make my decision much simpler, but also because Japan has this long history with blue and indigo and I also felt that I had this image of myself wearing jeans, passport in my back pocket, and setting off like some nomad – and my backpack has knitting needles in it and that's it. And I decided I'd buy one ball of wool to start me off, but it was a really free journey. Here I go and the whole journey is determined by the knitting. And the whole journey is about the knitting. It's the whole reason: it's the purpose for everything, to be there and the reason to do things ... You actually let things happen, instead of anticipating what will happen.[8]

For Pym, knitting became a reason to get up, to go to work, to move on. It gave her an excuse to meet new people and to see new things, as well as to chart and record her memories. Time – and time spent – became firmly entrenched within and made physical in the completed knitted object. Although Pym sees knitting as an expression of the 'useless', her work was purposeful; she was conscious of her journey and the narratives she was creating through her knitting activity. This became far more obvious to her when her work was exhibited in Japan:

All the little labels of the places in the knitting correspond to where I am in the week ... I think it was particularly interesting in Japan because visitors were really interested: 'Oh I live here', or 'My family's from here' – and they see the connection. This useless abstract thing, this section of dark blue wool – 'Oh, that's my home.' Or 'What does this marker mean?' It doesn't mean anything apart from the fact that I was there; I've been there and seen that, and I think there's an appreciation of that ... What are the things you report back on when you travel?[9]

Pym's sharing of the journey increased the significance of and the potential for narrative development. As signs, places and so on were recognized, the knitting, which was ostensibly abstract, became meaningful in different ways to the gallery visitors. Time and the representation of time spent became highly personalized and something that initially was about nothing acquired significance.[10] The relationship between the self and knitting offers not merely the physical manifestation of measured time, but also encourages a sense of being, of having been 'there', of witnessing events or moments, and of recording them. The collection of memories, yarns, etc. worked into this piece can be described as part of Judy Attfield's analysis of material culture as 'embodiment and disembodiment'.[11] The piece 'embodies' the identity and life experiences of its maker. It is made from specially selected yarns and recollections of people and places and therefore it is significant and personal. Yet it also represents a 'letting go', a collection of 'valued' and personal memories collected into one object, which may be recognized and remembered by others. The artwork therefore is a symbol of disembodiment in which the maker becomes detached from her 'special things', tidying them into a single item, distinguishing them from other memories and times.[12] This is an item of memory and remembrance, of holding on and letting go.

Biographical Objects: The Social Life of a Sweater

The following section addresses the biographical stages of the knitted object, investigating the cultural significance of memory, sentiment and narrative as cultural markers. Each area investigates the ways in which the knitted object relates, interrelates and addresses the life, needs and wants of its consumer, who may or may not also be the maker, once it has been 'made' (completed).

The circulation of goods, their use and exchange, value and significance in everyday life has been central to discourse in visual studies disciplines throughout the post-war period. In particular, the role of the commodity and the ways in which commodity status or value is changeable has been the focus of these debates. The anthropologists Igor Kopytoff[13] and Arjun Appadurai[14] describe the commodity as an object produced deliberately for exchange.[15] Commodity value is determined by exchange value, which is not static but political. Within the capitalist world of goods, exchange value may be interpreted as financial worth, as in Marxist discussions of the commodity.[16] Indeed, the commodity is frequently seen as a product of mass manufacture, a facet of the mass market. However, objects are not merely subject to monetary exchange. They can be given as gifts, tokens and so on. Knitted objects are deliberately made with a purpose in mind (an end to the means) – as gifts, as fundraisers, to decorate the home as a demonstration of identity, and so on. And therefore they have an emotional or sentimental exchange value – time spent = appreciation and/or formation or reaffirmation of the maker's personal identity.

Appadurai's assessment of exchange value and the 'life' of things is exemplified in his study of 'unnecessary' goods that have no actual use value, deemed *rhetorical* and *social*.[17] These objects are seen as embodying two types of knowledge: (a) an understanding of aesthetics and production techniques and (b) an understanding of what the object is 'good for'.[18] In relation to knitted objects, this can be interpreted as (a) knowledge of the time spent making a given object and an understanding of the object symbolically and (b) the way in which this object adheres to and/or reflects the identity of the owner (or those who share the living space). The knitted object is consumed therefore as cultural knowledge and as an expression of identity/world-view.

Although Appadurai's study refers essentially to the world of goods and the exchange value of the goods on the market, the symbolic value he identifies can be applied to domestically knitted objects. They do not circulate within the 'legitimate' marketplace – they are not produced with an eye to financial gain and have very little economic value. Frequently produced outside the sphere of capitalist employment, they are often made for the domestic environment. They are therefore part of a moral economy – a system of exchange that runs parallel to the financial world.[19]

The system of circulation and exchange of goods/objects within the household is as dynamic as those in the world outside. This is the 'consumption process', described by the anthropologist Daniel Miller as:

> The start of a long and complex process, by which the consumer works upon the object purchased and re-contextualizes it, until it is often no longer recognizable as having any relation to the world of the abstract and becomes its very negation, something which could neither be bought or given.[20]

Objects can be highly valued, ignored, displayed or thrown away; they can be used or not, and so on, and the objects' 'value' and 'social life' is determined by the systems of value in place within the moral (household) economy.

As Kopytoff acknowledged, identities in complex societies are both numerous and conflicting;[21] life is conditioned by the historical process and is therefore dynamic, fluid and changeable. Culture is also dynamic: technology, the media, style and fashion all contribute to a perpetual continuum that characterizes the contemporary, and change and transition is inevitable. Objects come and go, and are valued and ignored or discarded as part of this process.

The relationship between people and their objects is ultimately a relationship of identity. And as life changes, responses to specific objects also change. The objects' biography therefore reflects the biography of its owner (which may change), creating a fluid narrative, rather than remaining static.

The object is not only subject to consumption at the point of exchange. Once the object enters the possession of an individual, it becomes part of the owner's/consumer's life, part of a person/object narrative or classification system, and therefore objects can be seen as 'social' things. Objects can be favoured, cherished, hated, hidden, thrown away and so on. They can be used as the maker intended or in an entirely different way. The objects' biography therefore is intrinsically linked

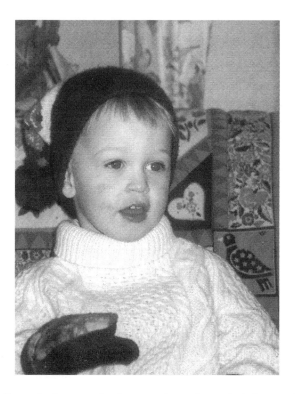

Figure 41 Respondent's son wearing the sweater her mother made for her as a child, 2000.

to the identity and biography of its consumer. The following case study investigates the biography of a sweater.

The current owner of the Aran sweater is thirty-four years old and has a child aged four and a toddler aged eighteen months. The sweater was knitted by the owner's mother and had been worn by the owner as a child. The sweater has recently returned to her possession after a period of over twenty-five years:

> My mum knitted the jumper when I was about three years old. I don't remember wearing it. You think that you do when you see your own kids in it, but I really don't. I must've worn it, though, because there are photographs of me in it. I remember them. We were living in Scotland at the time and my mum, gran and aunt all knitted. They were all very good. I had forgotten about the jumper until Mum gave it to me a few years ago. I was really touched that she had kept it.[22]

The sweater demonstrates a temporal link, a progression, in which the owner imagines a memory of childhood through the object. It is indicative of a relationship not solely between mother and child (owner and her mother), but of an understanding of family in which the owner remembers all of her female relatives knitting.

Similarly, the sweater is associated with a specific place, Scotland, a place that remains significant in terms of personal heritage and genealogy. This sense of place is heightened by the traditional style, pattern and wool utilized in the garment's construction.

The sweater has recently re-entered the life of its owner and is understood by the owner as a significant object. She notes that her mother kept it, rather than discarding it when it no longer fitted or was useful, stating that she felt 'touched'. The object is therefore loaded with a nostalgic sentiment, which informs its current use.

The sweater, now found and remembered, has regained its functional quality as an item of clothing now that the owner's son is of an age to wear it:

> I was a bit concerned at first because my son found it very itchy, so I always put a polo-neck jumper underneath it. He didn't wear a coat with it: it's just too thick and warm. I took the photographs because he looked so cute. I think it's nice for Mum as well, to see that the jumper is still useful.[23]

The fondness the owner feels for the sweater is not necessarily shared by its current wearer, her 4-year-old son, who finds it 'itchy'. Although functional, albeit uncomfortable, the sweater, in use/worn, is emblematic of a shared and continued relationship between the owner and her mother. The owner feels that her mother is 'pleased' to see that her work (knitting) is still useful.

The sweater is of a traditional design, is well made, durable and does not display the signs of ageing that other garments may do. The object seems to defy the rules of fashion and therefore seems ageless or timeless:

> I've had lots of comments about it. When my son's been wearing it, people have come up to me and asked where I got it from. It just shows that it's still fashionable. The pattern's lovely – a real traditional Aran – and I suppose things like that don't date. It's now in my daughter's drawer waiting for her to grow into it. I shall keep it and pass it on to them when they have children.[24]

The sweater as a non-fashion item increases its potential for future use and wear, as does its non-gendered colour and style. This is recognized by the people who have passed positive comment. Similarly, the owner hopes that the usefulness of the sweater will continue, by planning its long-term use and biography.

The familial bond exhibited in the respondents' testimony is embodied in the knitted object. The interviewee does not knit; she will not, therefore, pass these skills on to her children as a continuation of a family tradition, but the jumper (an otherwise ordinary object) will become an heirloom item. An understanding of the making process is demonstrated through memory, as is an understanding of the jumper as a 'traditional' item that indicates not only a familial link but a temporal and geographic link that places the owner within a whole genealogy.

The 'special' quality afforded to these items as souvenirs redefines the object as significant, different to similar – otherwise ordinary – objects. Fixed in time and space, the object becomes indicative of life progression, the distance between the here and now and there and then. Ultimately the object is symbolic of personal narratives, times, places, people and events to which its owner cannot return, existing only in memory. Memory and recollection become subjective over time, idealized or nostalgic, and thus the authentic experience is displaced and replaced by the inauthentic (the real/actual/doing replaced with the remembered). In this respect the authentic – the souvenir, or in this case the Aran sweater – is neither 'real' nor 'imagined', but part of a wider social and cultural discourse between object and owner/consumer, and therefore embodies an ongoing narrative. As Stewart suggests:

> The souvenir speaks to a context of origin through a language of longing, for it is not an object arising out of need or use-value; it is an object arising out of the necessarily insatiable demands of nostalgia. The souvenir generates a narrative, which reaches only 'behind', spiralling in a continually inward movement rather than outwards towards the future.[25]

This means that the souvenir is only part of a whole, i.e. it is a partial referent to other objects, but metaphysically is the physical manifestation of an experience. Therefore, as the experience can never be replicated, the souvenir exists as a partial referent, subject to change in time and through memory.

Knitted objects are consumed, by makers and consumers, and once 'made', re-informed by the making process. Indeed, the 'type' of object, a personal understanding of it, a cultural understanding of the making process, and the materials, all contribute to the ways in which the object is received and consumed. Unlike other things, knitted objects are frequently consumed intentionally as relationship markers, because even once the object has been 'made', it still maintains the identity and memory of the maker. This can be described as a means of making or 'leaving' one's mark, or as *poesis*.[26] Poesis is the rebirth or transformative process by which sensory memory brings the past into the present. By definition, such an act requires self-reflexivity, reinterpretation and recreation. The key, therefore, is 'How I remember' as well as 'How I want to be remembered'.

The consumption of the knitted object is largely indicative of the 'sentimental', and this can be as an extension of the self (identity/relationships), personal ideology and previous experience or expectation of knitted things (social/cultural), and/or understanding of the object within the world of goods. In these instances, the object can be described as 'sentimental', becoming more significant within its owner's life at times of great emotion, such as the death of a loved one or the birth of children. Therefore, such objects became most highly valued by their owner/consumer as commemorative items, physically marking life events and embracing narrative.

Knitted objects are often physical narratives; the embodiment of poesis, providing a link with the past in the present. These are not merely 'bygone' objects, as Baudrillard[27] would believe, but triggers for experience, an 'authentic' link with the past. These objects are kept – displayed, hidden, forgotten and found/recovered, associated with people, places, times, events and lives, and therefore can be described as sentimental. They act as personal mementoes, layered with variants of emotion, understanding and memory, and it is for these reasons that the objects are valued, and this of course, is subject to change over time.

Knit and Natter – Knitting and the Sociable Self

> Knitting circles across America routinely bring together young and old people, blacks, whites, Asians, Hispanics, those who speak English and those who do not, conservatives and liberals, men and women, and all kinds of folks who, if it weren't for the knitting, might just assume to avoid each other. Because they know from the start that they share a consuming passion, they are often able to look beyond their differences and think about what else they might have in common.[28]

In Wills's observation (above) one might assume that knitting is the great leveller: the one activity or practice that can bring people together and overcome difference, creating harmonious environments in which sociability is at the forefront, and from which knitting can establish a sense of utopia. This is certainly the way in which knitting in groups has been promoted in recent years, a fun and friendship-building practice, popular with celebrities and fashionistas.

The knitting group has developed significantly over the past few years. This has primarily been a response to its resurrection under the new name 'Stitch 'n' Bitch', deriving from 1950s craft groups and Debbie Stoller's book of the same name. As the name suggests, knitting is not the only activity on the agenda, and the groups offer an arena outside the domestic environment for 'light-hearted' discussion and conversation, fusing knitting and sociability.[29] Stoller started the movement in 1999 when she advertised in the feminist magazine *Bust*, of which she was also editor, for knitters who wanted to meet and knit together in New York City. They met in a coffee shop and, unlike traditional crafts groups that were hidden away in church halls, members' houses and so on, Stitch 'n' Bitch groups meet and knit in public.[30]

Rather than closing oneself off amidst the group, knitting in public becomes a performative activity, a means of expressing oneself in a public arena. This can be understood as the merging or infiltration of the private into the public, and as women reclaiming public spaces for themselves. Knitting has a new visibility.

Groups meet in coffee shops, pubs (traditionally a male domain), galleries, museums and parks; no space seems to be off-limits. These spaces are ostensibly connected with leisure, rather than work, and such arenas challenge the concept of knitting as 'women's work'. Indeed, knitting as leisure is predominantly the motivation for knitting now; yarns are expensive, glamorous and luxurious, and when combined with social occasions such as a trip to the pub and a chat with friends, knitting becomes an activity of choice rather than necessity. A knit-club organizer noted:

> I would like it to be a book club ... I would like to branch out so that as we knit maybe we introduce a book. But it's fun, and it's not meant to be too serious, and not competitive either, which is a relief. Because my career is really competitive, I felt a real need to do something, be enthusiastic about and get stuck into something that isn't about 'Are you the best?', 'Where is this going to take you?' Nowhere, hopefully.[31]

The above testimony highlights the ways in which knitting in groups can be assessed as the antithesis of women's social roles and responsibilities in contemporary society. It offers a creative outlet, which is devoid of the competition women face within the workplace and offers a form of leisure that directly connects them with other people. One might suggest that such relationships can be formed and maintained without knitting (one doesn't need knitting to go to the pub with friends), but like any club, it offers a group mentality and a form of belonging.

Although knitting in groups can be seen as the expression of the leisured self, it can also be seen as an extension of a capitalist concept of leisure per se; people need to work in order to access leisure, leisure has to be paid for, and therefore there is a need to return to work in order to complete the cycle. Meetings in coffee shops, pubs and yarn stores all encourage consumerism, the purchase of goods in order to maintain one's position within the group.

Historically, knitting circles were time- and location-specific meetings, solely the domain of women. This has changed, and although many groups meet at the same place and time, many do not, preferring to move away from a 'club' mentality, acting from a more spontaneous and performative standpoint, which might be described as a knitting 'event'. The British knitting group, Cast Off, exemplifies this distancing from the concept of the static group, offering varied venues to different groups of people at different times.

> Cast Off activities provide an alternative to the usual and often alienating networks in the world of handicrafts. By arranging fun and adventurous knitting meetings and workshops in a range of unusual public settings, Cast Off aims to introduce a wide cross-section of people to the craft. By providing materials and tuition to beginners and more advanced knitters, Cast Off aims to educate and spread the creative potential of knitting.[32]

Figure 42 Cast Off knit on the London Underground, Circle line, 2003. Photo courtesy of Rachael Matthews.

Cast Off has instigated public displays of group knitting (on the Circle line of the London Underground, in pubs, clubs, museums and other venues) in an attempt to extend the appeal of knitting; this is also seen as an experience, different each time one participates. This defies the 'boredom' factor inherent in regularly doing the same thing in the same place, and challenges the notion of a knitting club as comfortable and stable.[33]

The reasons why people choose to knit in groups is varied,[34] but the increasing popularity of affiliation with a group could be understood as a nostalgic and ironic search for 'community' which never existed,[35] or as a means of expressing and sharing skills with others in a time-poor, commodity-rich climate. Cast Off also avoids the consumerist ethic of other groups, providing needles, yarn and advice to all comers, and the diversity of location enables participation by anyone regardless of their budget. Spaces are transformed by knitters, who not only have fun, but also conform to contemporary notions of the nomadic self, i.e. knitting is portable and can be performed anywhere.

The influence and popularity of group knitting has been channelled by artists such as Shane Waltener; his piece, *Knitting in the Round*, is a testament to social interaction. Knitters, sharing circular needles and conversation, created knitted 'thoughts' or memories, which culminated in a knitted narrative of stories and craft. The result is a sculpture which bears witness to the testimonies of the makers, but also of the process of shared knitting activity. Waltener describes this as a 'low-tech version of the Internet' in which makers are brought together, recording a moment in time and therefore their own life narrative in stitch, whilst also referencing the traditions of group knitting in a public rather than private arena of a transient community of knitters.[36] The everyday experience of knitting becomes extraordinary, recorded and differentiated through each maker's contribution and through photography, later displayed in a gallery setting.

Figure 43 Shane Waltener, *Knitting in the Round*, 2007.

Knitting in groups is undertaken by individuals for a variety of reasons, and regardless of the personal choices for participation, the popularity of such groups has increased rapidly. Knitting in groups highlights the social aspect of the craft: it offers a forum for conversation as well as for making friends. It also encourages – and to a certain extent revives – oral craft traditions, and whilst contributing to personal life narratives, contributes to the narratives of knitting. To suggest that this return is merely the expression of some form of ironic retrogressive gaze is rather naive. As Minahan and Wolfram Cox suggest, for young women (and young men as well), knitting offers a new form of connectivity that challenges gendered roles and spheres, in which the creation of material culture is an expression of social cultures.[37] Knitting and natter contribute to personal and collective narratives of both makers and the making of objects.

Virtual Knitting

It is often said that technology has made the world smaller. Communication with people on the other side of the world is as easy and speedy as if they were on the other side of the room. The aim of this section is to investigate the ways in which technological communication, especially that engaged in via the Internet, has transformed traditional concepts of home, family and community, and this will be assessed in relation to a knitting blog, which effectively is a virtual community. In order to address these points, it is important to outline what is meant by 'community' under these conditions, but also to assess the ways in which technological development has transformed working patterns, and subsequently relationship networks and belief systems.

People tend to live among others – in neighbourhoods, friendship and kinship groups. Within these groups, values and beliefs are shared and members need to feel as if they belong as well as being reassured of their belonging. But belonging is reliant on a need to know that it is something worth belonging to and that one is engaging in a worthwhile discourse. By suggesting that in order to belong one must enter into a discourse, it illustrates that the need to belong is not static, but dynamic and constantly under review.

Virtual communities emerge from reality, from circumstance and from social and economic conditions that encourage their growth. Changes in working patterns, stemming from industrialization and expanding during the de-industrialization experienced during the 1980s,[38] resulted in altered demography and fragmented communities. Traditional communities dispersed and with them kinship networks. Technology, especially since the mid-1980s, has contributed to the further dispersal of community and family. This is not just in terms of geography, but in terms of space and time, mixing work and leisure patterns and the notions of the public and private. Before the computer age, people went out to work, returning home afterwards, providing a distinct division between work and leisure, and the public and the private. Post-computer, many more people work from home, bringing the public world of work into the private domain.[39] Much of this reality is met with concern in the media – that people will work far too many hours, lose their imagination and the ability to communicate face to face, or lack the desire to read books or to manually write letters.

The need to communicate, to belong, is still as strong – and the Internet enables the creation of communities globally, within the safety of one's own home. It also allows poetic licence – participants can present whatever persona they choose: no one knows who they 'really' are. Not only then do virtual communities fulfil some kind of need that can't be met in reality, such as real community/belonging, but they also add to or enhance a need for entertainment or wish fulfilment, and perhaps create an alter ego, a hyper-real self.

> At one level, the computer is a tool. It helps us write, keep track of our accounts, and communicate with others. Beyond this, the computer offers us both new models of mind and a new medium on which to project our ideas and fantasies. Most recently, the computer has become even more than a tool or mirror. We are able to step through the looking glass. We are learning to live in virtual worlds. We may find ourselves alone as we navigate personal oceans, unravel personal mysteries, and engineer virtual skyscrapers. But increasingly, when we step through the looking glass, other people are there as well.[40]

In his essay, 'The Virtual Community: Finding Connection in a Computerized World', Howard Rheingold[41] uses his personal experiences of life online to discuss the ways in which the participants become involved in a virtual life. Although initially he was sceptical about the ways in which the inanimate object of the computer screen could facilitate 'human' or 'warm' communications, he was quickly proved wrong, becoming increasingly involved with those he came into contact with online. He began to care for these people as if they were his 'real-life' friends, and became involved in community ritual within the confines of his own home.[42]

Rheingold demonstrates the ultimate distinction between real and virtual communities – the negation of sensory perception. Virtual communities enable communication, debate and resignation, and allow the declaration of a whole range of emotions, as well as providing a forum and environment in which to forge and maintain relationships. Virtual communities are therefore communities that exist outside the constraints of location, devoid of sensory perception.

There is no single type of online culture, more of a multiplicity of sub-cultures, dependent on the aims or agenda of the participants. Like Rheingold's community, the Knit List[43] boasts over 2,200 members worldwide, receiving an average of ninety messages per day. The community consists – as the title suggests – of knitters and this, it seems, is the single common element linking members. The age range is diverse as is background, nationality and occupational status, whereas gender is not – all of the contributors/members are women. This contradicts the popular belief that women and technology are incompatible.

On first inspection, the Knit List appears to be just a general information site, offering help and advice regarding patterns, yarn, magazines and supply details. The site is, however, much more than this. The sharing of information is significant – bargain buys, personal experiences of techniques, materials etc. all contribute to a sense of community, of education and identity. In this respect the Knit List offers a service of exchange and support, providing advice and encouragement to the other members similar to that found in 'actual' women's groups such as the WI or sewing circles. As one member demonstrates:

> Folks have been e-mailing me asking about the status of the 1995 gift page. Due to a houseful of sick folks, I got a late start on it. I thought I was about halfway done (there are over 100 files in this collection and I'm editing each of them), only to discover this morning that I'm going to have to redo the entire thing. I'm getting cracking on that, and thanks to the upcoming long weekend, I'll have it ready to go early next week.[44]

Like the traditional family, the passing on of knowledge to younger members of the group or even the 'real' community is celebrated, rather like a rite of passage. The major difference is that shared information on the Knit List, in relation to the acquisition of skill, is not merely inter-generational and reliant on the knowledge of family members, but is global, multicultural and draws from a whole world (literally) of knitting knowledge.

Knowledge and the sharing of information is demonstrated through the publication of patterns suitable for children or beginners, or through tales of accomplishment published in the List. One member tells of her experiences of teaching a neighbouring teenager to knit and how subsequently these newly acquired skills have led to an addiction: 'She's now knitting on the bus!' There are many more examples of tales like these – they justify what is essentially a hobby, whilst at the same time re-establishing traditional kinship rituals.

This sense of pride is representative of a passing on of knowledge, but also of a shared interest that secures or provides the basis for a future relationship. This suggests that a passing on of a skill is representative of the transition from childhood into adulthood, an activity that is a kind of rite of passage. The activity is an exercise in bonding and learning, giving pleasure to both teacher and pupil, and is performed within the sanctuary – or controlled environment – of the home; and even if the teaching is undertaken in a virtual community, it can achieve similar goals. This sharing is extended to the exchange of thoughts and feelings, which enhance the human aspect of the virtual community. Similarly, many members talk of their families, experiences in everyday life, work, holidays and, strangely, the weather, positioning the personal and the local within the global.

With any form of belonging, there is a sense of not belonging, and the Knit List is no exception. Knitting, of course, is the main concern and for non-knitters the site would be of little interest. However, for the casual observer, there are other forms of exclusion. The members use their own language, a kind of familiarized knit shorthand, not just to describe knitting techniques but to describe situations, family members, institutions (non-knit related) and places, for example 'D2' means 'second daughter', 'DD' is 'daughter's daughter', 'SS' is 'supply shop' and so on. The understanding of this language demonstrates commitment and a certain striving to belong to this group or community.

The Knit List exemplifies, reproduces and sustains a community mentality, which could be found within 'real' community groups. The difference here is that membership is global, albeit limited to English speakers. In this respect, the Knit List demonstrates the global popularity of knitting, the closeness in interests of nations, and therefore some common ground. It also exemplifies the shrinkage of the world and the ability to socialize without leaving home. Therefore, like knitting, this global community can be dipped in and out of, fitted in between chores, and can consume as much or as little time and space as required.

These new virtual communities are seen in some respects as impersonal and are often viewed with suspicion. The sociologist Roger Silverstone suggests that all communities are virtual and that regardless of electronic media, information society or no, communities are symbols of our sociability. This suggests that 'community' is reducible to a series of symbols, which can be reproduced in person or virtually, and systematically represent both personal and collective identity, i.e. community is a state of mind, based on expectations and experiences.

The main issue really is not whether it is possible to have 'meaningful' relationships online, but to investigate the ways in which technology encourages new forms of sociability, which appear to succeed where traditional forms and rituals are increasingly seen to have failed. Anthropological approaches have investigated the ways in which virtual communities facilitate cultural reproduction,[45] outlining how the Internet helps: 'Communities and people come closer to a realization of who they already feel they "really" are.'[46]

The growth of online knitting communities has been highlighted in a recent survey undertaken by the yarn manufacturer Lion Brand,[47] which claims statistically that 52.7 per cent of respondents read blogs and 50.4 per cent listen to podcasts;[48] whilst the Pew Internet Report, 'Hobbyists Online', reported that 83 per cent of Americans had used the Internet to pursue their hobby online. The most popular social networking sites are MySpace, Facebook, Flickr and Ravelry (which is knitting-specific), whilst the most popular blog is 'Yarn Harlot', whose author, Stephanie Pearl-McPhee, noted:

> The Internet has fuelled the socialization of knitters – it's great having an outlet where someone does want to talk about your new buttonhole technique or the beautifully hand-dyed merino you just got. It's become a huge knitting community – and while you might walk away from projects, you don't walk away from people, so the community continues to grow.[49]

The growth of an online knitting community is not merely the preserve of older women. Teenagers are becoming increasingly visible in online knitting communities, demonstrating the fusion of high-tech computers with low-tech hand knitting. This initial disparity is not quite as paradoxical as one might imagine: computer codes and knitting are both based on binaries, they both can be leisure pastimes, both are forms of self-expression and communication, both can be understood as 'escapist' as they enable the mind to wander, and both require skill and development.[50] One might also suggest that a desire to become actively engaged in both blogging and knitting exemplifies a desire for a sense of touch, of engaging in and maintaining connections in the sensory and interpersonal wider world,[51] contradicting Rheingold's assertion that virtual communities are devoid of the sensory.

It is important to note that the existence of the Knit List – as well as a myriad of similar knitting blogs, podcasts and chatrooms – provides a technological link between an established pattern of gendered and culturally conditioned behaviour, knitting, and the prospective anonymity and individualistic medium of the worldwide web. They also, as cultural theory acknowledges, establish an ideal – a realm or space, in which shared beliefs relating to an understanding of what knitting *is*, based on experience and expectation, can be explored and realized.

What is also relevant is that knitting is not a solitary occupation. It is an experience, which some feel needs to be shared. These blogs are indicative of a collective activity, performed in the privacy of one's home, but also of a 'private' sociability, where activity fuels friendship.

Out of the Loop? Repetition, Contemplation, Catharsis and the Inner Self

> When we knit, we dwell in our safe place – a quiet, focused, contemplative space. The ordinariness of the world gives way to a sense that everything holds a little bit of magic.[52]

This section examines the potential of knitting as a means of uncovering and communicating a spiritual or inner self. By addressing knitting as a means of contemplative practice as outlined in a 'new' genre of texts such as *The Knitting Sutra*,[53] *Mindful Knitting*[54] and *Zen and the Art of Knitting*,[55] which fundamentally centralize the meditative and mindful potential of creative practice and outline the processes by which the knitter can transcend the everyday by creating a mental space that can enhance well-being and act as a site for problem-solving. Essentially this might be understood as the fusion of knitting, spiritual awareness and self-help, enhancing a state of calm, 'wholeness' and balance.

Knitting is a repetitive activity, and like all activities involving repetition, creates a rhythm based on the coincidence of sound and gesture. Similarly, texts addressing knitting as a 'meditative' or 'contemplative' practice are equally repetitive; they say the same thing to the same audience, and with this in mind, and in the interest of balance, issues and testimonies arising from these texts have been juxtaposed with responses from amateur knitters in the UK, interviewed in 1998. The focus of this investigation intends to emphasize what might be seen as an innovative approach to traditional domestic practices (contemplation/therapy) in an attempt to capture new audiences; questioning this assumption by proposing such literature is highly revivalist, ultimately returning to and repeating popular concepts of the constituents of the meaning of knitting.

The crafts are often defined (and marginalized) as repetitious. They require the application of learned skill, and as such are consequently understood within an arts hierarchy as devoid of cerebral or conceptual (and to a certain extent creative) input. However dubious, this definition pervades the language of both art and craft. This seemingly inherent property of crafts practice will be discussed in three ways: firstly, as rhythm, sound and language, an aspect of the coincidence of hand/mind activity. Developing from repetitive activity is the creation of a transcendental or meditative state in which the maker can distance the self from the body through bodily practices in order to move from meaning to the void. And finally, repetition will be discussed as a return, a revisiting of traditional concepts of knitting, which places it at the heart of a postmodern and retrogressive yearning.

Knitting is a repetitive activity based on two stitches. Even if only one of them can be mastered, one can knit. This means that knitting is relatively simple and that most people can do it. Knitting is presented as 'easy', requiring little skill or application, and as such even belies the classification of 'craft'. Such an assumption negates the actual practice of knitting (it can be extremely complex, skilled and difficult), yet it is precisely this ease and repetition which is addressed as a means of creating a space for contemplation, of mindful creativity, and of self-healing.

> The act of knitting is inherently built on the formation of a stitch, the creation of fabric. When we knit, we place our attention over and over again on the natural rhythm of creating fabric from yarn – insert needle, wrap yarn, pull through a new stitch, repeat. Following this simple repetitive action is the basis of contemplative practice. It continually reminds us to stay focused, to stay in the moment. When we knit with this attention, we have an almost indescribable feeling of satisfaction and contentment. This is knitting as meditation.[56]

This opens the introduction of Tara Jon Manning's *Mindful Knitting*, and exemplifies clearly the relationship between knitting and contemplation. Here Manning focuses on areas one might associate with craft per se: repetition, focus, and the coincidence of hand/mind activity. We might assume, therefore, that all craft is 'mindful' or 'meditative', as although she suggests that 'The object of focus for the mindful knitter is repeated formation of the knitted stitch',[57] this could be applied to a wealth of other activities and practices.

Much crafts criticism relies on linguistic theory, or language- or story-based metaphors. 'Narrative', 'Myth' and 'Semiotic', are key terms that perhaps suggest that the crafts are eager to find a language of their own, as well as shake off the dominance of the visual, as in art history. The crafts writer Julian Stair acknowledges:

> Research in the physical and behavioural sciences acknowledges the importance of the body in the perception of self-identity, and its emotional embodiment in social interactions, and argues that even consciousness is a result of our physical experience in the world. It would seem that craft, which intuitively operates through these means, can be seen as a fundamental means of reinforcing our sense of self. If body and hand gestures are regarded as the precursors of verbal language, then what are craft objects but material gestures of the body, operating as externalized, pre-linguistic expression that through haptic engagement reinforce the very source they spring from.[58]

Stair's quote proposes that craft can be understood through practice as process, as a series of learned gestures. The implication is that maker and object are one, the self and the object resulting from the actions of the body.

The relationship between textiles, sensory perception and life refers to touch, the senses, and physical movement as a language, as an extension of the 'semiotic'. Unlike the structuralist definition of semiotics (sound/image/word),[59] crafts criticism addresses the term as a continuation of the psychoanalyst and linguist Julia Kristeva's 'Semiotic Chora',[60] where the semiotic occurs as a direct response to intense stimulation, i.e. the bridge between the conscious and unconscious, the real and the remembered or expected.[61] Fundamentally, Kristeva's 'semiotic' derives from the visual, but this concept of emotional and sensory response is further developed to address 'feeling' inherent in the crafts.

Central to Kristeva's semiotics, and to much crafts criticism that relies on her work, is the notion of rhythm, repetition and interruption. Historically, craft practice as repetitive, repeatable or rhythmic had distanced craft from art – seen as spontaneous, creative, cerebral and coming from a 'higher' being or sense of purpose.[62] Intent on addressing the properties inherent in craft, this new criticism, investigates activity as 'sound' as an aspect of semiotics.

Knitting of course makes a sound: needles click together as stitches are formed. And through repetitive practice, the sound of needles creates a rhythm. The more expertly the activity is performed, the more metered the rhythm. Rhythm here can be seen as contributing to a state of meditative contemplation in two ways; firstly, repetitive sound created through bodily action can be seen to mediate the heart rate and induce a state of calm, and secondly, that continued repeated action and sound can create a semi-hypnotized state that enables the creation of a mental space ideal for contemplation. Indeed, interviewees acknowledged that repetitive acts such as knitting encouraged a sense of 'otherworldliness', an emotional space of calm. One noted:

> When you are knitting you are left alone. You look busy: you are doing something. It's not like reading, when it looks like you are just filling time. Knitting gives you space. When I knit I don't think, I do it automatically; I can even do it in the dark, so it allows my mind to wander, to get away from the kids, the housework and all of the other rubbish I should be doing.[63]

Testimonies acknowledge the value of repetitive, engrossing craftwork during times of 'stress', an activity in which the combination of concentration and rhythm distances the self from the world outside. This 'invisible' space has been described by crafts critics as the distance between the interior and exterior self.[64] Indeed, one interviewee so disliked the space that making alone created, she joined a knitting group so that she wasn't haunted by her personal thoughts, which caused her great distress.[65] This suggests that knitting as rhythm can be seen as a form of introspection, either as a means of finding an internal 'quiet' space or as a more uncomfortable confrontation with the self.

The creation of this body/mind distance might be considered a state of transcendence, or an empty space which enhances the potential for meditative and contemplative practices. Indeed, this is the crux of contemplative and meditative knitting texts – the creation of a space in which one can exist in the here and now, focusing and directing thought. Alternatively, one might see this as a form of alienation, in which the knitter both physically and mentally distances herself from her surroundings and those within it. This is certainly evident in the testimonies of knitters who 'wanted to be left alone' or 'escape' from other chores. Yet the benefit of these practices often had consequences – the wrath of disgruntled family members who felt that knitters spent too much time on their hobby and not enough on them, or other domestic chores.

One could say that the experience of knitting as a form of contemplation and/or escape was actually what drove the respondents to continue to knit. Testimonies repeated that knitting was an activity undertaken outside other more specific tasks, so respondents spoke of 'sitting down and picking up' knitting[66] almost as a reflex action; a physical and psychological 'time out'. One interviewee, who had suffered bouts of depression for many years, expressed the ways in which 'the clicking of needles calms me down … I lose myself in the sound, although it irritates my husband to distraction'.[67] Indeed, for interviewees who used knitting as a form of escape or 'therapy', the act of making created a sensorial rhythm, a repetitive rocking motion, which was calming and stabilizing.

This meditative and contemplative approach is central to popular knitting texts that situate knitting within a model that is constructed from three areas, one historical, derived from a cultural appraisal of knitting as a gendered activity, one medical (occupational and psychotherapy), and one spiritual and loosely based on Buddhism, but encompassing a gamut of religious belief to accommodate any reader/knitter.

The historical impetus is particularly significant to the contemporary knitter, as it offers a return to a way of life that benefits from hindsight. It offers security – it is generally accepted that women knitted in the past under specific sociocultural conditions and for specific reasons, and although this is in no way homogeneous it offers a form of continuity in a world which is constantly changing and unstable. For women, whose roles have changed and expanded considerably to dimorphic proportions throughout the past century, such solace potentially addresses the problem of social and cultural confusion. Indeed, a lack of a sense of traditional social guidance, popularly understood as 'knowing one's place', often leads to a climate of anxiety. This anxiety is largely a twentieth-century phenomenon emerging initially after the First World War, building momentum as a consequence of economic instability, and coinciding with a general loss of faith in religion, science, progress and reason. Renata Salecl highlights the current sense of social anxiety as embracing a loss of identity through the dissolution or changed perception of traditional social roles, which is being redressed through a return to right-wing and overtly restrictive political and social doctrines in order to find structure and life guidance. She notes:

In today's culture, it again seems that economic uncertainty is not the primal cause of anxiety, since the latter is much more connected to the problems people experience with regard to their social roles, to the constant desire to change their identities, and the impossibility of finding guidance for their action. These uncertainties today also result in people turning to religious fundamentalism and to their embracing social restrictions, which introduce new forms of totalitarianism.[68]

Such an analysis does not assume that texts aimed at amateur knitters are on a par with religious fundamentalism, but there is certainly a parallel between the ethos of the texts and a contemporary need to find a sense of guidance for survival in the modern world. Knitting here may merely be a diversion, both in activity and subject, to promote a return to 'wholesome' and moral activities that fulfil a traditional sense of women's social role (the 'New Domesticity') or indeed satisfy the political ambitions of the Right. Indeed, from a feminist perspective, one might conclude that by promoting a traditionally 'feminine' pastime to women, with the additional emphasis on spiritual enlightenment and escape from the mundaneness and anxiety of everyday life, these texts might be disempowering women, returning them to a state of domesticity without questioning the continuing dominance of patriarchy. Indeed, the combination of testimony, projects to make, advice and humorous words of wisdom, juxtaposed with the perceived spiritual enlightenment within these texts, is highly seductive, subjective and somewhat dictatorial. Knitting becomes a metaphor for 'goodness' and moral purity, a state that one obtains, it seems, through meditative and contemplative practices.

Such an assertion is by no means new; indeed, the meaning of knitting in the contemporary world is largely based on definitions emanating from gender division, binary opposites and nineteenth-century codes of morality. Likewise, knitting has long been associated with disability, philanthropy and usefulness, historically offered as a pastime for injured servicemen, and as recuperative and restorative activity for those unable to find work in paid employment due to their mental or physical frailties. Knitting is also a useful activity and therefore has moral associations arising as a response to the Protestant work ethic, in which 'the Devil finds work for idle hands'. So, the contemporary knitting texts that have been outlined encapsulate a concept of the crafts as solace, whilst projecting an individualist ideology of self-help, combined with a series of spiritual practices that embrace a postmodern approach to non-organized religion. Knitting therefore becomes a metaphor for a retrogressive journey, travelling forward through the process of knitting row after row, whilst simultaneously looking backwards to the history and tradition of the discipline itself.

Indeed, this proactive approach had some resonance with the interviewees, who believed that knitting encompassed a sense of a journey in which they could see actual progress (the growing or forming of the garment/object), which psychologically demonstrated a transition from illness or unhappiness towards a certain extent of personal well-being.

Like the remits of occupational therapy,[69] the focus of knitting from a contemplative perspective (as outlined in popular texts) centres on experience. Experience here marks not just the journey (although this is significant) but the attitude which is applied to the process being undertaken.

Experience is initiated and consequently marked by the ability to create and sustain a state of stillness and calm, which is described as 'mindfulness'. Like meditation, mindfulness is far more directional and proactive, and encourages the meditative state to focus on progressive activity, combining both body and mind. Mindfulness exists in the moment; it has no past or future, and can be understood as the expression and experience of being.

Drawing from Buddhist thinking, the mundane becomes an arena in which the self, environment and the everyday can be endured, worked through and even transcended. This means that the knitter becomes aware of her place within a wider scheme (which may or may not have a religious imperative) and becomes more philosophical about her personal situation. An example of this is

Figure 44 A bear knitted whilst the maker was in hospital recovering from anorexia, 1993. Knitting was part of a cognitive behavioural therapy programme, in which time and progression from illness to health was marked from beginning to completion of each knitted project.

highlighted by Nancy's testimony, recounted in Bernadette Murphy's *Zen and the Art of Knitting*:

> Every project has its challenges. In each sweater there are times I get really discouraged or bogged down. There's great satisfaction in sticking with it, moving through the difficult times and getting to the end. Then you just have a thing, and things are impermanent and of little value.[70]

The testimony highlights the ways in which the process of knitting becomes a metaphor for daily life, but one that has a projected conclusion. Knitting, like life, is fraught with obstacles and difficulties to work through but, unlike life, has a set outcome – a sweater, scarf or other woolly object. In this respect, knitting is predictable, even if the journey/process encountered outside the making isn't. Indeed, the process itself seems to draw attention to the development of skill as a 'learning curve', the opportunity to put right that which is 'wrong' or could have been addressed differently, an opportunity not possible when dealing with life events. The potential to correct 'mistakes' is outlined by Sister Elizabeth, who suggests that knitting offers her the opportunity to restore calm to her stressful working life:

> I find I can't leave a mistake. I have to go back and rip no matter how far back and do it over again. My friend thinks I'm crazy when she sees me doing this. 'No one will notice that', she tells me. My answer is 'But I do.' I often think that if I could undo mistakes that I've made in life as easily, it would be just wonderful.[71]

The emphasis here is the acknowledgement of imperfection; the notion that to 'err is human' refocuses the knitter to accept that no one and nothing is perfect, and as a consequence it challenges her expectations of life.

This rather sentimental appraisal of knitting typifies the rhetoric associated with knitting as a contemplative practice; it highlights the spirituality that draws from the historical notion of making as familial and sociable, enhanced with elements of individualism and self-help. The made object is not valorized on the level of skill in its construction, nor on its aesthetic appeal, but on the time spent, and the emotional and spiritual significance embodied in its construction. This has certainly been the driving force within occupational therapy, and knitting within hospitals has been widespread, with visitors and patients engaged in knitting as a therapeutic practice.[72]

Conversely, the repetitive and soothing sound of the clicking of needles when knitting can be extremely irritating to those sharing the same space but not participating. And, the use of crafts as therapy in institutions is not necessarily the panacea to all ills. A mental health worker described his experiences of knitting within institutions, in particular knitting dishcloths. He described the simplicity of the object's construction – 'It was easy to make and required no skill' – and how the ordinariness and 'blandness' of the cloth reflected the maker's sense of self:

> There was no joy in making the cloths. They were ordinary and bland and not beautiful. The patients felt that this was all they were worth – dishcloths. It was really just about filling time, not about getting better. It was a soulless experience.[73]

The product of making seems here to be equated with social status and representative of the making of the purely functional rather than the decorative. The object said nothing to the maker about himself or herself. It was just 'something to do', a time-filler to alleviate boredom. The objects were not to be sold, given as gifts or donated to 'good causes', nor were they personal keepsakes, and consequently the maker felt as devalued as the object itself.[74]

As a constructed textile, knitting is measurable. One can see how much one has achieved by counting rows, a significant factor in marking time, time spent and for setting personal targets. It is manageable, or controllable (unlike life events), and the knitter can chart progress achieved through a meditative state moving from disarray to calm, from sickness to health/well-being or just to a state of acceptance.

The psychiatrist, Adolph Meyer, suggests that people 'learn to organize time and he (or she) does it in terms of doing things'.[75] This exemplifies the significant role 'doing' has on emotional and physical well-being as well as its impact on self-fulfilment. The value of time usefully spent demonstrates how the performance and completion of activities contributes to a sense of self-worth, of achievement and the desire to continue which, in turn, creates pleasure, satisfaction and pride. Therefore, doing or making, or generally being engaged in any form of activity, promotes self-esteem and confidence, which ultimately enhances quality of life.

'Quality of life' is a familiar facet of postmodern society. It acknowledges that our lives are increasingly chaotic but empty and yet we have the ability to fill the void of dissatisfaction. We search for meaning in the meaningless, which makes our quest never-ending. The sociologist Zygmunt Bauman recognizes the need for life direction, asserting that we need to make sense of who we are and where we're going, and describes modern life as a pilgrimage. The concept of pilgrimage is significant because it offers the potential for self-awareness, discovery and the ability to gain control over one's life. This is a form of identity-building, in which our past and future creates an objective language of space. The subjective here and now allows us to look back to our past and forward to plot our way into the unknown.[76]

It is evident that the performance of making, and the completion of each made project, is demonstrative of interpersonal communication between the real and the ideal self, and the self and others. Each worked project is representative of the imperfect current self, marking progress towards an ideal, thus acting as the physical manifestation of an internal dialogue. Therefore, mastery over a pattern or technique promotes mastery over the self. In a culture that valorizes human worth in terms of activity (i.e. 'What do you do?'), and places importance on the cult of individualism, doing it for yourself – in whatever form this may take – is indicative of control over the self, thus promoting self- and social worth.

Bauman asserts that we now live 'life in fragments', which has led to a sense of 'placelessness', of confusion, and with the dissolution of grand narratives, the place of religious belief has been superseded by 'New Age' thinking, prioritizing a proactive approach to spirituality that offers an escape from the pressures and mundaneness of everyday life. Knitting offers a practical application for this form of thinking; as a repetitive and rhythmic practice, it has the physical potential to elevate the mind to a state of contemplation whilst doing something that is both measurable and 'useful'. In this sense, traditional concepts of the cultural meaning and purpose of knitting (occupation, usefulness and philanthropy) merge with more scientific and rational practices such as occupational and psychotherapy, and popularized relaxation and meditative activities. As always, the path to enlightenment is fraught with obstacles: one might fall through the loops or simply unravel, and although knitting may offer a metaphorical language that is entwined with life narratives, whether that path is knitted remains to be seen.

CASE STUDY. Deadly Yarns and Knitted Fictions: Murderous Knits, Chick Knit Lit and the Twenty-First-Century Woman

This chapter has focused on the ways in which knitting can be both understood as a narrative, a journey through making, and as a biographical object once the making process is complete, as well as indicating the ways in which knitting contributes to the formation of personal identities and the biography of the knitter. This case study addresses the relationship between knitting and narrative in its most literal sense: through discussion, description and iconography in contemporary fiction. In recent years, knitting has become increasingly popular as a key theme within fiction, particularly in two specific genres – murder mystery and chick lit (or chick knit lit), and the purpose of this study is to discuss the generic components of the texts, discuss their relationship with earlier incarnations, and to assess what these novels offer to and say about their readership, primarily the twenty-first-century woman.

Historically, knitting and murder has been linked in literature through the writing of Agatha Christie and Patricia Wentworth, in particular the ways in which knitting is portrayed an innocuous pastime undertaken by clever but nosy old ladies such as Miss Marple and Miss Silver. Contemporary knitting mysteries, however, see knitting as active, aggressive even, often featuring murder victims skewered to death with knitting needles or restrained or smothered with knitting yarn. The murders are often perpetrated by women and the crimes solved by them; therefore the premise, protagonists and narrative are female-dominated and female-driven. Knitting in these texts is both pleasurable and horrific, exerting the potential to both heal and harm, and as a result extends beyond the hidden and unassuming as in earlier murder mysteries.

Chick knit lit is somewhat different and is aimed at a younger audience – the protagonists are twentysomethings, and the narrative is constructed around everyday issues such as relationships, family, sex, physical appearance, friendships, shopping and so on. The extension from chick lit is essentially the centrality of knitting to the narrative. Knitting here forges friendships: it develops alongside the narrative and offers the potential for positive activity amidst chaotic lives, for example 'Caught between life, love and pursuit of the perfect cast-on, these three friends learn that there are never any easy answers, except maybe one – when the going gets tough, the tough get knitting'.[77]

Contemporary chick knit lit embodies the traditional concept of knitting as a feminine activity, although not necessarily a domestic one. It celebrates the notion of female friendships (which could be argued are representative of a 'sisterhood') and challenges notions of knitting, and indeed reading, as passive and patriarchal pastimes. For the characters, knitting becomes not just a means of forging and maintaining dynamic female groupings, but it is also as a metaphor for life narratives, which unravel and are reknitted as part of the fiction. In addition, knitting becomes a motivator and skill set that enables women not only to take care of themselves, but also to solve crime and address personal crises in a pragmatic manner. Similarly, these texts offer the reader a form of escapism not dissimilar to other genres of fiction aimed at women, i.e. romance. However, knitting fiction offers more than wishful thinking: it offers escape through practical engagement, not merely with the narrative, but with the patterns and recipes additional to, but featured in, the texts. This suggests that the seemingly passive act of reading now offers the potential for interaction and activity.

In the twenty-first century, this new genre of fiction, which resurrects and celebrates 'traditional' women's pastimes, appears to be at odds with feminist thinking. This study intends to assess why knitting has become so central to fiction narratives as well as critiquing texts from feminist and post-feminist perspectives. What do these texts reveal about knitting and knitters in the twenty-first century? What do they owe to traditional textile stories, and to what extent are they representative of a 'new woman'?

Since the introduction of Miss Marple in Agatha Christie's murder mystery novels in 1930, knitting and crime detection have become tentatively interlinked. Marple, of course, is essentially a busybody for whom knitting is merely a guise, a means of appearing busy as she listens in to and watches the interaction between characters; she assesses motives, relationships and alibis whilst her clicking needles enable her to disappear into the background. Knitting is understood, therefore, as an innocuous activity, associated with dithering – if not curious – old ladies, a stereotype Marple distinctly plays up to in order to achieve her crime-solving objectives.

Miss Marple is an ingenious woman, whose character is largely derivative of feminine wiles, and whilst devoid of any concept of sexuality that this might imply (she is an elderly spinster and as such portrayed as distinctly sexless), embodies concepts of intuition, gossip and a faith in her instincts and knowledge of human nature. This clear emphasis on intuition rather than rationality is an extremely useful tool, particularly if the suspect has a strong alibi or appears motiveless, but nonetheless distinguishes the female from the male sleuth, assigning femininity to biological deterministic binaries of female/nature/irrationality versus male/culture/rationality. Similarly, Marple is an amateur, and although her crime-solving success rate is possibly greater than that of the police force, she receives no reward for her contribution, thus distancing her from the world of paid employment. Similarly, as an amateur, she has no actual power; she cannot make arrests or bring perpetrators to justice. For this she must rely on the cooperation of the exclusively male police force. Marple therefore becomes a sign of the paradoxical potential of women and expression of their powerlessness, functioning within a patriarchal framework. One might conclude that she is a product of inter-war society, and like the vast majority of ordinary women of the period, she is understood as valuable but is not valued. In the Miss Marple mysteries, after the hard work and the big reveal, the status quo remains unchallenged, harmony is restored and Marple returns to her knitting.

In new 'knitting' mysteries, the ghost of Miss Marple lingers, and although the women in these texts are equally products of the times, they bear witness to a history of female amateur detectives. Knitting is not merely an aspect of iconography, as with Marple, but a central theme running throughout each of the novels. Indeed, descriptions of the knitting of a particular item or garment runs parallel with the narrative, so as the story unfolds, the knitting grows,[78] as would be the case in traditional textile stories, which were performed orally. The correlation between narrative and the making process exemplifies the passing of real time, whilst also enabling the articulation of gesture and hand/brain coordination.

The focal site of each novel is a yarn shop and the narrative unfolds amidst this setting. Narratives may move away from this site, but it is always returned to as the conclusion is reached. Each yarn shop is situated in a small town (e.g. Fort Connor, Colorado; Excelsior, Minnesota) redolent of Marple's St Mary Mead, and is understood as the 'heart' of the community. Within these largely rural communities, knitting is often part of daily life: people keep sheep and alpaca, spin and dye their own yarns, and sell them to the yarn shop. Concepts of production and consumption are important elements within the setting – a firm emphasis on DIY and traditional methods of production, from animal rearing to hand-spinning, alongside knitting one's own clothing from one's own patterns, is juxtaposed with the opportunity for the purchase of kits, yarns and other knit-related ephemera, as well as lavish descriptions of the shop's layout and stock, to entice the reader into a state of consumerist desire. In the yarn shop, the reader finds a mix of the traditional with the modern, an ideal world in which local businesses support local suppliers, and where traditional practices and products merge with the latest fashions and yarn technology.

In these communities, everyone knows everyone else, and the yarn shop, which is also the site of knitting groups, becomes a place not merely for consumerism but discussion, highlighting the contemporary impact of Stitch 'n' Bitch groups whilst referring to the history of the knitting circle. In these instances, the yarn shop is significant for the formation of the narrative and characters, offering a predominantly female space which, unlike the communal focal point of the pub, as in British soap operas, is concerned with specifically female interests, and can be seen as respectable and seemingly non-threatening. In Maggie Sefton's *A Deadly Yarn*, the escapist potential of the yarn shop is described:

> Kelly concentrated on the deep rose circlet of yarn, stitches rhythmically adding row after row to the sweater-in-the-round. She'd been sitting at the shop's library table for over two hours this morning. Just like yesterday, she'd found herself unable to start on her usual morning routine at the computer. She'd work on client accounts later. Right now, Kelly wanted to be surrounded by the warmth of the shop, where she could talk to friends and people she'd grown to care about these last six months. She needed to be here.[79]

The yarn shop therefore provides a locale in which contemporary women can meet and engage in traditionally female pastimes, a place where they can feel safe, and as such creates an environment that is both comforting and nostalgic – the warmth of the yarn, the repetition of the stitches, the cosiness of knitted items, combined with a sense of an all-embracing community working in harmony together. This is knitting as an ideal.

This idyllic setting is thrown into disarray when a murder occurs. In several books, the murder takes place in the yarn shop, destroying the harmonious environment physically and metaphorically. For example, in Monica Ferris's *Crewel World*, Betsy Devonshire, the book's protagonist and reluctant amateur sleuth, returns to the yarn shop:

> Betsy could not believe the disarray. The floor was covered with yarn and floss. The spin racks were on their sides, magazines had been crumpled and ripped, baskets that had held knitting yarn had not only been emptied, but stepped on ... Behind the chair was a big heap of wool and books, and beyond them, as if they had been moved aside to uncover her, was a woman.[80]

The implied anger Betsy feels at the disturbance of the shop, in particular that the wool had been 'stepped on', suggests a moral outrage that seems more significant than the discovery of the body. The implication is that anyone who is so disrespectful of yarn could equally be responsible for murder. In *Crewel World*, the discovery of the body – Betsy's sister and the owner of the yarn shop – is an expression of chaos in a stable world. Here justice is to be sought, not merely as a means of retribution, but as a means of restoring harmony to the whole community.

For Betsy Devonshire, the discovery of a body in the yarn shop may well be the catalyst for the restoration of loss to what was once an 'ideal', but in other novels, knitting is a site of aggression, and therefore the threat comes from within. For example, in Mary Kruger's *Died in the Wool*, Ariadne Evans, proprietor of Ariadne's Web, finds a client dead in the shop: 'Ohmygod,' she gasped. A purple wool homespun yarn was tangled about Edith's neck and tied back to two sticks into a crude, but effective garrotte.[81]

Here not only the calm sanctuary of the shop is disturbed, but the victim is a knitter, and the killer has a clear knowledge of wool, which is intended to apportion blame to another (the maker of the homespun yarn). Here knitting is both active and proactive, utilized as a means of death and motivator for its punishment, exercising the potential for the hobby to both harm and heal, to destroy and restore. Knitting becomes the site, weapon, and thematic link between the key players in the narrative, and is therefore instrumental in unlocking or unravelling the mystery.

Knitting is also a sign of community: a group of people with shared interests working towards a common goal. This community is predominantly female, sharing an interest in knitting, meeting at the yarn shop for communal gossiping, eating, drinking and skill-sharing. Once the murder has been committed, the knitting group is mobilized, with each member exhibiting a skill or area of expertise which helps decipher a clue. This is more than a reliance on Marple's 'women's intuition'; the women in contemporary mysteries are amateur experts – in Mary Kruger's *Knit Fast; Die Young*, Ariadne Evans is able to identify a yarn with forensic accuracy.[82] This implies that women have useful and rational skills, albeit obtained through the knowledge of a traditional female pastime, which perform a vital role in solving a murder. Not only are women presented as having distinct individual skills, rather than accessing a homogeneous series of traits, they are also presented as flawed, making mistakes, feeling fear and so on, whilst also displaying a sense of fun and humour. This is evidenced in the language of the texts, which frequently utilize puns:

> While Josh pieces together the details of the crime, clues about Ariadne's ties to Miss Perry come to light … and a bizarre pattern unfolds. Now it's up to Ariadne to do some sleuthing of her own. Can she untangle the investigation without getting snarled up into too much trouble? That depends on whether the killer is as crafty as she is …[83]

One might suggest that the humorous use of rather corny puns implies that these mysteries are fun or light-hearted, rather than exhibiting gritty realism, the preserve of the male detective. Although crimes are often gratuitous (stabbing with knitting needles, smothering with fleeces, falling from high railings, etc.), their description is limited, leaving the details to the imagination of the reader, implying a sense of propriety and decency, which sanitizes and feminizes murder. The emphasis on the female 'detective' as an amateur is also a refection on a desire to 'clean up' crime, offering a rather domestic and nostalgic return to the women in murder mysteries of the past, rather than emulating contemporary and popular professional women investigators such as Kay Scarpetta in Patricia Cornwell's novels.[84]

The premise in all of the novels is the creation of a safe community, symbolically represented by the yarn shop. From this haven, chaos reigns when a murder is committed, and is witnessed or discovered by the book's protagonist, who has a specific interest in knitting. The protagonist becomes detective, amassing clues and evidence seemingly ignored or overlooked by professional law enforcers, and ultimately the women uncover the 'real' perpetrator. Such a premise may be reminiscent of Christie's Marple (intuitive, reliant on gossip and engagement with the community, belief in her knowledge of human nature), but the amateur women detectives have, to a certain extent, moved on.

In each novel, the central character displays traits pertinent to a stereotype of a 'modern' woman. Each woman is financially independent, either employed in business (as in Maggie Sefton's *A Deadly Yarn*, in which the main character, Kelly Flynn, is an accountant and amateur knitter), or is the owner of a yarn shop (as in Monica Ferris's and Mary Kruger's mysteries). Similarly, each of the women is divorced and single; therefore each displays a sense of financial control that does not rely on the income of a male partner. These women are independent in other ways: they rarely have family obligations[85] and are freely able to pursue amateur detection without the constraints of children, ageing relatives, nine-to-five work schedules,[86] and so on. The women are constructed to demonstrate business acumen, but also display an emotional independence, exemplified in their contentment with a single – as opposed to married – life.

Whereas Marple was a confirmed 'old maid', these women are single; however they have all, at some stage in the past, conformed to societal and heterosexual norms and been married. Now divorced, one might suggest that these women are rejecting these norms, and challenging them by exerting signs of success and independence. However, this is problematic, and although these women appear strong and independent, existing in situations that are on the whole female-dominated, the insistence of a heterosexual past implies a particular norm, in which no space is created for homosexual women. In Monica Ferris's novels, there is a male gay character, Godwin, who is so stereotypical he appears merely for comedic value rather than social critique –

I'm sorry sleuthing is making you so miserable, because I love it when you prove you're so much more clever that everyone else, even the police. And I love it that you're so good about telling me first. In a gossipy town like Excelsior, that makes me Queen.[87]

So initially, marriage is presented as a means of communicating that characters are heterosexual, and the end of marriages presented as the result of poor choices that are currently being redressed. This creates an arena in which the potential for heterosexual romance is ever present. Although not a central element of the narrative, romance is certainly an aspect of the novels that is deemed to speak to a female readership, reflecting what might be described as life narratives, whilst working structurally as a device to tie up loose ends creating a sense of 'wholeness' in the scenario. It appears that a single woman, however successful and independent, is still an awkward and out of place entity, who can only be completed or resolved by her possible joining to a man.

In the knitting murder mysteries, the possibility for romance is never completely fulfilled. In each novel, romantic interest is presented in the form of a rather benign 'good man', often a policeman involved in the solving of the crime. Love is chaste and there is no sex. The seeming impotency of the male romantic persona, re-establishes the potential empowerment of the female protagonist, yet she is neither femme fatale nor slut[88] and becomes the embodiment of a 'good woman': hard-working, honest and largely without desire. Lack of desire therefore can be assessed as a means of either transcending female stereotypes that emphasize a reliance on overt sexuality to achieve their aims, or as a means of promoting traditional values that oppose promiscuity. Either way, the absence of sex in these novels creates an unreality, reminiscent of a retrogressive gaze into a nostalgic world.

An absence of sexual contact does not imply a lack of sensual or sensory pleasure, and it is through these concepts that a notion of desire is both constructed and fulfilled. Desire operates as a stimulant for consumerism, expressed through the fetishistic descriptions of yarns and food, both of which encourage notions of touch and pleasure of the mouth, which can be understood as a substitute or metaphor for sexual acts. Indeed, each novel is packed with references to food: huge phallic sandwiches, steaming bowls of messy foods such as spaghetti or chowder, which need to be slurped and are dribbled, contributing to a sense of gastro-porn for the reader: one imagines the sensation of eating, has one's appetite stimulated, but is left hungry, desirous for more. Food and its provision has historically been the remit of the woman,[89] and characters are all expert bakers, with recipes included as an appendix for readers to make at home. As readers are perceived as identifying with characters and the narratives of these texts, the presumption that they will want to reproduce the mouth-watering offerings so richly described emphasizes identification with traditional female roles and occupations, as well as encouraging the consumption of products/ingredients and the food itself.

The descriptive prevalence of food consumption in these texts is representative of women with 'hearty appetites', which both literally and metaphorically contribute to the dilemma inherent in the contemporary female body – of excess and constraint. The female grotesque, as discussed by Lorraine Gammon, is understood as a sign of overindulgence, of wantonness and unquenchable lust, a threat to the status quo.[90] And likewise, characters in knit mysteries are mindful of the pleasures of overconsumption, frequently commenting on a need to cut back or diet, as well as demonstrating an obvious restraint of sexual urges.

Similarly, references to yarn border on the fetishistic, with descriptions of colour, texture and feel stimulating a sensation of perceived touch in the reader. As these yarns are intended to be worked into garments or accessories that will adorn the body, the sensation of touch is further stimulated and simulated through the association with its proximity to the flesh. It appears that whilst women are precluded from engaging in the pleasures of the flesh, desire becomes admissible when it is performed or achieved through the consumption of goods. Women cannot and do not take control of their own bodies through sexual relationships, but they can control the appearance of their bodies through its adornment in sensuous fibres and garments. As with the inclusion of recipes, patterns for garments discussed or made throughout the narrative are included as an appendix, encouraging reader participation.

The female protagonists may appear to embrace traditional feminine virtues such as abstinence and nurturing, and occupy their time with similarly traditional activities such as knitting and baking, but they also display a fearlessness and tenacity which often endangers their lives. Following warnings from the police, which go unheeded, the amateur detective puts her own safety at risk, confronting the murderer. As each woman becomes closer to 'the reveal', her life becomes increasingly threatened, and in some cases she comes to blows with the perpetrator. Unlike their predecessors (Misses Marple and Silver), these women literally fight back, kicking, punching and utilizing weapons that come to hand to save themselves and to further the cause of justice. Female protagonists are therefore constructed as entities straddling the past and the present, both feminine and fearless, domesticated and independent, and as such can be labelled post-feminist.

Knitting mysteries, although including youthful protagonists, are ostensibly rural and steeped in a nostalgia that assumes an older reader. Conversely, chick knit lit has an urban setting, more fashionable characters and, by association, presumes a younger audience. The term 'chick lit' refers to a genre of novels aimed at and written by women, emerging as a response to Helen Fielding's *Bridget Jones's Diary* (1996). Largely derivative of the romance, emphasizing the importance of female friendships as well as finding a man, hungry for glamour and independence, juggling the pressures of a successful career whilst dealing with life's ups and downs, chick lit offers a scenario deemed familiar to the contemporary woman.[91] Humour is at the forefront of these novels, which assumes that the genre is light-hearted and, by association, light reading, offering a fantasy or escapist arena for the discussion of everyday life. Such an assumption presupposes that writing for, about and by women is itself less serious than other forms of writing, an approach highly contested by authors and readers alike.[92] Regardless of the seriousness of the genre, it has been extended to include a variety of hobbies and interests deemed suitable for a female readership. Therefore, chick knit lit throws knitting into the mix, which is not incidental and acts as a catalyst for change, personal development, meeting ground, means of independence or self-sufficiency, and so on.

Each text has a narrative derivative of the dual genres of the romance and the fairy tale. This enables the mundane and everyday to become a site for both opportunity and escape into a fantasy. For example, Olivia Goldsmith's *Wish Upon a Star*,[93] is essentially Cinderella with a twist; the 'handsome prince' is rejected and replaced with the character initially perceived to be the villain, whilst also referring to other favourite tales such as Rumpelstiltskin: 'I never expected knitting to be so relaxing and fulfilling but to take a ball of wool and turn it into something useful – well, it's like spinning straw into gold.'[94]

Other narratives are not so explicitly derivative, dealing with death, financial hardship, loss and loneliness, but ultimately each includes fantastic chance events, for example celebrity endorsement[95] or meeting with and being welcomed into the social circle of the aristocracy or fabulously wealthy,[96] which transforms the lives of the protagonists.[97] These events provide a mechanism that allows the female protagonists to survey their situations, ethics, friendships and futures. Essentially, they can establish who they are, what they want, where they want to go and with whom. The 'event' therefore is a catalyst for empowerment, opening up options for self-betterment and self-discovery.

The protagonist(s) in each text is/are female, frequently a disparate group of women working in equally disparate professions ranging from the sciences to the media, drawn together through a shared interest in knitting and an ideological commonality. This shared belief system revolves around kinship, achieving potential and the confusions around finding a man to settle down with. The emphasis on individuality and achievement distances these women from traditional romantic heroines, bearing witness to the features of the genre and indeed to concerns of the contemporary woman, described as 'the Bridget Jones effect', in which the distinction and miscommunication between the sexes is emphasized.[98]

Men in these texts are considered 'the Other', thus reversing rather than questioning the patriarchal 'Othering' of women. One might see this as a step towards equality, albeit rather tenuous, or as a return to biological determinism, evidenced in contemporary popular sexual psychology[99] contributing to the text's drive towards finding a partner. The women in knitting novels appear to represent a generation who find feminism stereotypical and its ideals at odds with a social and personal desire to settle down. Post-feminism enables women to find some equilibrium, the opportunity to 'have it all', satisfying a concept of gender equality whilst acknowledging sexual difference. This is evident in the novels, where women choose to knit for themselves, rather than for others, distancing themselves from the domestic and housewifely associations of the craft. Knitting is more frivolous, expensive and glamorous; it is an expression of one's own creativity, achievement and personality. In, for example, *Knitting Under the Influence*, when Lucy starts to make a sweater for her boyfriend, she is met with horror from her friends:

> 'You should only ever knit for yourself,' Kathleen said. 'That's the first rule of the single girl's knitting handbook. It's the *only* rule.' She put down her work and held up her hand. 'You try to knit a guy a sweater, then one of two things will happen' – she raised her index finger – 'either he'll break up with you just as you're finishing it, which means you have to destroy all your work or spend the rest of your life trying to find another guy exactly the same size, or' – another finger went up – 'even if you *do* get to give it to him, he won't like it or even wear it and it'll make you so mad, you'll end up breaking up with him. And some future girlfriend of his will find it someday and tear it to pieces. Trust me, you only want to knit stuff for yourself.'[100]

Built around a group of friends, either established or made during knit club attendance, the women in the novels are indicative of a support group, offering advice, companionship and friendship without judgement. As each character is introduced and her background revealed, the reader becomes part of this group, and the women representative of the ideal friends and relationships readers don't – but would like – to have. The women are presented as potential role models, active and successful, achievers, people who engage in life rather than passively watching the world go by, whilst sharing the frailties and concerns of the reader, i.e.

> I'm really enjoying it. It's so nice in the evenings when I'm watching telly. It makes me feel like a proper mum, sitting there knitting. And it stops me eating crisps too … I like it because it helps to pass the time while you're waiting for something exciting to happen.
> You'll end up with a very long scarf if you're waiting for something to happen around here.[101]

The praxis at which traditional female roles merge with the new, as outlined in the above quotation, highlights a contemporary dilemma faced by young women: of achieving personal and societal goals whilst actively participating in and determining their own lives. Indeed, knitting becomes a metaphor for life, something that takes a great deal of skill to master, something which requires effort and dedication to achieve perfection, whilst something that can be remedied by unpicking and redoing:

> She liked perfection, but it seemed achievable only in very small things. When she looked at her life and the lives of others she saw nothing but disappointment, compromise, dropped stitches and twisted yarn … Of course it was only a scarf, but she had made it with her own hands, her own vision and her own intelligence. Perhaps the secret to a perfect life (or something close to it) was to keep it small and pay attention.[102]

Whilst feminists debate the recent revival of knitting as a pastime[103] as a sign of a return to patriarchal values, novels that feature knitting as a theme do little to counterbalance the argument. The fictitious heroines of these novels may display characteristics of independence, but largely they are seduced by the possibility of romantic liaisons, traditional female relationships and the lure of consumer goods.

The popularity of chick lit and the new fashionability of knitting have created a market for young women, in which they are offered the opportunity to buy kits, instruction on how to knit a jumper in a day, and access to both cheap and very expensive yarn, enabling the highly portable pastime of knitting to fit into busy schedules, suit any budget, and satisfy fashion trends. Therefore, these books, like so many other aspects of women's lives, address women as consumers, not only through the purchase of the books themselves, but through their language and rhetoric, and the ways in which they romanticize accumulation.[104] Lifestyles can be achieved through the purchase of goods, and the inclusion of patterns and recipes as standard enhances and encourages reader participation.

The stories told bear witness to genres historically aimed at women, such as romance and its contemporary sister, chick lit, and light mysteries (or 'Cosies') offering well-worn formulas that reinstate rather than challenge the dominance of patriarchy. One might conclude that whilst traditional stories are revived alongside traditional crafts practices, we are witness to a revitalization of activities presumed lost as a result of both industrialization and modernism,[105] and from a feminist perspective, this can be viewed as a means of uncovering hidden histories,[106] previously deemed part of a folk culture, domestic and inherently feminine. Indeed, in each example of chick knit lit discussed, both women's creative practice and their ability to make something from nothing become synonymous with women's struggles with daily life. Making provides meaning for the women as well as supplying the means through which their problems are communicated, worked through and overcome. Knitting becomes both a metaphor for daily life, an indicator of life narratives, but also a tool for making space, making special things and for making friends and communities, activities and ideals otherwise hidden, forgotten or lost.

Conversely, one might see these revivals as the reinstatement of women's traditional roles, a reinvestment in patriarchy, in which old stereotypes are given an aggressive makeover, the housewife becomes the 'mumpreneur', the single girl about town or the professional woman; the same character, but nicer sweaters. A return to knitting may merely be the replication of domesticity, a means of keeping busy, of doing, rather than engagement in potential political struggle.

Conclusion

The sociologist Paul Willis, in his assessment of 'common culture', questioned the role of 'art' in everyday life. 'Art', he believed, was a term loaded with institutional exclusivity, presupposing that everything outside a 'gallery' was 'not art'. For Willis, 'art' existed as a necessary component of daily life, as 'symbolic creativity', a means of making the ordinary special, and marking individuals as different from the masses.[107] Willis argues that symbolic creativity (the expression and drive of creative practice) can be verbal (joke-telling), performance (acting), or non-verbal (like making).[108] This is an essential part of everyday life, a means of communication, a demonstration of the real and the ideal self (what I am and what I could be), an acknowledgement of culturally and historically determined perceptions of identity (of class, race, age, gender) and the experience of them, and of personalities and vital capacities.[109] Knitting therefore can be understood as demonstrative of the makers' personal identity and relationships with others (real or ideal), the knitters' experience/perception of their class, gender, race (or perhaps their understanding of 'home' or 'motherhood' or 'family'), and also their achievements, the ways in which the knitting demonstrates learning, time spent and aesthetic sensibility or 'taste'.

Knitting can be understood as a form of narrative; it has a beginning, a middle and an end, each distinct and involving the working through of ideas, patterns, thoughts and identity over time. Knitting can offer the knitter a sense of self, the creation of a personal identity, either through standing out from the crowd or fitting in with it. It offers an outlet for personal creativity whilst signifying one's personal role within kinship and friendship groups; knitted garments can act as an aide-memoire, offering a connection with people, places and times, and establishing a sense of personal biography, a place within a lineage.

Stories and knitting are interwoven into the experience of the everyday, becoming metaphors and markers of life events and experiences. Modes of communication have changed, the stories are different and participation in knitting is no longer a necessity, yet the relationship between knitting and narrative continues to be told.

–6–

Knit Power: The Politics of Knitting

Stop making scarves. Start making trouble.[1]

This chapter aims to investigate the ways in which knitting can be understood as an alternative: an alternative to the world of mass-produced goods, machine production and global capitalism in general, as well as being an alternative lifestyle. The term 'alternative' in this instance implies not merely difference, but subversion, which has far-reaching political undertones. In this respect, the investigation questions the significance of knitting as an act or site of rebellion that challenges the dominant ideology and provides a means of conveying political and social protest and comment.

Employing a Marxist and post-Marxist approach to knitting, the chapter aims to establish a dialogue that addresses and questions the balance of power and resultant inequalities existent in contemporary society. Focusing on concepts of globalization, environmentalism and anti-war protest, the ways in which knitting can be understood as an extension of Marxist philosophy are addressed.

Marxism and Post-Marxism

Marxist thought covers a whole range of ideas pertaining to an understanding of social organization that questions the unequal power relations arising from capitalism. The writing of Marx is prolific, and has been influential throughout the twentieth century in addressing and bridging the gaps between rich and poor, strong and weak, and as a means of formulating oppositional societal and economic structures. The influence of Marxism is far-reaching, and in relation to knitting, can be seen to permeate discourses surrounding thrift, philanthropy, globalization, ecological and ethical practices and discourse, as well as informing acts of social protest.

Marx was influenced by Hegel's *The Philosophy of History*, which discussed the ways in which societies progressed through conflict between the oppressed and their oppressors, which pivoted on the notion of religion, spirituality and the conflict of ideas. This implied that regardless of how oppressed a person was socially or physically, the mind and spirit had no boundaries and were ultimately free (this is the basis for dialectics – reasoning, argument and discussion). Challenging (but following) the structure of Hegelian dialectics, Marx upturned these ideas, focusing on society rather than philosophy and religion. The central focus of Marx's philosophy was the acknowledgement of the potential for social (rather than spiritual) progress through struggle, concentrating on historical societal progression and development from a feudal to capitalist form of social organization.

This changing structure was pertinent to Marx as it was essentially a commentary on his own times. He had been influenced by German philosophy, which had questioned the concept of freedom and power relations, informed by writing and political thought arising from the French Revolution; he had read Engels's texts on the English working classes, and had witnessed the results of mass industrialization. Industrialization had transformed working practices; demographic change had created urban overcrowding, rural poverty, social dissatisfaction and had established unequal power relations. In turn, such inequality had enslaved man to machine, worker to employer, poor to rich, and so on. In relation to the manufacture of knitted goods, one can assess this as the result of the development of technology as a means of instigating new methods of social organization and working practices.

Historically, knitting had been part of a guild system, which could be seen as an early form of trade union that trained, supported and protected manufacturer and workers alike. Workers were largely independent, working from home or studio environments, with working practices dominated by seasonal demand rather than the demands of the market.[2] Although appearing rather idyllic, work was hard, hours were long, and workers were often poorly paid. Industrialization, initiated by technological development, particularly the stocking frame, had, by the seventeenth century, increased production for the home market and for export, but also squeezed out the work of the hand-knitters.[3] Additionally, legislation largely hindered any form of social mobility, enforcing *de jure* a master/servant divide.[4]

The shift to a capitalist system was pivotal as it created new working practices, which Marx believed alienated the worker. Alienation occurred as a direct result of working for someone else – the worker works not just for his pay, but for the pay of his employer.

> The alienation of the worker is expressed thus: The more he produces, the less he can consume; the more value he creates, the less value he has … Labour produces fabulous things for the rich, but misery for the poor, machines replace labour, and jobs diminish, while other workers turn into machines …[5]

The worker was therefore distanced from the products of his labour, whilst labour was dehumanized, and man and machine merged. The value of human life and work was negated, whilst the value of the market grew. The products of labour were no longer for the benefit of the producer or worker, but for the benefit of the wealthy few. Through exploited labour, Marx believed that the worker had become a possession, or commodified, something to be bought and sold like any other 'thing', and as such man was no longer free, but a cog in the wheel of capitalist production, of no more value than any other commodity. This is central to Marxist dialectics and the praxis of struggle: the employer is reliant on the worker, yet has all of the power, whilst the worker is reliant on the employer for money, but has no power. Capital and labour have an interdependent but unequal relationship.

From this perspective, Marxism questions the relationship between the economic base and the way in which it determines the superstructure. This means that capitalism and its mechanisms (production and consumption) determine the culture and conventions of a society, i.e. everything a society thinks, believes and does. For Marx, the superstructure is dominated by ideology, which includes not merely patterns of belief, but organized and institutional structures such as government, the law, education, religion and so on. A capitalist ideology dictates social organization and behaviour, which perpetuates the centrality and continuation of the economic base. This is the dominant ideology: an ideology which according to Marxist thought is an expression of the ideals of the ruling classes, i.e. the people in power make the rules by which everyone lives.

Ideology is a system of beliefs that are considered to be true: laws, rules, ideas and so on. Knitting is part of an ideology, which situates it as a domestic activity, largely undertaken by women, and as such, exists in a very lowly position within a capitalist economy, i.e. it is not perceived to be about making money. However, the dominant ideology does express certain truisms surrounding knitting, which in recent years have been central to texts aimed primarily at the amateur knitter, i.e. domesticity, harmony, spirituality, philanthropy and so on, which confirm gendered binaries and support the continuation of patriarchy, another form of social, cultural and economic inequality.

Marx believed that social inequality could be challenged by overthrowing ideology, something that neo- or post-Marxists believed was impossible, but for Marx, writing in the midst of rapid industrialization, the defeat of ideology would lead to revolution and the rejection of capitalism. Ideology offered a 'false consciousness', which once removed, would enable people to seek the truth. Therefore an ideological perspective of knitting would be one of domestic and familial bliss, in which the woman/wife/mother happily knits for others, giving her time and energy to the pursuit of warmth, comfort and love, for those around her and the less fortunate in general. This implies that knitters are generous, nice even, altruistic and giving, and although this may well be the case, it is certainly set within a rigid framework. For example, such an analogy does not consider the non-self-sacrificial knitter, the male knitter, the poverty and hardship of the pieceworker, nor the vast amount of time, skill and difficulty of knitting itself. Equally, knitters are seen as a homogeneous group, as are women, and the two are interchangeable; like women, all knitting is not the same, and such a static and sentimental viewpoint consigns both knitters and knitting to a cultural and social backwater that reinforces gender and class stereotypes. Ideologically, knitting can be seen as rather quaint and homely, an expression of familial love and thrifty housewifery, ideals of femininity that perpetuate production, which lead to the creation of a 'false consciousness', which conceals the reality of production.[6]

In the nineteenth century, industrialization had led to the evolution of a new working class, the proletariat – a group of people who owned nothing. Before industrialization, the working classes had owned their tools; the proletariat only had themselves to sell and as such could be mobilized into a 'workforce'. One way in which this could be achieved was through collectivism: individuals working for a collective aim such as social and political revolt.

Although frequently understood as an activity undertaken alone, knitting historically had been established as a collective activity, undertaken by individuals working towards a common aim.[7] In relation to domestic knitting, this is best exemplified by the knitting circle, which has an extensive history drawing on agitation, but also of bringing like-minded people and communities together. Such historical reference demonstrates a Marxist understanding of a 'workforce', a group of workers mobilizing in collective political dissent. Indeed, knitting has been described as a positive social force – 'When you are knitting, you are ready to listen',[8] and contemporary political groups draw on this concept of community activity through knitting. For example, the Revolutionary Knitting Circle's (RKC) Manifesto states:

> By sharing in the skills and resources of our communities, we shall become free to cast off dependencies on global trade for our subsistence. In so doing, we shall all be able to enter fairly into meaningful and equitable trade of not only goods, but also those cultural intangibles that are necessary if we are to bring about understanding, justice and peace to truly enrich our individual lives and our communities.[9]

The emphasis here is on community independence, a move away from a reliance on mass manufacture and global corporations. What is also significant is the focus on self-sufficiency, on making rather than buying, but also on challenging the status quo through direct action and political protest, also known as 'craftivism'.

Interestingly, contemporary forms of knitting protest do not display the Luddite tendencies of their predecessors, frequently utilizing technology and machinery to mobilize a global 'workforce', thus extending the potential geographical and numerical membership. The organization MicroRevolt, based in New York and founded by artist Cat Mazza, uses the Internet to communicate the problems inherent in sweatshop labour. In 2003, she started the Nike Blanket Petition, engaging over 500 knitters from the USA and twenty other countries to produce a blanket featuring the Nike 'swoosh' logo, constructed from donated 10 cm (4 in) knitted squares, which is to act as a petition supporting Nike workers.[10] On completion, the blanket is to be presented to the board chairman of the Nike corporation. In this example, the knitting circle has gone global, with global citizens and knitters able to express their dissatisfaction with sweatshop manufacture employed by multinational companies. MicroRevolt has questioned the status quo in three ways: firstly, by adopting part of the language of corporate identity (logos), the protest communicates to the company on its own terms, secondly, by utilizing the collective activity of knitters as a 'workforce', the vastness of concern is acknowledged in terms of scale that a written petition would not, and finally, the medium of knitting refers directly to garment manufacture and the plight of those employed in these industries. This is not a hollow gesture: from a Marxist perspective the needs of the worker are being addressed by a workforce (albeit a different one) and a statement is being made through the expression of a non-capitalist process using the language of capitalism.

Knitting has a history that is intertwined with the history of women and women's work – a marginal group, in relation to discussions relating to cultural production and indeed to social status. The significance of women's work has been questioned by feminist artists and writers since the 1960s. The sociocultural and economic inequality of women, particularly in respect of labour in the textile industries, has been a focal point of a variety of feminist art and design historians, with authors such as Christina Walkeley commenting on the relationship between textile work and prostitution in the nineteenth century.[11] These discussions have been returned to, albeit in a more humorous manner, by the textile artist Kelly Jenkins, whose knitted prostitutes' calling cards emphasize the lack of economic power afforded to women in the twenty-first century. Here, like Marx's proletariat, women only have themselves to sell, and the rendition of such a common sight in phone boxes nationally and internationally in knit, juxtaposes domesticity, a history of poorly paid piecework, and the woman as commodity.

Since the Second World War, the most significant group to provide a critique of society based on the writings of Marx was the Frankfurt School, a group of émigré philosophers whose writing has been categorized as post-Marxist. The group's main concern was the ways in which post-war society was driven by a dominant ideology that created false needs. The post-war cultural climate was dominated by the rise of the mass consumerism and obsolescence, the rise of the mass media, subliminal advertising and the global domination of certain branded goods. What the Frankfurt School saw emerging was really an industry of persuasion, hegemony in visual form, and the dominance of media conglomerates offering false hope, false realities and impossible but alluring promises in order to maintain inequalities of power.

Figure 45 Kelly Jenkins, *Knitted Chatlines*, 2004. Photo: Dominic Tschudin. Image reproduced with permission from the artist.

Knitting and Alternative Lifestyles

The term 'lifestyle' has been used by post-war sociologists and anthropologists to understand the consumer choices people make.[12] Consumer goods are seen as having 'magical'[13] or symbolic qualities that attract and/or appeal to specific groups of people, and which consequently 'reflect' the 'type' or 'life' the consumer has or aspires to have. This can be understood as a 'world-view', the way in which an individual places him/herself within the world and how the world sees him/her.

The representation of lifestyle through the consumption of goods is probably most noticeable in clothing, where apparel – as acknowledged by Colin Campbell[14] – is most closely associated with the creation of an identity, albeit most frequently constructed through the media and peer groups, rather than as a conscious act of self-expression. The sociologist, David Chaney,[15] attributes this person/commodity/life relationship to aggressive marketing and advertising techniques and noted:

> That products are imbued with symbolic or social value through being positioned implicitly consistent with other lifestyle values. Personal lifestyles in this view generate demands through individuals seeking out goods, services or activities that form a perceived pattern of association.[16]

Although lifestyles are largely perceived to be culturally constructed, Pierre Bourdieu's study of 'habitus' addresses the ways in which object/person relations are socially and behaviourally constructed and repeated so that they become natural.[17] Bourdieu's work on lifestyle, applied to the study of knitting, highlights the ways in which 'lifestyle' may be a series of behavioural practices that are socially and culturally determined, and which simultaneously establish ideals, aspirations and 'norms'. Therefore the term 'lifestyle' is inherently interwoven with the products and ideology of capitalism; people mark who they are by what they buy, but also what has been assimilated from their class backgrounds.

In terms of craft, which frequently is seen to occupy an opposing position to that of commercialism and the capitalist marketplace, a craft lifestyle can be understood as oppositional, if not subversive. To make, rather than buy, is to reject the dominant ideology and to react against consumerism per se. This form of protest has been dominant in knitting revivals from the 1970s onwards, which emphasized alternative ways of living, rejecting mainstream culture.

By the 1970s, knitting and craft in general had become associated with what the feminist craft historian Gillian Elinor has described as a 'hippy ethos'.[18]

> Craftwork was then embraced as a most suitable 'alternative' activity, this having had, in my view, two important outcomes for craft in the present. Firstly, there has been the association of craft with lifestyle. The 'drop-out' living of the early 1970s was the determinant for much craftwork. Craft represents still that alternative mode, on the one hand in opposition to the dominant values of the late twentieth-century capitalism, and on the other, a dream of a rusticated harmony of being.[19]

Elinor outlines the association of craft practice with lifestyle alternatives as a rejection of the values of contemporary society by 'dropping out', portraying the crafts as a 'subversive' activity, seemingly rejecting technology and establishing a way of life based on a utopian rural idyll that has romantically permeated the literature of the crafts, particularly the popular crafts, from the mid-nineteenth century.[20] However, craft and making as a lifestyle alternative was further popularized on a mass scale through television, which by association suggests that craft was also a mainstream interest.[21] Craft and alternative lifestyle was popularized most notably in the recently revived 1970s sitcom, *The Good Life* (1975–7), in which a suburban couple (Tom and Barbara Good) reject the values of Middle England and turn to self-sufficiency. The televisual escape from the humdrum rat race typified by suburbia[22] appealed to viewers[23] and, although total self-sufficiency was near-impossible, the lifestyle was imitated nationwide, with vegetable plots and allotments becoming increasingly popular.[24] Knitting, and indeed other domestic practices such as wine-making, dressmaking and the like, were popularized and adopted as a means of thrift in hard times, but also as a sign of anti-Establishment feeling, embracing a political and ecological form of dissent.

This perspective was evident in women's magazines of the 1970s, which ran biannual features about the significance of domestic craftwork as a means of making extra (or 'pin') money during times of hardship. Such an approach was nothing new; domestic crafts such as knitting had, since the Second World War (which was still part of a collective social memory) and beyond, been firmly associated with making do and mending, philanthropy, and to a certain extent, political engagement, as in the drive to knit for fighting troops overseas during times of conflict. By the 1970s, however, notions of class or poverty and a socially collective motivation to knit were being eroded to make way for personal benefit during hard times. The OPEC oil crisis and ensuing power cuts and three-day week, the impact of decimalization and entry into the Common Market, and wider global concerns such as environmental issues brought to light by the grounding of the Torrey Canyon and political instability characterized by the war in Korea and (later) Watergate, left the British public at least watching the pennies and tightening their belts. As an editorial in a British craft magazine stated in 1976:

> Lovely to see knitting shrug off its undeserved fuddy-duddy image and take over the fashion scene in such a creative and colourful way. But the price of those handsome garments in the shops leaves us breathless. Even knitting for yourself can involve quite an outlay, but you can still have something with a really exclusive look for considerably less than when buying ready-made – and have the satisfaction of creating it yourself.[25]

The early 1970s encapsulated times of hardship, which to a certain extent mirrored the climate of the Second World War without the country being at war; the enemy now was much more vague and the threat came not merely from outside, but from the government too. This correlation between contemporary mood and a wartime ethos was emphasized in knitting patterns and yarns; some manufacturers launched 'nostalgia' ranges during the period. Sirdar, for example, launched Majestic, a 100 per cent luxury double knit wool, to be used in the construction of 1940s-style patterns. One advert for the product, from 1980, was promoted under the strap line 'Socks aren't the only things they knitted for the troops

Figure 46 Sirdar advertisement for Majestic Wool, 1980. Courtesy of Sirdar.

in the 1940's',[26] highlighting the continued popularity of hand knitting, but also the ways in which current fashion was derivative of that of the Second World War. The product and imagery was indeed in a 1940s style: the advert depicted troops in uniform waiting to board a train, looking admiringly at two women wearing very tightly fitting sweaters knitted with the Majestic wool. However, the image had been updated to appeal to the post-permissive generation: luxury was emphasized, nipples appear erect through the sweaters, demonstrating an overt sexual appeal, and the admiring glances and sexual promise are heightened with the text: 'It'll be appreciated as much as now as socks were then.' The past had been reappropriated to address the needs of a post-war – but thrifty – population, and granny's make do and mend was now presented as sexually alluring, made for the presentation of the sexual self rather than for the warmth and comfort of men away from home.

To find a means of surviving outside the dictates of government red tape and legislation, was appealing to many, and the desire to move away from the perceived social problems of the times, as well as wider global issues, encouraged a new interest in environmental concerns. Certainly, environmental disasters were featured regularly in news reports, but the interest in the environment was not merely a knee-jerk reaction. Since the late 1950s, the onslaught of mass consumerism and the culture of obsolescence that fuelled such developments had been seen as problematic by social, political and design critics in the USA.

Such texts were certainly within the public consciousness, although often the lure of cheap, mass-produced goods proved too strong. Nonetheless, some design companies encouraged restraint, not necessarily from an ecological perspective, but as a means of expressing personal taste and creating an 'individual' sense of design.[27]

Craft became appealing to the general public and sparked a vogue for self-sufficiency. This was reflected in women's magazines through readers' stories, such as 'The Family Who Swapped Flowers for a Farm',[28] in which Joanna and Alan Smith discussed how anyone could create an alternative way of living by transforming the back garden and aiming for self-sufficiency. Warnings were given, however, to readers who might be seduced by the romance of 'getting away from it all':

Being a full-time craftsman may look romantic – up to your waist in wood shavings, shearing sheep, supper by candlelight … We could go on, but it's extremely hard work, and though very rewarding to those who are well suited by temperament and talent to being craftsmen, it is also usually not very rewarding financially.[29]

The editorial acknowledgement that craft was rarely a huge moneymaker further distanced craft from the world of paid employment. Craft, therefore, in this context becomes a symbol – the ultimate suburban dream – escape, not just from the rat race, but from the concerns and issues of the contemporary world. Tinged with a nostalgia reminiscent of the crafts narratives of the pre-industrial world, the utopian idealism surrounding the potential for the amateur to work or participate in the crafts as seen on TV can be interpreted as a symptom of a postmodern diaspora – a placelessness, a search for authenticity amidst the inauthentic.

The feminist historian, Leonore Davidoff, recognized this quest as a symptom of the alienation of the workforce and the rise in multinational corporations, which turned the seemingly 'static' arena of the home into an idealized state. The idealized version of 'home' ignited, within its occupants, a need for 'creative homemaking' – which Davidoff sees as 'farmhouse cookery', 'organic gardening', 'wine-making' and so on – a suburban substitute for authenticity.[30]

The desire for a sense of achievement through the resolution of a search for 'reality' or 'authenticity' in a world increasingly dominated by 'hyper-real' experience[31] places craft practice, and knitting, as different or outside the contemporary world of manufacture and the world of goods. They are not necessarily treated as serious – *The Good Life* was a comedy, and the tone of magazine articles addressing self-sufficiency was humorous, such as 'These families live with mud like we live with carpets'.[32] Similarly, knitting, although often seen as a business opportunity, was presented as a means of making 'pin money' or raising money for 'good' causes. Knitting, when seen as a lifestyle but not a way of life, is reduced to a commodity, whereas knitting as a hobby or pastime can be seen as a sign of stability in a changing world.

By the 1980s, ecological concerns had given way to a climate of de-industrialization, and heavy industry was rapidly being replaced with service and information industries. The move from hand to cerebral work had many implications – primarily, a poorly trained and equipped workforce led, in regions traditionally associated with manufacture, to mass unemployment. Conversely, other areas, notably the south of England, witnessed an economic boom time similar to that experienced in the 1930s. Yet, with manufacturing taking a downward turn, workers from traditional industrial occupations often turned to other forms of manual work either as a hobby or business enterprise to maintain skills or make money. This was particularly evident in areas where industrialized craft manufacture, such as furniture production, was in decline. This resulted in the development of small, craft-led businesses or craft fair stalls maintained by ex-factory workers turned hobbyists. The move from manual or 'dirty' work to cleaner forms of employment had implications on the notion of class structure and by the beginning of the 1990s, politicians were talking of Britain as a 'classless' society. Once again, notions of stability had been called into question and a mood of instability was prevalent. One might see these developments as a return to Marxist ideals, a more humanized form of labour that is more ethical, regional and spiritually empowering. However, such changes were minimal, making little impact on the economic structure or base of contemporary society. A move towards de-industrialization did not mark a move away from capitalism, nor did the notion of 'classlessness' indicate the eradication of rich and poor.

Thrift: Make Do and Mend

Knitting is frequently associated with thrift and as a result has been popularly perceived to be a working-class necessity rather than as a means of leisured occupation, such as embroidery.[33] Because knitting results in 'useful' objects, it is frequently cited as a means of making do during times of hardship. From wartime make-do-and-mend campaigns, which encouraged the unpicking and re-knitting of old or outdated garments,[34] through to knitting items for 'pin money' or raising money for charitable causes, knitting occupies a position which is neither work nor leisure, but more an example of thrifty housewifery. Such conceptions establish knitting and knitters as both enterprising and exploited, as articles in women's magazines from the 1970s suggest.

From the 1970s, knitting as an aspect of thrift found itself in a precarious position. With the advent and impact of second-wave feminism, knitting largely became seen as an act of compliance and submissiveness, and was derided. This was not an image of the contemporary woman, who was perceived to be commodity-rich and time-poor, and knitting was therefore indicative of an old-fashioned woman. To knit for oneself, family or others became a sign of meanness, the insignia of poverty and an inability or unwillingness to engage in consumer culture and fashion.

In recent years, a growing public concern with environmental and ethical issues has led to the reassessment of knitting, not necessarily as an aspect of thrift, but as an aspect of Green politics and an anti-consumerist backlash, in which a craft revival has been central.

Ethical Knitting

Since the late 1950s, the education of the consumer has been of primary importance in determining choice of goods amidst the post-war consumer boom. Publications such as *Which?* and *Consumer Reports* have offered advice regarding purchase to a public overwhelmed by a mass of products, which in turn has led to legislation protecting and guiding the consumer. The educated and powerful consumer was now able to make serious decisions about what to buy based not merely on aesthetics, marketing hype or personal preference, but also in relation to manufacturing processes, sustainability and social responsibility or ethical issues. As a result, designers looked to wider social issues, returning, to some extent, to the ideals of the modernists, and investigated ways in which design could address the needs of society, the working conditions for those employed within the manufacture of goods, and address problems arising from environmental decay.

This form of 'responsible' design was championed by Victor Papanek, whose text, *Design For the Real World*, outlined the ways in which design could become a holistic discipline[35] whereby the designer, the consumer and the environment were paramount. Such an approach highlights a trend towards design for society, addressing needs (and to a certain extent, wants), and which has been extended to the development of fashion in recent years. For example, the knitwear designer, Caterina Radvan, has developed a means of addressing the fashion needs of a female disabled clientele. Her research had identified that clothing for the disabled was unfashionable, ugly, and although practical, excluded disabled people from the fashion process and the experience of fashion, heightening their social marginalization. Studies surrounding fashion and the disabled had identified the

Figure 47 Caterina Radvan, clothing design, 2007. Photo: Moose Azim. Image reproduced with permission from the artist and photographer.

body as a site of discourse and in relation to fashion, a specific Western ideal or 'body order' had been imposed on the population. It appeared that clothing designed specifically for the disabled was largely for the convenience of those administering care, and that the 'dated' designs emphasized a social and personal stigma in which the wearer felt 'out of date' and by association 'out of circulation'.[36] For the disabled, clothes had become a sign of oppression, and old-fashioned clothing only increased the social perception of the wearer's 'outsider' status.[37] Radvan notes:

> When I spoke to the woman who owns the mail order company (for clothing for the disabled), she was so negative. She said: 'Please send me any ideas you've got, but … you know they need to have certain items of clothing and they need to be comfortable.'

Figure 48 Caterina Radvan, clothing design, 2007. Photo: Moose Azim. Image reproduced with permission from the artist and photographer.

> But when I see this kind of clothing, this pair of trousers with these hidden poppas going all the way down, it's all very sickness-oriented, I feel. It's really depressing.[38]

Acknowledging that the market consisted of two opposed spheres of clothing (expensive bespoke or cheaper, but uninspiring, practical garments), Radvan started to challenge both approaches by designing fashionable clothes suitable for both disabled and non-disabled wearers. Research into designing fashion garments for the disabled had been addressed previously, but frequently these models had focused on pattern-cutting, which ostensibly had meant that bodies were made to fit garments; Radvan, conversely, fits garments to bodies. She started working with the artist Alison Lapper, who was born with phocomelia, a condition that left her without arms or legs. Radvan comments:

Alison [was] talking to me about her clothing needs and … her way of life. She has a child and … [she is just] is a single mother who has a normal life, so to speak, but with difficulties, obviously. And that's how it started. It didn't start from any altruistic point: it started from an aesthetic point or the challenge of making abstract garments … [to fit] a more abstract body.[39]

Such an approach can be seen to encompass the clothing concerns of both the disabled and the non-disabled; very few people adhere to an ideal body shape, and an opportunity to escape the dominance of such an ideal is appealing. Indeed, all of the garments she makes are photographed on disabled and non-disabled models to demonstrate the inclusiveness of each garment. For Radvan, this is significant, as her work is the expression of inclusive or universal design, a technique or approach central to architectural design, which centres on the needs of the user and is ultimately user-friendly.

I suppose, in a very broad sense, it is one size fits all – because what they're saying is that we're no longer going to have the entrance to shops or the entrance to houses here and then if you're in a wheelchair you have to go round the back and up there; if you're building something new from now on it has to be useful … [for] everyone so that everybody uses the main entrance. So I suppose it is one size fits all from that perspective. But, I suppose, maybe I'm cheating in a way – because the whole point of this is that this is fashionable clothing, and there are some rules that I'm allowed to bend. One thing, for example, is that most women will put up with a little bit of discomfort in some clothing for some of the time, so you would wear high heels in the evening to a party, because you know it's only going to be for a couple of hours. And so I think a disabled woman would also do that just for a little while.[40]

The focus here is therefore twofold: disabled women should be able to wear fashionable clothing and express their identity through what they wear as other women do, and they should also be able to experience the discomfort of glamour, as this too is part of dressing up and being fashionable. The garments are about choice, differentiation and the ability to take part within the fashion system.

Radvan's designs develop from a basic knitted tube, which exploits asymmetry, and include a variety of slashes through which the head and/or limbs can be placed, which enable the wearer to dictate how the garment is worn. Equally, the garment can be worn in a variety of ways, which heightens its sustainability. Working with a group of people with a variety of disabilities has enabled her to develop the designs in accordance to the needs of the user, whilst maintaining her position as a fashion designer and creating garments that are suitable for all women.

Ethical implications and their effects on the fashion and textile industries have recently been questioned as an aspect of wider debates surrounding global capitalism. Consumers are now voting with their feet and demanding more ethical goods and services. Fair trade is central to the notion of ethical production and consumption and 'Fairtrade' is a term most frequently applied to the production of goods in the Developing World. However, it is also a term which has recently been applied to the production and classification of goods produced in the Shetland Islands. The association between a group of Shetland knitters under the Fairtrade ethical shopping label and an Edinburgh-based company, Thistle and Broom, who promote Scottish goods in the USA, has been forged as a means of demonstrating genuine Fair Isle knits and discriminating between locally produced goods and cheap imports.[41] Pieceworkers had been paid very poorly in the past[42] and this collaboration (The Fair Isle Knitting Project) has enabled workers to retain two-thirds of the retail price of each garment.[43] Similarly, Shetland Knitwear is a local, non-profit-making cooperative, which makes garments to sell on Shetland, for a largely tourist market, and online.[44] In each case, education and sustainability have been at the forefront of these initiatives: poor pay and bad working conditions had discouraged younger knitters from entering the industry, and as a result the industry was potentially dying out as knitters aged and were not replaced. In essence, new approaches to working practices and financing have revived both the industry and an interest in it.

Issues of sustainability have been addressed by the designer Amy Twigger-Holroyd, whose knitwear company, Keep and Share, promotes ethical design and consumption. Equally inspired and appalled by the culture of obsolescence that surrounds the consumption of clothing, Twigger-Holroyd devised a means of establishing a sustainability for garments, which relies on versatile design and an extended biography of the object. Garments are designed to be worn in a variety of ways, which offers more potential usage; they are also designed to be worn by other users at a later date (hence the name, 'Keep and Share'). She describes this as 'slow fashion': garments with longevity and the potential for multiple ownership. Keep and Share also express commendable levels of social responsibility by employing ecological and ethical approaches to their business and products. Although the yarns used in construction are not wholly organic or environmentally friendly, this is the aim in the future; but locally sourced and naturally coloured organic yarns are used in their EcoEdition range, and recycled scraps in the Offcuts line.[45]

It is apparent that a renewed interest in holistic design, which addresses the needs of the consumer whilst providing attractive design solutions, has created a market in which the ethics of production and consumption are at the forefront. Knitting is very much part of this movement, because it has the potential to provide hard-wearing, flexible and slow fashion, which can accommodate all consumers. This emphasis on equity with regard to participation in the fashion system may not eradicate the inequalities currently dividing production and consumption (workers and wearers), but it does offer access to alternative forms, modes and approaches to knitted apparel.

Philanthropy

Knitting has a reputation that has been tainted with poverty. Primarily, such associations have developed as a result of thrift, and the using of 'scraps' or leftover materials as a means of raising money or helping those less fortunate. Knitting can therefore be seen as an expression of philanthropy.

Knitting was most prolifically promoted in women's magazines of the 1970s and 1980s as a means of either thrift or as raising money for 'good' causes. Knitted goods were presented as 'bazaar novelties', and included patterns to make soft toys, cosies and covers such as knit-covered coathangers, tissue boxes and toilet rolls. These items were small and could be made from oddments of leftover fabric and wool, or from household 'rubbish' such as yoghurt pots, toilet rolls, cardboard and so on. The emphasis on recycling materials that would otherwise have been 'wasted' or thrown away, and their transformation into goods to raise money for the 'needy', continued a history of craft and charity that dates back to Victorian philanthropy[46] and aligns the middle-class virtue of thrift with poverty and 'making do'.[47]

Figure 49 Knitted novelties, such as these crinoline lady toilet roll covers, typify a popular understanding of knitting in everyday life. Winchester, UK, 2000. Photo: Jo Turney.

Similarly, the objects themselves could be recognized as examples of an established popular and 'feminine' understanding of 'home' craft: the decoration of the 'useful'[48] and the domestic. In terms of style (and indeed the type of goods for which patterns were available), the objects had a heritage feel which referred to the history of feminine pastimes and domestic taste, illustrating the interconnecting relationship between the fancy, dainty goods made by Victorian 'ladies of leisure'[49] and the bazaar goods being made at the end of the twentieth century.

The emphasis on 'fun' inherent in the bazaar novelty detracts from the serious social implications of the bazaar and fundraising in general. From the nineteenth century onwards, the bazaar has remained a predominantly female event, with organized events developing from philanthropic fundraising and WI stalls and sales.[50] Historically, the bazaar has offered women the opportunity to organize and contribute to a public event, and assume traditional male 'work roles'.[51]

The duties and responsibilities involved in a bazaar, in the main shouldered by women, demonstrate an area of life in which the inequalities inherent in patriarchal society are not mirrored. Women dominate every area of this bazaar 'culture', from the production/making of the goods for sale to the organization of the event, and the sale of goods; they are also largely the consumers of bazaar goods. A Mass Observation respondent, bazaar contributor and reader of *Woman's Weekly* wrote in 1988:

> I spend many, many hours knitting as part of my group's fundraising organizing a handicrafts stall. My friend and I do knitting for people and the money they pay us is used to buy materials for the stall and to pay for the site, etc. ... The Guildhall at Windsor is a favourite.[52]

This is a continuous culture, existing nationwide as a variety of local events. Sales are themed by seasonal and religious occasions – spring, Easter, summer, autumn, Harvest Festival, winter, Christmas – to tie in with gift-giving festivals; they are also promoted as 'a day out' in the case of those held in the summer. Such cyclical persistence creates a sense of timelessness, of a culture that is representative of the past in the present and, combined with a proliferation of goods unavailable in shops, situates the bazaar or fête as nostalgic and outside the changing world of fashion and its accoutrements.

Most significantly, the bazaar is a political tool, and is linked to the popular definition of making as a 'subversive' lifestyle alternative. Fundraising in itself is a political activity – recognizing the failure of the state and society to support its less fortunate members, or indeed to support communities and community services, such as the school fête that raises money for activities and equipment not covered by government funding. Bazaars, therefore, can be seen as a reaction to social, political and economic situations and a means whereby individuals can instigate some monetary response to circumstances.

On a national scale, knitting as a means of charitable fundraising as well as a means of political activism was most successful when applied to the African famine appeals of the 1980s, in particular in response to those made by the charities Band Aid and Oxfam. Television brought the plight of the starving directly into British living rooms, an event that acknowledged the shrinkage of the world and the influence of media technologies. In March 1985, *Woman* magazine launched the Band Aid appeal for knitted squares to be made into blankets and jumpers for famine victims, as night-time temperatures were extremely low. Simple patterns were included.[53] The response was phenomenal, raising a total of £12,000 and huge amounts of knitted goods.[54] The magazine later printed a series of readers' letters in response to their experiences of knitting for Ethiopia, one of which stated:

> Living as I do on a basic, small pension, I have felt very guilty because I could only afford to buy the Band Aid record and send a small cash donation. What a delight then, to hear that blankets were needed: I already had a large bag of knitted squares, made up during the winter from balls of leftover wool, so I made up two blankets.[55]

The responses to the magazine appeal, as exemplified by the above letter, demonstrate the way in which making is seen as a way of responding to the plight of others. Knitting in these circumstances enables more people to contribute to a particular cause, indicating that knitting is accessible to everyone regardless of their financial situation. This form of global altruism developed into a variety of projects developed as a result of media coverage of global citizens in crisis. In 1993, the UK knitting magazine, *Knitting Now*, launched its 'Knit Now for Romania' campaign, in which readers were asked to knit jumpers for sick children in poorly funded hospitals in Romania. The request stated:

> Every once in a while, we are reminded of the suffering around the globe that makes our daily anxieties seem trivial in comparison. News clips of famine-ridden bodies and children with Aids activate our sympathy glands and many of us feel, even momentarily, the need to do something. Here is a chance to help out – by knitting NOW for Romania.[56]

In addition to the request for jumpers, readers were also offered the opportunity to contribute money to a variety of Romanian charities. The power of the press in these instances is evident; television images and newspapers enter the home on a daily basis, they are part of the fabric of everyday life and as such have the ability to communicate human suffering in unprecedented ways. By the July/August issue of *Knitting Now*, jumper donations had reached 750,[57] and the success of the campaign had, by September of the same year, sparked a new knitting challenge – knitting for Barnardo's.[58]

These examples of knitting for 'good causes' are only a few of many hundreds of groups and charities that knit or rely on knitted goods to promote and sustain their causes. In Betty Christiansen's book, *Knitting for Peace: Make the World a Better Place One Stitch at a Time*,[59] Christiansen provides testimony of many groups and charitable organizations that knit for good causes, outlining the purpose and response to these knitted gestures. She also includes patterns and charity contact details for those readers inspired to contribute.

Although there is no doubt that knitting for charity is a formidable, sentimental and sometimes a necessary means of expressing support, the altruistic potential of such endeavours is not always quite as charitable as one would imagine, communicating more about the knitter than the cause or intended recipient(s). Indeed, in interviews and observational fieldwork studies of amateur knitters conducted in the south of England between 1998–2002, testimonies showed elements of deliberate self-sacrifice, personal aggrandisement and a competitive altruism, which emphasize the importance of the maker rather than the seemingly generous act of making. These rather pious character traits were manifested in three ways, each of which was aligned with the maker's understanding and presentation of the self, i.e. role within a family group, role within a community group, and role within a social group.

Knitters who had established a sense of personal identity within familial relationships frequently viewed their knitting as an expression of provision and love for that group. When their knitting was no longer appreciated (or indeed wanted), the knitters felt rejected and felt that their position within the family as, rather sentimentally, the provider of 'warmth' and 'comfort' was destabilized. As a result, these knitters turned to others who appreciated their knitted gifts as a form of self-preservation and as a sign of their own family's 'rejection'. One respondent commented:

> I make jumpers and cardigans for my grandchildren, but they're not too bothered by them, so I make them now for that country where all the trouble is [Kosovo] ... terrible ... Women are giving birth to babies by the roadside.[60]

The obvious empathy many of the interviewees had with less fortunate global citizens can also be seen as a reflection of a search for a wider family. No longer needed to make clothing for her family, this interviewee found a niche for her skills, people who will appreciate her efforts, and who visit her daily on the television news. Similarly, familial appreciation and bonding through making has encouraged other interviewees to increase production to include families who miss out on this kinship network. One interviewee knits jumpers for Oxfam, using the same care and attention as she would for her own family, in the hope that these gifts will bring the same pleasure to the 'poor children in Africa'[61] as they brought to her own family.

Figure 50 Balaclava, UK, 2007. Photo: Jo Turney.

For interviewees who identified themselves within community groups, knitting for good causes was primarily for the good of their own community, taking the form of goods made as fundraisers for the local needy, and was sometimes to the benefit of the knitters themselves. In these instances, knitters were competitive, proudly commenting on the volume and the quality of their production in comparison to other contributors to the cause. Similarly, some members of knitting clubs were keen to discuss their own achievements amongst the group in order to solidify their own position within the group's hierarchy. These forms of altruistic self-sacrifice have been identified by the social anthropologist Daniel Miller, who outlined the ways in which women would afford themselves luxuries if they believed they would benefit a wider group, even if after purchase, the consumer indulged alone.[62] It appears, therefore, that women are aware of a sense of gendered social propriety which discourages them from self-promotion, whilst simultaneously relying on such behaviour, under the guise of altruism and self-sacrifice, to formulate and maintain a specific identity within a familial or social group.

Globalization and a Question of Standardization

Globalization has been said to have instigated the 'shrinkage of the world'. Such commentary arises as a response to developments in information technology and a rise in global capitalism, which has, to a certain extent, made communications between peoples and nations much easier and quicker, whilst the dominance of global corporations, products and brand identities has overtaken and in some cases eradicated local cultures. One might assume that this has been an egalitarian merging of ideas, practices and beliefs, but as dress historian Margaret Maynard suggests, the relationships forged have been unequal, particularly between First and Third World countries, to the extent that globalization could be redefined as Westernization.[63]

As industrialization, through machine production, enabled and increased the production of standardized goods, globalization has created a network of homogenized identities and products that circulate around notions of lifestyle preferences.[64] For dress historians, globalization has created a generic form or 'sameness' in dress, which has enabled the production of vast quantities of clothing cheaply; this has been sustained and perpetuated through the media, in particular advertising, television and film.[65] This homogenization is encouraged, whilst diversity is discouraged, which in turn leaves the consumer with little choice other than the branded goods and styles produced by trans-national corporations,[66] the result of which is a 'world' style – i.e. jeans, T-shirts and trainers that bear recognizable logos.

Fashion and dress has always exhibited aspects of differentiation, primarily because fashion is, by definition, fuelled by the new, but also because dress is performative: the ways in which it is worn communicate the identity of the wearer.[67] A standardized 'world' style negates the significance of the role of fashion in the creation of personal identity, and although there are many minor differences (personalization) within what can be described as a 'world uniform', it remains restrictive, offering the consumer little choice. This, combined with the rise of discount 'fashion' chain stores such as Primark, encourage a sense of obsolescence, in which cheap fashions are worn and, because styles change so quickly and quality is often poor, are swiftly thrown away.

On the one hand, one can view the accessibility of mass-produced fashion as a form of democratization: everyone, regardless of income, has access to fashionable clothing. On the other, one must question the ethics of such cheap clothing[68] – if a sweater costs £10 in a UK High Street shop, how much did it cost to make and how much did the maker receive?[69] Such questions sit somewhat uncomfortably with

Figure 51 Ralph Lauren, knitted navy blue jersey dress with stars and stripes motif (bugle beads and sequins), 1991. Fashion Museum, Bath. Image courtesy of Bath and North East Somerset Council.

contemporary consumers, who are educated about environmental, ethical and global issues. Similarly, fashion trends have started to reject cheap, disposable fashion, with many style commentators promoting more expensive and more ethical key wardrobe pieces, as well as vintage or self-customized clothing.

> Historically, fashion has always offered a highly accessible way of engaging with visual culture, but the 'cheap chic' phenomenon means that individualism is seeping out of the style silhouette. In an era of mass-produced design, the fashion playground of colours, fabrics and shapes is now saturated with similarity. Interestingly, as consumer pressure groups force design houses to consider ethics, we may see High Street fashion

at least flirt with ecologically sound style, which could slow down trend turnover and encourage us all to experiment again ... Prices may soar, but value can only truly be measured by a collective vision that treats everyone, from garment workers to style slaves, with respect.[70]

Fashion, it appears, has moved towards quality rather than quantity, extolling the virtues of searching for better quality and more ethically sound goods as well as the personalization or revamping of one's 'old' clothes. The emphasis here is on the 'educated' consumer, but also on the experience of shopping, making and wearing clothes.

And it isn't just teaching yourself how to felt that's going to make you feel warm and fuzzy – because, as well as being a licence to play, craft cocks a snook at our lousy consumer society. Who needs the cheap high of buying disposable, mass-produced tat, when you can experience the slow-burning gratification that comes with making it yourself? Your handmade things certainly won't be flawless but they will be unique and precious.[71]

The Guardian's assertion (above) that craft is an alternative to consumerism is not new, as previously indicated. However, what it suggests is that making things for yourself offers an experience of the world of goods, which is different to, and has a greater longevity or 'feelgood factor' than, that experienced when shopping. This approach is different to earlier craft revivals as it doesn't assume that crafting is cheap or an extension of thrift, but central to a sense of the 'unique' and 'precious', terms more frequently associated with exclusive or luxury products. The linkage of DIY craft with luxury elevates its status, equating the consumer with discernment, rather than slavishly and randomly consuming the 'tat' offered by the mass market.

The Guardian has highlighted a significant move away from the mass market, distant from the rather limited, alternative interpretations of crafts practices of the past. Contemporary approaches to craft don't challenge the make-up of society by offering alternative ways of living, but emphasize the intelligence of the consumer and the rights of the individual to consume intelligently, and part of this choice is to choose not to consume, but to make.

The emphasis away from standardization has also been the focus of yarn shops, with new stores such as Prick My Finger in London, stocking only yarns that have a provenance. The co-owner, Rachael Matthews, commented: 'Each ball of wool has to have a story before we stock it.'[72] The ethical accent adopted by Matthews, and many other yarn store owners, highlights a consumer desire to engage in consumption opposed to the mass market. She stated:

When I started Cast Off, people were naive, they weren't sure why they wanted to join, but knew that they wanted something handcrafted, but not necessarily why this was important. With the encroachment of the High Street, people started to become more interested in having something different, something more ethical.[73]

Similarly, the exclusivity of the yarns on sale expresses a move away from the traditional concept of knitting as an act of thrift. Here, yarn is selected and sourced and therefore presented as luxurious, expensive and limited, which contradicts stereotypes of both knitting and 'ethical' goods.[74] The 'stories' the yarns tell are significant; they add an element of exclusivity to the product, a narrative which transcends the silence of mass production.

Attempts to dissociate knitting from connections with thrift and necessity is not a particularly new approach, as large yarn companies such as Rowan and Colinette[75] had been producing high-quality, luxurious products since the 1980s, the properties of which were promoted through 'heritage' as well as fashion-led advertising, with patterns devised by contemporary knitwear designers that are suitable for the home knitter to reproduce. What differentiates contemporary yarn producers and merchants is a clear knowledge of consumer demand combined with an understanding of why people knit. This fusion of past, present and future is expressed through the in-store provision of knitting clubs and lessons, which continues a tradition and draws on the sociability of the craft, an awareness of the needs of the contemporary consumer, and sustainability through organic and thoroughly sourced yarns. This commendable fusion does not come cheaply, and therefore the necessity of knitting has been replaced with a luxury price tag, and the thrifty practicality of knitting is now part of the leisure of the middle classes.

Regardless of the changing meaning of knitting (its move from a form of thrifty housewifery to one of an ethical lifestyle choice), elements of the significance of knitting remain. An emphasis on quality of materials and the experience of making, as distinct from purchasing from the mass market, bears witness to a history of knitting which pre-dates consumerism. Knitting, according to Grant Neufeld, founder of the Revolutionary Knitting Circle (RKC), is the expression of 'community independence', as he states:

> We need as communities to be able to take care of ourselves because when we are not able to take care of ourselves, we end up dependent on others – in this case the corporation – to survive. And when we're dependent on them, they can tell us what to do, like eating genetically modified foods or clothing made in child-labour-dependent sweatshops.[76]

Neufeld's sense of community independence refers to Marxist dialectics and a concern for the position of the worker within a capitalist society. If a community demonstrates a sense of self-sufficiency, it has a choice as to whether to make or buy, to rely on the mass market or to reject it by producing goods of its own. Although it is incredibly difficult to be completely self-sufficient, small measures of defiance, such as knitting a sweater rather than buying one from a multinational corporation, appear to be gaining popularity, and certainly the sentiments that accompany such moves are central to the work of many artists working in the medium of knit.

Kimberley Elderton knits installations that comment on the onslaught of the consumer society and the problems inherent in distinguishing between need and want in the contemporary West. Her main focus has been to knit everything that she wants, an exercise in which she discovered that, if she had to knit what she wanted, and considering the time and energy involved in doing so, she actually didn't want very much at all. The work raises questions and makes judgements

Figure 52 Kimberley Elderton pictured with her work *Knit What I Want: PlayStation 3*, Cardiff School of Art and Design degree show, June 2007. Image reproduced with permission from the artist.

based on the relationship between desire and longevity; was her desire for something equal to or greater than the time it would take to knit it? Indeed, much of her portfolio consists of started but unfinished projects – the desire for possession frequently faded in the wake of the momentum needed to complete the projects. Such an approach creates a discourse between need and want, work and rewards (a theme at the heart of a capitalist ideology) and, in a culture overwhelmed with goods and a desire to obtain them, such a project offers an insight into contemporary consumerism. She commented:

> My brother, who's into computers and gadgets, had been desperate to get a PS3. This really grated on me. He was getting his PS3 … [at] midnight just as it was released, so I thought I'd knit something that everyone else wants – so that I could have it before the general release and before everyone else. I only had four days and this wasn't long enough to knit one, but I did finish it. Even though it was later than the release, the hype was still there – it was still an object of desire.[77]

The knitted PS3 (PlayStation 3) was displayed on a plinth under stark lighting and surrounded with a knitted a red barrier, making a comment about collective – rather than personal – greed. The emphasis is on greed and touch: these are possessions, things to hold or to touch, to covet and own, yet the gallery setting is the antithesis, with the perceived message of 'Do not touch'. Such instruction, through the exclusion demonstrated by the barrier, increases the temptation for possession, but also draws attention to the significance of the object on display. As this is an art piece it demands contemplation, even awe, yet it is a knitted PlayStation, something high-tech and desirable in terms of consumerism, mixed with something woolly, homely and low-tech, a combination that would not normally receive this level of reflection. It also comments on what constitutes leisure – knitting is seen as a leisure activity, as is playing games on the PS3, but one is very male and market driven and the other is its polar opposite. What is leisure and who is it for? Is leisure something you have to pay for and is enjoyment about possessing the latest fad?

Elderton's work can be seen as an expression of the writings of Herbert Marcuse. Marcuse, a key thinker and member of the Frankfurt School, believed that because people function within ideological and capitalist structures such as the economy, they could never be free. This means that people find it difficult to distinguish between what they need and what they want. So, because people function within a specific economic structure, they work beyond what they actually need to meet their daily requirements. This means that people consume more than they should, literally buying into the dominant ideology, by assuming that if they work harder and/or longer, they can make more money and buy more things, which will, if the adverts are to be believed, satisfy their heart's desires – the things that capitalism has seemingly taken from them, such as time, love, beauty, happiness, valuable relationships, a sense of wholeness and so on. Indeed, the dominant ideology encourages people to feel inadequate – so much so, that they need to work harder in order to meet some kind of social ideal, i.e. one 'needs' the right clothes, the right house, the right type of friends, in order to 'fit in'. The popular sociologist, Vance Packard, addressed this theme in *The Hidden Persuaders*,[78] outlining the ways in which advertisers stimulated a sense of desire or want in consumers that lured them into buying things they didn't need. By creating a state of constant want, built on a sense of filling the void of personal lack, advertising was perpetuating a desire for new things at a rapid rate. This built a culture of obsolescence – a throwaway society – that enabled the production and consumption of goods to engage a much wider portion of the population. In turn, this created debt and ultimately trapped people in a cycle of work–purchase–pay in an unprecedented way.[79]

Elderton's PS3 is exemplifies the impact of Theodor Adorno's *The Culture Industry*,[80] which discussed the ways in which culture has become an industry, an arm of the dominant ideology promoting enlightenment through mass deception. He concludes by noting that by keeping people passive, by giving them what they think they want, and by dumbing down culture, you can manipulate them. This means that by keeping people 'happy' through low popular cultural forms, access to 'luxury' goods and the promise of something better, the populace will be impotent and unable to act or challenge the social hierarchy. This reaffirms the dominant ideology and keeps the wheels of capitalism turning. The PS3 is a luxury product; it gives consumers what they want and is a passive 'activity' – users may shoot 'baddies' as they work their way through the levels of computer games, but they are so engrossed in this fantasy mission that they are unable to or uninterested in challenging or fighting for justice in the 'real' world. Similarly, this is a dumbed-down form of entertainment – it doesn't enlighten, challenge or really engage the consumer/user intellectually. It encourages people not to think.

Environmentalism

> I decided to learn how to knit, a skill that I soon realized would not only get me and my fellow survivors through a long, cold, nuclear winter – it may actually prevent that horrible post-apocalyptic world from ever coming to fruition.[81]

Environmental concerns have been the focus of consumers and producers recently, and knitting has been cited as offering a greener approach to both production and consumption. The emphasis on green design has sparked interest from fashion designers, which has sparked a trend for environmentally friendly designer goods. The launch of Anya Hindmarch's eco bag, produced for the supermarket Sainsbury's to coincide with its first 'Make a Difference Day', created a consumer demand that witnessed hundreds of shoppers queuing outside stores for the reusable bag. Priced at £5, the bag appeared as a trendy designer product at a very low price, and its limited production fuelled a desirability that later saw the bags selling on e-Bay for at least four times the retail cost. One might assume that this huge interest in a bag is partially the result of two factors at work simultaneously: the designer-branded item at low cost, and limited availability combined with media hype. Nonetheless, the popularity of Hindmarch's bag and its ecologically friendly construction and ideology has impacted on and inspired knitters globally, receiving much press attention. Supermarkets give away 17.5 billion carrier bags to customers in the UK alone, and this wastage has been central to addressing the ways in which consumers can make a difference to the environment. One knitter (and art student), Elizabeth Edwards, so worried about the ecological impact of discarded carrier bags that she knitted old supermarket carrier bags into a reusable bag suitable for carrying groceries. Her design was featured in the national press, with editorials asking for readers' designs and comments.[82]

The current interest in knitting as an aspect of environmental and ethical consumer practices does not challenge consumerism itself, as yarn has to be purchased (unless it is collected from one's own animals and/or spun by oneself), and so on, but it does emphasize thoughtful consumer practices. As a response to consumer demand, suppliers of yarns and patterns have developed ecologically sound products. For example, Lion Brand and Blue Sky Alpaca have created organic, Fairtrade cotton yarns, and Cascade Yarns have developed a range of Eco Wool.[83] Web and blogging sites also address consumers' environmental concerns by outlining how knitters can be more environmentally friendly, focusing on the themes of using locally produced yarns, recycling and sustainability.[84]

Textile waste is estimated to exceed 1 million tonnes annually in the UK. Of this amount, only 25 per cent is recycled.[85] This is a huge environmental problem, as many textiles, specifically synthetics, do not biodegrade and as a result stay in landfill sites. Advice offered by environmental agencies to domestic consumers offers the following solutions: (a) recycle through donation to overseas charities, jumble sales, etc.; (b) reuse, through wearing second-hand clothes or customizing existing outdated garments in the wardrobe; (c) consume ethically, by purchasing less, by purchasing environmentally friendly, locally produced products, or by wearing clothing for longer.

Recycling is not a new idea in relation to knitted goods. As previously outlined, knitting – as a thrift craft, and because of its structure and the potential for unravelling knitted items – enables old or unwanted items to be re-knitted. Examples of this practice dominate discussions of wartime make do and mend, and the making of knitted toys suitable for sale at bazaars, children's clothes and so on. Such practices give yarn a new life, transforming one item into another.

Environmental concerns are not only addressed through the recycling of clothes; knitting also offers an opportunity to comment on biodiversity and the changing environmental landscape. In the work of Laurel Roth, suits that replicate extinct birds are knitted and crocheted for pigeons, demonstrating the propensity of one species at the expense of another.

CASE STUDY. **The Revolution Will Be Knitted**

Everything that is created within a society is the product of the social institutions of that society.[86] When people knit, they are knitting as a response to the socio-cultural conditions and behaviours of that society. Knitting may be an act of conformity, or of subversion of the values or ideology of the society in which it is undertaken. The meaning of knitting is determined by its social and cultural perception, and therefore the ways in which people knit and the type of objects knitted will reflect or reject the dominant ideology.

The term 'craft' occupies a rather paradoxical position within both language and culture, and as a consequence can be understood as two opposing factors at the same time. Firstly, if one adopts an institutional understanding of craft, which

Figure 53 Laurel Roth, *Biodiversity Reclamation Suits for Urban Pigeons – Dodo*, 2007. Crocheted yarn, 30 × 20 cm (12 × 8 in), hand-carved pigeon mannequin, walnut stand. San Francisco, USA. Photo: Andy Diaz Hope. Image reproduced courtesy of the artist.

perpetuates an arts hierarchy, craft is understood as rather backward-looking, skilled and repetitive but not creative, and manual rather than cerebral. This has distanced craft from the fine arts, attributing to it a second-class status. Secondly, and historically, the term 'craft' is employed to define the forward-moving, as in 'hovercraft', something that has a forward trajectory that cuts through obstacles. This, combined with the political and rather devious definition of craft (as in 'crafty'), offers the potential for progressive and active change. The paradox of craft is pertinent to a Marxist interpretation as it deals simultaneously with inequitable power relations, a group of (traditionally) manual workers, non-alienated labour, and the potential to act as a vehicle and group moving towards social change.

Political protest in relation to knitting has been solidified by the enduring image of Dickens's grotesque character, Madame Defarge, in *A Tale of Two Cities*, in which the author situates knitting as both mawkish and revolutionary. Worker for the Revolution during the Reign of Terror in eighteenth-century France, Defarge quietly and vengefully knits the names of the Revolution's intended victims into a list, which increases as the Revolution intensifies. Capitalizing on the iconography of the *tricoteuse*, the woman who knitted by the guillotine, Dickens creates a character that is both part of, and seemingly oblivious to, the hatred both within and around her. Although the historical existence of the *tricoteuse* was in evidence, Dickens employed a large amount of artistic licence,[87] yet his creation informed subsequent novels set in the period, such as Baroness Emmuska Orczy's *The Scarlet Pimpernel*,[88] in which the Pimpernel disguises himself as a wine-selling *tricoteuse* in order to help aristocrats escape from Paris. The fictional caricature of the *tricoteuse* is somewhat far-fetched, but nonetheless informs an understanding of knitters as social observers, whose 'innocent' pastime acts as a guise to collect information and to engage unnoticed in subversive activity. The bloodthirsty *tricoteuse*, for example, has been transformed to include Agatha Christie's Miss Marple, a mild-mannered amateur sleuth who uses her knitting as a pretext to listen in to conversations and observe wrongdoings. Knitting therefore can be seen as a cover, a literal means of hiding (one can hide behind a piece of knitting as one might do with a newspaper or book), but also as a disguise, a means of concealing oneself in public places and, as such, can be utilized as a means of information gathering.

Drawing from the Dickensian iconology of knitting and from a history of political protest clothing and accessorization, such as the banner, button and slogan T-shirt, contemporary knitters are communicating their social and political dissatisfaction in a variety of ways. One might see this as the development of the contemporary *tricoteuse*: Reign of Terror versus War on Terror.

Knitting has a history as a subversive, even devious activity. However, craft activity has a historical association with secrecy and deviousness (i.e. 'crafty'), which originated as a response to the ways in which traditional guilds were organized as 'closed', exclusive bodies, often with a political intent.[89] Similarly, the knitting circle, largely the domain of women, has an equally subversive history, which recognizes the power of group work, discussion and activism.[90] Indeed, from a Marxist perspective, engagement in practical and creative activity, such as knitting, acts as a tool for changing society.[91]

Since the 1970s, knitting, as a political tool, has been elevated as a means of articulating feminist ideals, drawing attention to what had ostensibly been described as 'women's work'. Like women's lives, knitting acted as a communicative tool, expressing histories that had hitherto been hidden, marginalized or ignored. In this vein, knitting has now become the chosen medium of the anti-capitalist protester, a means of demonstrating the power and discontent of the ordinary and individual in an increasingly homogenized world. The muteness associated with knitting has now come to signify the muteness of populations in the wake of the domination of multinational corporations. Here, knitting demonstrates the potential power of the individual working for a collective aim, establishing a voice for the silent majority. Making therefore makes a statement.

Much of this knitting has arisen as a response to globalization, climate change and the destruction of the natural environment, or as a reaction to the war in Iraq. This study aims to investigate the forms 'revolutionary' or 'activist' knitting takes, and questions the ways in which knitting as a medium communicates messages of political and social change.

The word 'revolution' here is used to describe the practice of knitting in two ways: firstly as an increasingly mass performative activity, involving public displays of knitting, engaging new or non-traditional participants, as demonstrated in knitting clubs and groups, either in set locations or on the Internet and, secondly, as a form of social engagement aimed to instigate political, cultural and social change. Therefore, this study addresses knitting as an act of sociability and of the social, a means of presenting the self as a social being with a social conscience. Such an investigation also acknowledges the notion of scale, not in terms of objects produced, but volume of participants and a focal move from the local to the global, and from the private to the public.

> Social craft action. Craft activism. Craftivism. Along with answering to various names, I also tend to talk about the intrinsic connection between craft and activism no matter what name it's given. I also believe that craftivism is about more than 'craft' and 'activism' – it's about making your own creativity a force to be reckoned with. The moment you start thinking about your creative production as more than just a hobby or 'women's work', and instead as something that has cultural, historical and social value, craft becomes something stronger than a fad or trend. I started writing along this theme in late 2002, and have delighted in the ways that people have been empowered and enlivened by the handmade, and knitting in particular. I started a blog site called craftivism.com to pay attention to two culturally stigmatized words, 'craft' and 'activism', to better spotlight the ways in which we can use our craft production to make the world a better place to live.[92]

'Craftivism' is a term used to define the synthesis of craft activity and political protest or commentary. Essentially relying on the power of the individual to create, whilst systematically promoting a sense of collectivism and collaboration through the inclusion of many, craftivism can be seen as a means of making both personal and collective statements with a view to social enlightenment and/or change. The collaboration between hand work and political intent can be assessed as a form of literally 'making' change, symbolically harnessing the power of the individual to make a difference. The emphasis within craftivism is primarily the message, the political intent or agenda, whilst craft, or the knitting (as most craftivist projects are knitted), is a vehicle or medium for the expression of that message.[93]

The most famed craftivist group is the Calgary-based Revolutionary Knitting Circle (RKC), which promotes anti-capitalist and environmental policies through non-violent knitting protest. Campaigning against the G8 summit in Calgary in June 2002, the RKC circulated a call for action via the Internet claiming:

> The G8 claims to be a gathering of democratic leaders. The Revolutionary Knitting Circle proclaims that they are anything but. The G8 is a meeting of the wealthiest of the world to decide the fates of the vast majority of the world who are in no way represented by these 'leaders'.[94]

Such a stance and use of rhetoric is reminiscent of earlier Marxist gatherings, with the novelty of demonstration including a knit-in rather than a more passive sit-in. Similarly, the mobilization of participants through new technologies such as the Internet implies that communication via what is essentially a capitalist tool can be utilized as an underground network to ultimately overthrow the system within which it operates.

Unlike Marx, who believed that societies were deterministic, Habermas believed that economies developed societies, not citizens. Revolution is therefore not a natural and progressive conclusion, and ideology cannot be bypassed or overturned. As a result, he saw contemporary society as in crisis, because the manipulation of individuals left their needs unaddressed. Traditional forms of protest were seen as not working, primarily because these too were in the hands of the ruling classes, so revolution was ultimately impossible. The closing of access to potential revolt was met with 'Communicative Action', a concept based on rationality and reasoning, enabling communication and protest through groups of people. This is demonstrated, for example, through the formation of community groups, charitable bodies and pressure groups such as the RKC, who regularly meet with local, regional and national government representatives in an attempt to reach agreement on a variety of political issues.

Similarly, quiet protests by large numbers of people, drawn together as a response to major situations, have become increasingly popular in recent years and the familiarity and accessibility of knitting offers the potential for large numbers of people to literally make social comment. For example, the Danish artist Marianne Jorgensen has, as a protest against the Iraq War, covered a series of tanks, each in a cosy made from 4,000 donated knitted pink squares. Jorgensen states:

> The possibility of 'knitting your opinions' gives the project an aspect that I think is important. The common element in the project gives importance beyond words. Most people can knit or crochet a square of 15 × 15 centimetres, and most people have some pink yarn to spare, and a lot of people are willing to use the time it takes to knit a patch that size and to support the project with the money it costs to mail the patch. I am thankful that people of many age groups, both sexes and several nationalities have been willing to use their time to support the project and I am hopeful. Unsimilar to a war, knitting signals home, care, closeness and time for reflection. Ever since Denmark became involved in the war in Iraq I have made different variations of pink tanks, and I intend to keep doing that, until the war ends. For me, the tank is a symbol of stepping over other people's borders. When it is covered in pink, it becomes completely unarmed and it loses its authority. Pink becomes a contrast in both material and colour when combined with the tank.[95]

Figure 54 Marianne Jorgensen, *Pink M.24 Chaffee*, 7–11 April 2006, Nikolaj Contemporary Art Centre, Copenhagen, Denmark. Photo: Barbara Katzin. Image reproduced with permission from the artist. The Second World War combat tank was covered in 15 × 15 cm (6 × 6 in) pink knitted squares donated by knitters from Denmark, Europe and the USA as a protest against Danish, British and American involvement in the war in Iraq. Jorgensen believes that the potential for 'knitting your opinions' takes protest to a level beyond words, connoting home, care, closeness and a need for time for reflection.

Knitting in this example embraces the absurdities of war, whilst referring to the iconography of both craft and femininity. Such a statement challenges concerned feminist critics who have showed displeasure at a resurgence of interest in knitting, suggesting that such a resurgence is a sign of a re-domestication of women, forcing them back into a condition of patriarchal servitude.[96] It also offers the potential for the growth of a global community of dissent, one which crosses cultural and political boundaries, and offers contributors the opportunity to think about the cause whilst knitting.

Habermas's Frankfurt School contemporary, Max Horkheimer, focused his philosophical social critique on reason and its use as a tool for manipulation in everyday life. For Horkheimer, reason was divided into two distinct areas: objective and subjective reason. Objective reason was a universal truth that determined whether an action was right or wrong; subjective reason encompassed the shades of grey positioned between the black and white of objective reason. Subjective reason is far more discursive: it requires consideration of circumstances, conditions and norms that might make an action 'reasonable'. The form of reason employed most frequently is subjective reason, which appears quite democratic, flexible and inclusive, accommodating the interests of everyone. In 'The End of Reason: Changes in the Structure of Political Compromise', Horkheimer discussed the ways in which the Nazis had risen to power using a campaign based on subjective reason.[97] This analogy explains the ways in which the presentation of an argument that appears to be 'reasonable' will be accepted more willingly and therefore the population is more responsive to manipulation, as to reject the idea may be construed as being 'unreasonable'. These ideas are materialized in the work of a variety of artists and amateurs who make statements about global and local issues through knitting. As both a practice and object, knitting is innocuous; it is perceived to be generally unthreatening, homely and safe, and to make a statement through harmless means seems perfectly reasonable. As Grant Neufeld, the organizer of the RKC's knit-in in 2002 noted:

> Talking with the general public has always been a challenge for activists, because when [activists] start out with [talking about all these problems in] the world, most people just shut down because they feel so overwhelmed. So finding a way to ease them into the discussion is pretty necessary. Also, the knitting creates a much friendlier environment for a dialogue. It is hard to associate knitting with anything really bad.[98]

Neufeld's statement highlights the subversive and seductive potential for knitting; his comments demonstrate how knitting is easily understood as a passive and non-harmful activity that offers a means of seducing others into a dialogue that satisfies the group's aims. Here, knitting tempts bystanders into political activism through the offer of a shared familiar practice, 'friendliness' and humour.

Recent global events, from the bombing of the Twin Towers to the consequent war in Iraq, have questioned the dominant role of global capitalism. The continual news footage of war and the subsequent moral panic surrounding the terrorist threat has been central to knitters globally. As the craftivist Betsy Greer comments: 'Atrocities are happening in our front yards and on our televisions and we need to find ways to react against what is happening without either giving up or exploding.'[99]

The postmodern theorist, Jean Baudrillard, described how contemporary terrorism is rooted within and is a condition of globalization. Distinguishing between the 'universal' (the universality of human rights, freedoms, culture, democracy) and the 'global' (the globalization of technologies, the market and tourism), he suggests that the rise of the global devalues and destroys the universal.[100] This effectively results in a monoculture, a homogenized system in which the flow of capital supersedes everything else. The local is lost in the global, and people become commodified. But this is also a climate in which rebellion is possible, an arena in which the universal can be potentially reclaimed:

> However, matters are not cut and dried, and globalization has not won the battle before it begins. In the face of homogenizing, dissolving power, we see heterogeneous forces rising up everywhere – not merely different, but antagonistic. Behind the increasingly sharp resistance to globalization, social and political resistance, we should see more than mere archaic rejection: a kind of painful revisionism regarding the achievements of modernity and 'progress', a rejection not only of the global technostructure, but of the mental structure of equivalence of all cultures. This resurgence can assume aspects which, from the standpoint of enlightened thinking, seem violent, anomalous, irrational – ethnic, religious and linguistic collective forms, but also emotionally disturbed or neurotic individual forms It would be a mistake to condemn these upsurges as populist, archaic, or even terroristic.[101]

Baudrillard's assertion that terrorism is a symptom of globalization follows post-Marxist social theory, which sees economies as deterministic. For Marcuse, for example, the success of capitalism simultaneously undermines it, stimulating a desire for socialism.[102] Protesters who knit may not always be seeking socialist ideals, but they are certainly seeking change and an alternative to the choices on offer. Protesters no longer seek to mobilize a workforce to overthrow the dominant order, but they do utilize technology to mobilize hundreds of thousands of knitters globally via the Internet to make petition squares or objects that will make a statement of protest, with the intention of change, if not revolution.

Lisa Anne Auerbach knits messages into sweaters and banners. Like her predecessors who made statements through accessories such as slogan T-shirts, buttons and the like, Auerbach makes a series of political comments through each piece. In *Warm Sweaters for the New Cold War* (2006), a series of seven knitted sweaters, Auerbach addresses the war on terror in four ways: rhetoric and language, iconography, public and individual response. Each garment, knitted in red and black (the

Figure 55 Lisa Anne Auerbach, *Warm Sweaters for the New Cold War*, 2006. One of seven sweaters. The text on this sweater is from George Bush's radio address on 2 September 2006.

colours of revolution) and playing on the rhetoric of 'Code Red', explores and recreates the responses to the events of war.

The communication of the iconology and ideology of the war on terror has been articulated through the mass media. The nature of modern warfare, in particular with the Gulf War and the war in Iraq, not only culturally distances East from West, but there is also geographical distance, which means that for many in the West, war is an abstract concept in which images, films and discourse are played out like a scripted fiction through the media. The war, therefore, is communicated not through lived experience, but a series of simulations[103] in which the real and the hyper-real exist as signs. The complexity of distance and the effects of war on individuals in the West is the subject of three of the series of seven of Auerbach's collection, in which she has knitted responses to the question: 'What is your favourite thing about the war on terror?' A rather tongue-in-cheek question instigated equally flippant comments, such as 'Getting patted down by women at the airport. I like that it's OK to be touched by another woman in public', implying that overt security had led to a relaxation of social and moral norms.

The significance of the sign is evidenced in Auerbach's sweaters: one features the juxtaposition of a transcript of President Bush's radio address on 2 September 2006, with the iconic image of a hooded prisoner being tortured by US troops in Abu Ghraib prison, Iraq. The concomitant image and text express the duality of 'truth' in contemporary society as played in the media. The theme of 'broadcast' is performed through the wearing of the sweaters, demonstrating the conflict not merely between messages, but also the personal and the public.

> I like sweaters as a vehicle for a political message for a few reasons. Even with the most obnoxious slogan, a sweater is still soft and warm and cosy. It's a bit disarming, I think, because people seem to see the sweater first, before reading the slogan. A sweater [can]

be worn in situations where a T-shirt might be inappropriate or even censored (I have worn some pretty outrageous sweaters at airports, for example, a bastion of garment prudence, but have never even received a comment). But at the same time, the message is powerful because it is so intentionally integrated into the fabric of the garment. So it runs the line between being more intense by virtue of the medium and [is] also over-shadowed by the medium.[104]

The main vehicle for Auerbach's message is the humble sweater, a warming garment with longevity. She states: 'T shirts represent something you can just throw away when you don't believe in them any more. Sweaters are forever. Sweaters with messages become historic.'[105] The longevity inherent in this phi-losophy captures the moment; it marks time and monumentalizes the zeitgeist. She says:

> I'm interested in today's news, tomorrow's history. I make sweaters about what I think is problematic, hypocritical, fucked up. I think most of us in the USA would prefer not to engage with what is going on outside our borders. We lie to be afraid, but we don't like to be bothered with details. In 2005, I made sweaters that had the number of US casualties –on the day I designed the sweater – knitted into the garment. I was inter-ested in seeing how these numbers would weather time. After a few years, would a couple of thousand casualties sound like the peak or just the beginning? Bringing this kind of specificity into a sweater gives it a connection with a certain time, and while the statistics or facts from that time don't change, our perspective, looking back, cer-tainly does.[106]

The concept of the longevity of specific knitting in relation to media events and temporality was explored in April 1995 by the Canadian artist, Janet Morton, in an installation piece called *News Flash*. Part performance, part public display, part time capsule, *News Flash* consisted of Morton knitting the news headlines from three Toronto daily newspapers for a whole month. Working for eight to ten hours per day, situated in the window of a main street Toronto store and watched by thousands of passers-by, Morton recorded daily events in knit. The final piece (a 2.75 × 7 m/9 × 23 ft blanket) was a testament to both personal and collective experiences and events occurring during that one month, including the Oklahoma bombings.[107] The recording, inscribing and thus monumentalizing of everyday events solidify and witness the atrocities of war, the rhetoric of government, and contemporary horrors that refer back to and replicate the actions of the Revolutionary Mme Defarge. Defarge was undoubtedly tainted with the macabre and personally involved in the downfall of her fellow citizens, which of course these contemporary artists are not. However, these works do demonstrate a col-lective responsibility, and fingers sub-texturally point to the voters who elected governments and to those who sat and watched their televisions passively as events unfurled. These works are testament to the dead but are also a monument to the guilt of those who witnessed the terror. Time has passed, but nothing has changed.

The concept of knitting marking time is central to Auerbach's *Body Count Mittens*, a pair of mittens which memorialize the number of US soldiers killed in Iraq. The mittens have been made into a pattern and published on the Steal This Sweater website, encouraging knitters globally to keep tally of the rising death count.

> These mittens memorialize the number of American soldiers killed in Iraq at the time the mittens are made. Since the numbers escalate daily, each mitten has a different number and date. Seen together, the pair of mittens shows a span of time and the increase in killed soldiers over that time. Each pair of mittens will be different, as the numbers and dates will vary. Some of us knit faster than others, and this too will be reflected in the finished pair, since the date on the mittens is the date each one was started. This makes an excellent project to knit in public. It's small and portable, and the intricate-looking mittens attract attention and encourage conversation both about the knitting and the occupation/war.[108]

Figure 56 Lisa Anne Auerbach, *Body Count Mittens*, 2005, ongoing project. The number of US casualties is memorialized in each mitten, but as casualties increase, the numbers commemorated in the pattern do too. Image reproduced with permission from the artist.

For Auerbach, the marking of time and the commemoration of significant events are evidenced in the mittens; she questions and historicizes the way in which cultural memory becomes selective, and news events distanced over time. The mittens provoke discussion, whilst also literally 'bringing home' statistical and reported data, monumentalizing the speed at which the death toll rises and the obsolescence of the garments themselves.

The textile artist, Adrienne Sloane, also makes visible the devastation of the contemporary world in her knitted body parts representative of the casualties of

Figure 57 Adrienne Sloane, *Line of Fire*, 2007. Knitted wire. Photo: Adrienne Sloane. Image reproduced with permission from the artist.

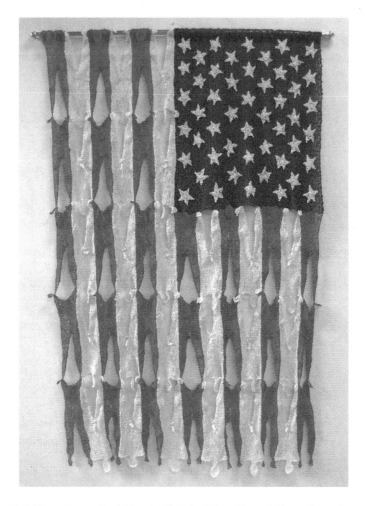

Figure 58 Adrienne Sloane, *Fated Glory*, 2008. Knitted linen. Photo: Adrienne Sloane. Image reproduced with permission from the artist.

war. The knitted figurative sculptures, such *as Body Count, Dirty Laundry, Cost of War II*, and *The Faces of Good and Evil*, are transparent; the viewer is able to see the hollowness of the structure and make judgements about the emptiness of war and also perhaps about the seeming hollowness of one person's actions in the face of global conflict. In *Dirty Laundry*, for example, a clothesline on which twelve knitted hands and feet hang is representative of the colloquial phrase 'Airing one's dirty laundry in public', whilst drawing reference to the 'hidden' or not talked about aspects of war such as killing.[109]

The visualization and materialization of the realities of war are also indicative of the contemporary climate of fear, which focuses on the body, not merely the prospect of penetration by weaponry, but of invisible body invaders, such as disease, germs and viruses for which there in no known cure. Terror, therefore, is not only abroad in society, but potentially inside the unsuspecting individual, transmitted in the food we eat and the air we breathe. Renata Salecl comments:

> Terrorists appear very similar to viruses and bacteria in that they are at first invisible, then suddenly erupt at one place or another; afterwards they hide again and one never knows how they have multiplied or what mutations they have made after they came under attack. As bacteria become resistant to antibiotics, terrorists, too, seemed to resist the warfare that was supposed to annihilate them.[110]

Katie Bevan, curator of the UK Crafts Council exhibition, 'Knit2gether', commented on the resurgence in popularity of knitting as a response to global events, stating: 'There's a sort of zeitgeist: a make-do-and-mend spirit during this war on terror or whatever it is. Everyone wants to go home and knit socks',[111] but the comforting potential of knitting also has uncovered a paradox in which knitting has the potential to both harm and heal. Knitting, like viruses, is based on a binary code, and like a virus can spread, transmute and have a devastating effect.

The contemporary fear of viral infection and infestation was the starting point for the Viral Knitting Project, a group of academics, activists and artists who aimed to draw together the anti-war movement and the RKC through the communicatory possibilities of the Internet. The project exploits the binary coding of the devastating computer virus that attacks the indexing system of Microsoft Windows, turning it into a knitting pattern. Knitting the virus has endless possibilities, mutating as any virus would, but in its most simple form can be made into a scarf, which offers warmth and comfort, transcending national boundaries and 'infecting' communities globally.[112] The spread of viral knitting through the making of patterns into objects highlights the disquieting prospect of life in the contemporary world: things that offer comfort and might have healing properties may also be harmful and extremely dangerous.

The Viral Knitting Project has also mutated into a series of four video performances, unending and continuous rhythmic knitting, which encourages knitters to participate in the performance by watching and knitting the virus in red, yellow, orange and green, simultaneously, reflecting proportionally the number of colour-coded (Code Red, Code Yellow and so on) days the USA has been on a terrorist alert since 9/11. The looped videos, juxtaposed with the loops of the knitting, suggest an endlessness: fabric is created, but it has no beginning or end, symbolically representative of the tireless wheels of capitalism and the ceaselessness of war and the threat of terror.

Knitters use recycled wool or yarn, reclaimed from unwanted or discarded sweaters, and by doing so intend to demonstrate one way in which the destruction and wastefulness of capitalism can literally be undone and remade. These performances include a variety of elements of protest: the fusion of the 'old' and 'new' technologies of hand knitting with the Internet, computer technology and video screenings, the recycling of the products of capitalism through re-knitting, the mobilization of a 'workforce' through a shared common interest, and the making of statements about the relationship between capitalism and war, whilst commenting on the real but invisible fear currently gripping Western societies.

Like Mme Defarge, contemporary artists are harnessing the ordinary practice of knitting to communicate and list the atrocities of the times. In each example, horror is commemorated and solidified, but as the atrocities continue, each object is stuck in time, obsolete as the death toll and casualty numbers increase. This is perhaps the potency of the message; whilst art communicates, action must be instigated, otherwise the message is rendered hollow, merely an aspect of the circulation of images, one of many within a highly visual media society.

Conclusion

The history of knitting as an act of agitation continues to inform contemporary knitting. The accessibility and simplicity of mastering knitting stitches, combined with the relative low cost of yarn, particularly when it is reused, makes it the perfect inclusive group activity. Knitting is egalitarian and when undertaken by hand is always unique, thereby offering an antidote to mass production, mass consumption and a global economy and monoculture. Embracing environmental and ethical concerns, knitting offers an alternative, a means of problem-solving, as well as providing a critique of issues and events. Essentially, as knitting is seen so frequently as an alternative or marginal culture, it has the power to challenge the dominant ideology.

Knitting employs both individual and collective effort in order to make a political comment. As this chapter has demonstrated, collectives have the potential to create statements on a mass scale, whilst the contribution of individuals is central to this. Small acts of knitting can change lives, raise funds or show concern, and in this respect the individual is not without power. Drawing from the history of knitting as a collective activity associated with the dual concerns of thrift and philanthropy, groups step in where business and the state fail to do so. Knitting here enables the social being to express a social conscience.

Although knitting is classified as a low-tech form of manufacture or making, knitters make extremely good use of high-tech media in order to communicate their messages, call like-minded knitters to action, or as an inspiration for works of art and social and political commentary. High-tech media and the language of capitalism are being used to challenge the dominant ideology, as a means of subverting from within. Capitalism is challenged through the use of its own language and media, and knitting – a traditionally 'mute' and humble activity – gives those who seemingly have no say a voice.

Activism and knitting for good causes is not without its problems; activities and objects are still part of the dominant ideology, as nothing exists outside society. Yarn has (even if it is recycled) to be purchased as a commodity, and some knitted goods are produced for large-scale sale and as such are an expression of capitalism. People who knit for good causes, however passionate about their cause or altruistic, effectively take the pressure off government funding, which heightens the division between government concern (through proper funding provision) and the concerns of the electorate.

Similarly, ethical and environmental yarns and Fairtrade products are extremely expensive, distancing them from the reach of the average consumer, whilst simultaneously challenging the notion of knitting as a working-class economy. Such consumer division illustrates class separation in relation to economics, whilst also distancing knitting culturally from 'work' to 'leisure', and from necessity to pleasure. Indeed, it is not only the move from necessity to leisure that has proved problematic, as Lisa Anne Auerbach notes:

> I used to think that DIY was always good, that people were making their own stuff; just by the fact that they were making, it gave them freedom from the market and from the vagaries of fashion and the prison of consumerism. But watching this knitting trend grow has proven otherwise. I'm glad people have a connection to what they are producing, but I'm not convinced that this is changing the world in the direction I'd like to see it change. I just see more petroleum acrylic made into more ugly Afghans and horrible scarves. Sweater-in-a-day patterns mean that yarn companies sell more yarn and the sweaters just get uglier.[113]

It appears that knitting and pleasure have opened up more opportunities for consumption, less opportunity for discernment, with more emphasis on speed rather than learning and skill. The world is, indeed, as Auerbach states, full of ugly sweaters, and the meaning of making becomes lost as the fashion for knitting increases. Knitting is not always ethical, environmentally friendly or political in its intent. Frequently it is just a hobby, something to do, a time-filler, which requires no form of aesthetic or ideological motivation.

Nonetheless, as the development of craftivism, the display of overt political knitted statements in museums, galleries and other public institutions, and as the revival of knitting draws increasing media attention, allowing knitting to develop the potential to become visibly and actively part of a political and social dialogue. Whether this popularity and press coverage will destroy the potency of both act and object, commodifying it for a mass market through mass-produced kits, patterns and causes, and in turn erase its marginal status, making knitting mainstream, only time will tell.

Conclusion: Is the World
Full of Ugly Jumpers?

Knitting is currently undergoing a revival in its popularity. More and more people are picking up needles and starting to knit. Whether this is as a means of relaxation, socialization or celebrity emulation, or as the expression of fashionable dress, as an art installation or as the demonstration of new approaches to new materials, knitting as a practice has certainly been revisited. This may just be a passing fad, a trend that will die out and be replaced with the next 'new' best thing. But there are a great many people who have an investment in knitting that transcends the novelty and situates knitting at the heart of everyday contemporary life.

On the one hand, we may understand knitting as the 'new' yoga, the 'new' celebrity hobby, as an expression of the 'new' domesticity, but on the other, what we are being offered is the old knitting in new packaging. If the activity is the same, why does it need to be rebranded? Essentially, knitting can be seen as having been party to a bad press; it had fallen out of favour, was a bit too sentimental and outdated and needed a change of image to sustain its continuation.

Traditionally, knitting has been seen as the domain of women; whether this was part of piecework to make a bit of extra money, as part of domestic chores and thrifty housewifery or, indeed, as a purely home-centred leisure activity, concepts of what it is to be female and what 'home' represents have been central to discussions about knitting. This preconception assumes that knitting is distanced from systems of value one would associate with patriarchy: the world of work, culture and commerce. Knitting remains somewhat tainted by these concerns, and is often a starting point to challenge or make visible women's otherwise hidden work and creative practice within the domestic sphere. Knitting came to represent the 'old' woman, not necessarily in terms of age, although that is also an issue, but as a sign of non-liberated femininity, of women tied to the domestic environment by a round of thankless chores.

As feminism informed education, and arts education became dominated by a quest for work-based and industrially 'useful' skills, hand knitting became further eschewed with domestic hobbies. And even though post-feminists have sought to reclaim knitting as a site of women's pleasure, sociability and creativity under the banner of the 'new' domesticity, challenges to old stereotypes are bypassed and it very much remains a leisure-based pastime; whilst cooking (another prime example of the new domesticity) is a life necessity, knitting is not.

The emphasis on knitting as leisure, as relaxation or even meditation or therapy has dominated much of the contemporary texts addressing knitting practice. With the reformist zeal of self-help manuals, these texts suggest that knitting cannot merely busy idle hands, but heal your soul and uplift your spirit. As a repetitive practice, knitting offers a rhythm that can be calming, mediating the beat of the heart rate. Equally, as a constructed textile, knitting can demonstrate and mark the passing of time – the distanced travelled, counted in knitted rows, which has beneficial effects for those who find it difficult to structure their lives. Both the new domesticity and the meditative approach exemplify knitting as a means of embracing quality of life, of a more 'authentic' way of living, of filling the void left by heavy work schedules, busy family lives, the overconsumption of goods, and the stresses and strains of modern-day existence. Knitting, it appears, offers a means of creativity, of confidence in one's own ability to 'do', as well as occupying a space in which one can just 'be'.

Knitting is the physical manifestation of the adage 'Making something out of nothing'; with very little material, one can make exceptional objects, and knitting therefore becomes an expression of the coincidence of hand and mind, of imagination and skill, demonstrating the value of hand work in an era that is dominated by the hyper-real, the virtual and the technological. Likewise, knitting becomes part of wider social debates on ethical production and consumption, environmentalism and alternative lifestyles. To make or to knit is therefore about demonstrating a personal creativity in everyday life, and under these circumstances making is to make special. Likewise, to knit is perceived as an ethical choice, and as an alternative to the impersonal world of goods.

The iconography and meanings attributed to knitting infer that it expresses a non-changing activity and aesthetic, a general and popularly held view of craft per se: stability and continuity. Indeed, as the book has demonstrated, certain motifs, styles and patterns have a long history, such as the popular crinoline lady or the 'traditional' Fair Isle sweater, which are easily recognizable and representative of a stylistic genre. However, although the motifs are continuous, they are constantly updated, reinvented and restyled to appeal to a contemporary audience and market. Similarly, the resurrection of hand-knits, beading or embroidery in haute couture fashion collections contributes to a popular understanding of knitting as simultaneously high-fashion innovation and low-level traditional kitsch. This is one of the many paradoxes of knitting, indicative of its ability to situate itself within two seemingly separate and opposing spheres at the same time.

As a result of the consumer revolution, and tainted by poverty, knitting not only fell out of favour, but became firmly established as a sign of something distanced from the fashion system and commodity choice. Recently, this perception has been addressed in two ways: firstly, knitting is presented as a deliberate and political stand against mass manufacture and the global circulation of goods; alternatively, knitting has also been promoted as a luxurious, exclusive and expensive activity, which also distances the knitter from a reliance on mass-manufactured goods. In both cases, knitting is self-consciously referring to its heritage, embracing the constituent elements that have previously marginalized it.

This self-referentiality might be seen as indicative of a postmodern cultural shift in which the ordinary is celebrated and the past informs the present. Such a climate creates a space for retrogressive gazing, for nostalgic yearning, assigning cultural signs to objects, practices and words, which refer directly to their heritage. Indeed, knitting is so entrenched with symbolic meaning pertaining to class, gender, location, value, aesthetic and so on, that it is difficult to move the discipline on.

Interviewees provided interesting responses to the medium of knitting, which also added to this disparate view. Artists working with knit tended to distance themselves from the medium, emphasizing that knit was merely a means of expressing ideas – a vehicle, and nothing more. Such proclamations appear to be culturally loaded; knitting is perhaps not serious enough, is too tainted with the feminine and the domestic to be considered an 'art' in its own right. Equally, textile media in general attracts much less funding, has access to fewer prestigious venues, and despite the attempts of the Crafts Council, remains distanced in terms of exhibition and support than other 'fine' media. Knitting therefore remains firmly embedded as an 'outsider', a populist pastime, and is distanced from serious aesthetic and academic consideration. This distancing is telling: it would be highly unlikely that a fine art painter would make the same kind of statements about her relationship with paint. The paradox is – and for knitting there are no absolutes – that in examples of fine art knitting, the medium is fundamental to the message, exhibiting a self-referentiality that enhances and gives form to the concept. One can never escape from the culture of knitting.

A concern for the seriousness of knitting was also evident in the testimonies of designers, who were keen to discuss the ways in which knitwear had frequently been negated within fashion histories. Scarred by a history of novelty jumpers, innovation in knit has seemingly been overlooked, and knitting has become the butt of jokes. Knitting, the designers believed, had been seen as fun, frivolous and something to be laughed at, when actually it was big business, and as well as being a wardrobe staple (everyone owns something that's knitted, even if it's just their underwear) it was highly innovative, experimental and fashion-led. Again, it seemed that knitting had been consigned to a life on the margins, whilst quietly pushing ahead and challenging stereotypes.

If knitting is subject to a revival, one must assume that it is near death and in need of some form of resuscitation: new life has to be breathed into it before knitting takes its last gasp and is gone forever. The relationship between knitting and potential loss equates with much writing on the contemporary crafts; without new approaches, new methods, technology and so on, hand work will ultimately be lost

Figure 59 Rachel John, *Extreme Knitting*, demonstration, 'Unravel', South Hill Park, Bracknell, UK, 2006. Photo: Jo Turney.

or confined to the iconography of the past. And as mills close down at an alarming rate, what is the future of hand knitting?

Knitting beyond two basic stitches is difficult, skilled and takes time to master, and although knitting is frequently promoted as simple and quick, the transition from making a simple scarf to a wearable garment requires a huge conceptual and practical leap. And this is a problem in terms of sustaining practice. How many scarves can one person make and wear without becoming bored or frustrated? Craft takes both time and knowledge. How can this be addressed when life is lived in fragments in a quick-fix MTV culture?

For designer-makers and craftspeople, the practice of hand knitting raised questions pertaining to hand work and activities deemed 'traditional' in contemporary life. The concerns expressed emerged from two distinct, but interrelated areas: the value of hand work, its sustenance and longevity, and the expansion of the boundaries of the discipline. Many interviewees expressed a need to reintroduce activities such as knitting into the school curriculum, putting a new generation literally in touch with making, building self-confidence through self-sufficiency, prioritizing reflective and relaxing practices, and developing an understanding of materials through personal creativity. Conclusively, knitting had to be valorized, needed, wanted and learned for it to continue in the long term, and craftspeople have been addressing these issues.

To dissociate knitting from the domestic and from the constraints of leisure, craftspeople have started to see its potential for industrial collaboration, as a means of challenging the constraints of materials, forms and uses. Knitting as a discipline has expanded its boundaries in terms of scale, function and artefact, with traditional yarns replaced with high-tech threads, metals and ceramics, and forms extended into the domains of furniture, architecture and engineering. Likewise, the constituent elements of knitting, its tactility, repetition, rhythm and its portability have been championed as examples of thoughtful, contemplative, sensory practices that offer a connectedness between people and things – a relationship seemingly under threat as Western society relies more and more on the computer interface and the virtual as a means of experiencing the world.

The experiences of amateur knitters have been central to this investigation, and oral and written testimonies have featured throughout. It has often been difficult to remain (as an interviewer and observer) totally emotionally separate from the respondents, as frequently their testimonies were so sentimental, emotive, personal or private that it was impossible not to feel sympathy or to empathize. Equally, as knitting appears to elicit such responses, it has been important to highlight it as such, and in a manner that remains faithful and sensitive to the original testimonies and wishes of the contributors.

The emphasis of the personal, emotional and subjective testimonies of the respondents intimated that knitting was a journey, in which frequently the travelling (knitting) was more important or emotionally significant than the arrival at the destination (knitted object). The emphasis on process and change, evident in narrative structure (beginning, middle and end) was equally evident in the progress achieved through making (raw materials, making process, completed project). So knitting can be understood as a journey, undertaken for a variety of reasons, in which the knitter consciously transforms one set of materials into another. This transformation can be understood as material culture as process, a journey marked by not only the transformation of objects to object, but indicative of a shifting relationship between maker, making and made object. The process of transformation – of raw materials to completed project – is often a parallel to life transformations, of distance travelled and time filled 'usefully'. The knitter is alchemist, timekeeper and pioneer.

Knitting, as this book has testified, is an extremely complex series of practices undertaken for a variety of reasons, with varying results, outcomes and contexts, produced for a variety of disparate audiences. Whatever the reasons for knitting and whatever the result, knitting is very much part of our visual and material world, and its existence generates discourses that provide evidence of practices otherwise marginalized or ignored. The ordinariness of knitting and knitted objects seemingly defines its discussion or analysis. Too easily it is dismissed as 'just knitting'. But it is precisely this ordinariness that makes it special, elucidates such responses and evokes memories of times, people and places. Knitting allows makers to not 'just' make things, but to communicate ideas, forge relationships, and make sense of and comment on the world around them.

Knitting is culturally significant because it questions and comments on contemporary cultural values. Similarly, knitting is representative of and evident within the distance between cultural binaries, demonstrating its permeation throughout a huge area of everyday life. This proliferation or saturation of familiar and ordinary practices and objects allows knitting to 'mean' as little or as much as the individual spectator/knitter/consumer requires. The world is indeed full of ugly jumpers, but it is also full of wonderful, innovative, frightening and challenging knitted objects.

Notes

Introduction

1. Sheila McGregor, *The Complete Book of Fair Isle Knitting*, B. T. Batsford, 1981, p. 7.
2. 'Men and Boys Knit Up a Storm' CBS News, Chicago, 4th February 2005, http://www.cbsnews.com/stories/2005/02/04/national/printable671644.shtml.
3. http://www.knitrowan.com.
4. http://www.bhkc.co.uk/.
5. David J. Spencer, *Knitting Technology*, Woodhead Publishing Ltd., 1998 (3rd edition), 2.1.
6. In conversation with Alison Kelly, 2007.
7. Montse Stanley, 'Jumpers That Drive You Quite Insane: Colour, Structure and Form in Knitted Objects', in Mary Schoeser and Christine Boydell (eds.), *Disentangling Textiles*, Middlesex University Press, 2002.

1 Knitting: A Gendered Pursuit?

1. Sharon Aris, *It's My Party and I'll Knit If I Want To!*, Allen and Unwin, 2003, p. 130.
2. Kate Millett, *Sexual Politics*, Virago, 1977, pp. 25–6.
3. John Storey, *An Introductory Guide to Cultural Theory and Popular Culture*, Harvester Wheatsheaf, 1993, p. 125.
4. Betty Friedan, *The Feminine Mystique*, Penguin, 1992 (new edition).
5. Debbie Stoller, *Stitch 'n' Bitch Handbook: Instructions, Patterns and Advice For a New Generation of Knitters*, Workman Publishing, 2003.
6. Debbie Stoller quoted in Zoe Williams, 'Close Knit', *The Guardian*, 8th January 2005.
7. Joanne Hollows, 'Can I Go Home Yet?', in Joanne Hollows and Rachel Moseley (eds.), *Feminism in Popular Culture*, Berg, 2006, pp. 106–7.
8. The Victoria and Albert Museum's website asks users to outline how they learned to knit. See www.vam.ac.uk.
9. Kim Tucker, interviewed 18th May 1999.
10. Ellen Dissanayake, 'The Pleasure and Meaning of Making', p. 44.

11. Roszika Parker, *The Subversive Stitch*, The Women's Press, 1996, pp. 187–88.
12. Pat Kirkham, 'Women and the Inter-War Handicrafts Revival', in Judy Attfield and Pat Kirkham (eds.), *A View From the Interior*, The Women's Press, p. 177.
13. Cristina Walkley, *The Ghost in the Looking Glass*, Peter Owen, 1981, pp. 3–5.
14. Cheryl Buckley, 'Made in Patriarchy: Towards a Feminist Analysis of Women and Design', *Design Issues*, Vol. III, No. 2.
15. Penny Sparke, *As Long As It's Pink*, pp. 151–2.
16. Barbara Burman, 'Made at Home with Clever Fingers', in Barbara Burman (ed.) *The Culture of Sewing*, pp. 44–6.
17. Richard Stewart, *Design and British Industry*, p. 47.
18. M. Ross, 'The Last Twenty-Five Years: The Arts in Education, 1963–1988', in M. Ross (ed.), *The Claims of Feeling: Readings in Aesthetic Education*, The Falmer Press, 1989, p. 10.
19. Culminating in the Department of Education and Science's draft 'The School Curriculum', 1983, the launch of GCSE in 1986 (first exams in 1988), and the Education Reform Bill, 1987. Training schemes included the Manpower Services Commission's 1981 'New Training Initiative' and the 'Technical and Vocational Education Initiative' (TVEI), 1983.
20. The closure of heavy industry included steelworks, shipyards, mines and docks.
21. Professor David Keith Lucas, Design Council Report, 1980, quoted in P. H. M. Williams, *Teaching Craft, Design and Technology*, Routledge, 1990, pp. 1–2.
22. Examples of Design Council initiatives are listed in J. M. Woodham, 'Managing British Design Reform I: Fresh Perspectives of the Early Years of the Council of Industrial Design', *Journal of Design History*, Vol. 9, No. 1, 1996, pp. 55–66; and J. M. Woodham, 'Managing British Design Reform II: The Film Deadly Lampshade – An Ill-Fated Episode in the Politics of Good Taste', *Journal of Design History*, Vol. 9, No. 2, 1996, pp. 101–16.
23. Herbert Read, *Art and Industry*, Faber and Faber, 1934.
24. 'Curriculum 11–16', Her Majesty's Inspectors, 1977.
25. 'A Statement on the Value of Crafts in Secondary Education: Discussion Document', Crafts Council Education Committee, CCE (81) 2/2.
26. Pen Dalton, 'Housewives, Leisure Crafts and Ideology', in G. Elinor et al., *Women and Craft*, p. 34.
27. M. Williams, *Teaching Craft, Design and Technology*, p. 6.
28. Ibid., p. 9.
29. Crafts Council Education Working Party, est. 1977, under the chairmanship of Robert Godden, to investigate the teaching of crafts in secondary schools.
30. Crafts Council memorandum to the House of Commons Select Committee on Education, Science and the Arts, May 1981.

31. The Warnock Report, HMSO, 1975.

32. Stephen Wagg, 'Here's One I Made Earlier', in Dominic Strinati and Stephen Wagg, *Come on Down? Popular Media Culture in Post-War Britain*, Routledge, 1992, p. 153.

33. Lesley Burgess and Kate Schofield, 'Shorting the Circuit', in Pamela Johnson (ed.), *Ideas in the Making*, pp. 122–30.

34. Analysis of questionnaires on the training of craft teachers in England and Wales, Education Working Part, Crafts Council, p. 6, Appendix B, CAC (79) 1/3.

35. Tanya Harrod, The Crafts in Britain in the Twentieth Century, p. 392.

36. Quick and easy packet, ready-made and microwaveable meals were ubiquitous products advertised in women's magazines throughout the period, i.e. Knorr powdered soups and sauces, etc. Cookery features in magazines also emphasized speed of preparation, i.e. 'Speed Is the Essence', *Woman*, 14th October 1978, pp. 20–22.

37. Shirley Conran, *Superwoman*, Fontana, 1980.

38. Recent studies by educational psychologists have stated that four out of ten British schoolgirls can't boil an egg. This statistic was commented on by Vanessa Feltz in the *Sunday Express*, 10th February 2002, p. 41; Suzanne Moore, the *Mail on Sunday*, 10th February 2002, p. 35; and India Knight, 'Oh, Go Boil an Egg, Girls', *The Sunday Times*, 10th February 2002, p. 5.

39. C. Frayling, 'The Crafts in the 1990s', *The Journal of Art and Design Education*, Vol. 9, No. 1, 1990.

40. Interview with Janet Morton, 10th October 2007.

41. In 1978, 9.1 million women were in paid employment.

42. Margie Proops, *Fresh Start: A Guide to Training Opportunities*, Equal Opportunities Commission, 1978. Advertised in *Woman* magazine on 2nd September 1978.

43. Frank Mort, *Cultures of Consumption: Masculinities and Social Space in Twentieth-Century Britain*, Routledge, 1996, Introduction.

44. 'How to Mind Your Own Business', *Woman*, February 25th 1978, pp. 30–31; 'People are Getting Craftier', *Woman*, March 11th 1978, pp. 24–7; 'How to Help Yourself', *Woman*, 17th February 1979, pp. 20–21; etc. Or how home craft makers/ workers were an exploited workforce: 'Slave Labour', *Woman*, 4th November 1978, pp. 26–7; 'Who's Making Money From Our Homeworkers?', *Woman*, 6th October 1979, pp. 20–22. Each article had a dual focus on 'real-life' experiences – successes or failures, depending on the emphasis of the feature.

45. 'The Dismal Decade', *Woman*, 22nd December 1979, p. 26.

46. Fashion spreads showing the difference in prices, include articles such as 'How to Look Good, Though Hard Up', *Woman's Weekly*, 8th January 1977, pp. 14–15.

47. Dressmaking patterns and readers' pattern offers appeared weekly in *Woman's Weekly* from 1975 onwards.

48. Janice Winship, 'The Impossibility of Best: Enterprise Meets Domesticity in the Practical Women's Magazines of the 1980s', in Dominic Strinati and Stephen Wagg, *Come On Down? Popular Media Culture in Post-War Britain*, Routledge, 1992, p. 83.

49. Shirley Conran, 'Who Wants To Be Superwoman?', lecture, the Women's Library, 21st March 2002.

50. Conran disputes this – speaking at the Women's Library on 21st March 2002, she stated that she'd never said that it was possible to 'have it all', but to have pieces of everything. An academic perspective is provided by Penny Sparke in: *As Long As It's Pink, The Sexual Politics of Taste*, Pandora, 1995, p. 232.

51. Margaret Thatcher interview, *Woman*, 28th July 1979, pp. 40–43.

52. 'Behind the Headlines: Anne Scargill', *Woman*, 6th April 1985, pp. 2–3; and 'After the Miners' Strike: The Women Who Hold the Key to Peace', *Woman*, 11th May 1985, pp. 18–19.

53. Claire Francis, *Woman*, 3rd February, 1982, pp. 40–43.

54. 'The Dismal Decade', *Woman*, 22nd December 1979, p. 26.

55. 'Superwomen? But Can They Cook?' *Woman*, 25th August 1979, pp. 20–22.

56. Ibid., pp. 20–22.

57. Ibid., p. 20.

58. Penny Sparke, *As Long As It's Pink: The Sexual Politics of Taste*, Pandora, 1995.

59. *Woman*, December 2nd 1978, pp. 40–44.

60. In the mid-1970s, 'The average Briton watched sixteen hours of television a week in the summer, twenty hours in the winter', quoted in Jan Boxshall, *Every Home Should Have One: Seventy-Five Years of Change in the Home*, Ebury Press, 1997, p. 101.

61. Credit cards were first introduced in the UK in 1972.

62. Gillian Elinor, 'Feminism and Craftwork', *Circa*, No. 47, Sept/ Oct 1989.

63. Jennifer Craik, *The Face of Fashion*, Routledge, 1994, p. 48; Leonore Davidoff, *Worlds Between: Historical Perspectives on Gender and Class*, Polity Press, 1995, p. 20.

64. *Woman's Weekly* had a header that rotated weekly – 'Famed for its knitting' and 'Famed for its fiction'.

65. Easy ready-to-sew patterns include 'Honey Bears' in *Woman's Weekly*, 15th October 1983, p. 12.

66. Jennifer Craik, ibid., p. 49.

67. Janice Winship, 'The Impossibility of Best: Enterprise Meets Domesticity in the Practical Women's Magazines of the 1980s', in Dominic Strinati and Stephen Wagg, *Come On Down? Popular Media Culture in Post-War Britain*, Routledge, 1992, p. 84.

68. In 1983, *Woman* and *Woman's Own* underwent a 'makeover'; consequently

there was a reduction in crafts and fiction.

69. 'Toys Galore', *Woman's Weekly*, 6th October 1979, pull-out feature.

70. *Woman's Weekly*, 25th December 1982; *Woman's Weekly*, 31st December 1983.

71. Betsy Wearing, *Leisure and Feminist Theory*, Sage, 1998, p.viii.

72. Henrietta L. Moore, *Feminism and Anthropology*, Blackwell Publishers Ltd., 1988, p. 49.

73. Interview with Liz Padgham-Major, 16th October 2007.

74. Charlotte Abrahams, 'Bring on the Knit Wits', *The Guardian Weekend Magazine*, 5th March 2005, p. 58.

75. M. Barrett and M. McIntosh, *The Anti-Social Family*, Verso, 1982; S. Jackson and S. Moores, *The Politics of Domestic Consumption*, Harvester Wheatsheaf, 1995; P. Corrigan, *The Sociology of Consumption*, Sage 1997.

76. M. Csikszentmihalyi and E. Rochberg-Halton, *The Meaning of Things*, Cambridge University Press, 1975; D. Miller, *Material Culture and Mass Consumption*, Blackwell, 1994.

77. J. Attfield and P. Kirkham, *A View From the Interior: Feminism, Women and Design*, The Women's Press, 1989; J. Bird et al. (eds.), *Mapping the Futures: Local Cultures, Global Change*, Routledge, 1990; A. Forty, *Objects of Desire: Design and Society 1750–1980*, Thames & Hudson, 1989.

78. S. Jackson and S. Moores, ibid.

79. Stephen Miles, *Consumerism – As a Way of Life*, Sage, 1998; Robert Bocock, *Consumption*, Routledge, 1993; M. J. Lee, *Consumer Culture Reborn*, Routledge, 1993.

80. Crolin Sorenson, 'Theme Parks and Time Machines', in Peter Vergo (ed.), *The New Museology*, Reaktion Books, 1989, p. 61.

81. Gloria Hickey, 'Craft in a Consuming Society', in Peter Dormer (ed.), *The Culture of Craft*, Manchester University Press, 1997, pp. 83–100.

82. MO respondent D1559.

83. As described in the Crafts Council papers, CCE (81) 2/2.

84. Ben Highmore, *Everyday Life and Cultural Theory*, Routledge, 2002.

85. *Market Review 2000: UK Leisure and Recreation*, report, p. 5. States that hobbies are too disparate to conduct accurate market research.

86. *Market Review 2000: UK Leisure and Recreation*, p. 2. 'Overall, watching television (TV) is the most time-consuming leisure activity, but time use surveys show that more people than ever manage to fit in reading (books, newspapers and magazines are all important markets) and listening to music or the radio.'

87. The autumn 1988 MO Directive included a BFI day diary. The Directive stated to prospective respondents: 'An unusual package this time. The British Film Institute has asked for our cooperation in their first November "Television Day Diary" project – an idea inspired by Mass Observation in the first place'. Respondents were asked to catalogue all of the programmes that they viewed in one day.

88. Penny Sparke, ibid., pp. 151–52.
89. MO respondent, C108.
90. MO respondent, C139.
91. MO respondent, C1922.
92. MO respondent C.1939. There are many more examples i.e. respondents B1785, B1721, B1771, C1225, B1915, B2046, B50, B663, A1473, D666, and so on.
93. MO respondent L333.
94. MO respondent B633.
95. MO respondent A1412.
96. MO respondent D159.
97. Thorstein Veblen, *Theory of the Leisure Class*, Augustus M. Kelley, 1899, p. 35.
98. Ibid., pp. 35–9.
99. Ibid., pp. 43–55.
100. John Urry, *Consuming Places*, Routledge, 1995, pp. 112–28.
101. MO respondent C1922.
102. MO respondent G1003.
103. MO respondent B36.
104. MO respondent, B1180.
105. MO respondent D666.
106. Rosemary Deem, 'Leisure and the Household' in S. Jackson and S. Moores (eds.), *The Politics of Domestic Consumption*, Harvester Wheatsheaf, 1995, pp. 137–8.
107. Cynthia Cockburn, 'Black and Decker Versus Moulinex', in S. Jackson and S. Moores (eds.), *The Politics of Domestic Consumption*, Harvester Wheatsheaf, 1995 pp. 213–16.
108. Rosemary Deem, ibid., pp. 137–8.
109. MO respondent G1241.
110. MO respondent H1806.
111. Others include talk of hiding work from husbands, sneakily doing things while alone, and so on.
112. David Chaney, *Lifestyles*, Routledge, 1996, p. 33.
113. Rozsika Parker, *The Subversive Stitch*, The Women's Press, 1984.
114. Anne L. Macdonald, *No Idle Hands: The Social History of American Knitting*, Ballantyne Books, 1988, p. 330.
115. Judith Durant, *Never Knit Your Man a Sweater Unless You've Got the Ring*, Storey Publishing, 2006.
116. Peter Corrigan, 'Gender and the Gift: The Case of the Family Clothing Economy', in Stevi Jackson and Shaun Moores (eds.), *The Politics of Domestic Consumption: Critical Readings*, Harvester Wheatsheaf, 1995, pp. 116–134.

117. Naomi Wolf, *Promiscuities: A Secret History of Female Desire*, Chatto and Windus, London, 1997.
118. Valerie Steele, 'Clothing and Sexuality' in C. Kidwell and V. Steele (eds.), *Men and Women: Dressing the Part*, Smithsonian Institute Press, 1989, p. 61.
119. Jennifer Craik, *The Face of Fashion*, Routledge, 1993, p. 176.
120. M. Pumphrey, 'Why Do Cowboys Wear Hats in the Bath? Style Politics for the Older Man', *Critical Quarterly* 31:3, autumn, p. 96, referenced in Jennifer Craik, *The Face of Fashion*, Routledge, 1994, p. 191.
121. Donald F. Sabo Jr. and Ross Rinfola, *Jock: Sports and Male Identity*, Prentice Hall Inc., 1980, p. 7.
122. Garry Whannel, *Media Sports Stars: Masculinities and Moralities*, Routledge, 2002, pp. 64–5.
123. Paolo Hewitt and Mark Baxter, *The Fashion of Football: From Best to Beckham, From Mod to Label Slave*, Mainstream Publishing Company, 2006, p. 79 and p. 85; Tara Jon Manning, *Men in Knits: Sweaters to Knit That He WILL Wear*, Interweave Press Inc., 2004, p. 2.
124. Jennifer Craik, *The Face of Fashion*, Routledge, 1994, p. 190.
125. Judith Butler, *Gender Trouble*, Routledge, 2006.
126. Tim Edwards, *Men in the Mirror: Men's Fashion, Masculinity and Consumer Society*, Cassell, 1997, pp. 41–2.
127. Sean Nixon, *Hard Looks: Masculinities, Spectatorship and Contemporary Consumption*, Routledge, 1996, pp. 12–13.
128. Although the 1960s had afforded fashionable men to return to a behaviour and dress style indicative and reminiscent of the eighteenth-century dandy, and youth groups and sub-cultures had adopted forms of sartorial narcissism previously unseen in the twentieth century, it wasn't until the mid-1970s that an overtly sexualized masculinity became mainstream. Such developments were evident in popular cinema, as in *American Gigolo*, in which Richard Gere's character displays a narcissism previously unseen, and in *Saturday Night Fever* (1977), where the opening scene captures a young John Travolta strutting whilst presenting himself as a fashionable and sexual being. These characters were aware of their sexuality, their sexual power and their appearance, which very much contributed to their identity.
129. Joanne Entwistle, *The Fashioned Body*, Polity Press, 2000, p. 174.
130. Richard Martin and Harold Koda, *Jocks and Nerds: Men's Style in the Twentieth Century*, Rizzoli, 1989, p. 26.
131. Anthony Easthope, *What a Man's Gotta Do: The Masculine Myth in Popular Culture*, Unwin Hyman, 1990, p. 47.
132. M. Gottdiener, *Postmodern Semiotics*, Blackwell, 1995, pp. 209–13.
133. Dan Rivers, *Congratulations, You Have Just Met the Casuals*, John Blake Publishing Ltd., 2007, p. 285.
134. Phil Thornton, *Casuals: Football, Fighting and Fashion – the Story of a*

Terrace Cult, Milo Books, 2003, p. 281; Paolo Hewitt and Mark Baxter, ibid., pp. 177–203.

135. Sean Nixon, *Hard Looks: Masculinities, Spectatorship and Contemporary Consumption*, Routledge, 1996, pp. 18–19.

2 Knitting the Past: Revivalism, Romanticism and Ruralism in Contemporary Knitting

1. Susanne Pagoldh, *Nordic Knitting: Thirty-One Patterns in the Scandinavian Tradition*, Interweave Press, Loveland Colorado, 1st edition, 1987, foreword.
2. Christopher Frayling, 'The Crafts', in Boris Ford (ed.) *Modern Britain: The Cambridge Cultural History*, Cambridge University Press, 1992.
3. David Lowenthal, *The Past is a Foreign Country*, Cambridge University Press, 1985 (1986, 1988, 1990).
4. Pamela Johnson, 'Can Theory Damage your Practice?' in Pamela Johnson (ed.) *Ideas in the Making: Practice in Theory*, Crafts Council, 1998, p. 15.
5. During the 1970s, this concept of 'popular' craft was best demonstrated in the poet Edward Lucie-Smith's *A History of Craft*, Phaidon Press, 1981.
6. Tanya Harrod, *The Crafts in Britain in the Twentieth Century*, Yale University Press, 1999.
7. Raphael Samuel, *Theatres of Memory*, p. 61.
8. Maggie Andrews, *The Acceptable Face of Feminism: The Women's Institute as a Social Movement*, Lawrence and Wishart, 1999, pp. 123–45.
9. P. Knox, 'The Restless Urban Landscape: Economic and Sociocultural Change and the Transformation of Metropolitan Washington DC', *Annals: Association of American Geographers*, 81, 1991, pp. 181–209; P. Jackson and N. Thrift, 'Geographies of Consumption', in Daniel Miller (ed.), *Acknowledging Consumption: A Review of New Studies*, Routledge, 1995, pp. 204–37; Steven Miles, *Consumerism as a Way of Life*, Sage, 1998, p. 53.
10. John Urry, *Consuming Places*, Routledge, 1995.
11. Nicholas Green, *The Spectacle of Nature: Landscape and Bourgeois Culture in Nineteenth-Century France*, Manchester University Press, 1990, p. 3.
12. Henri Lefebvre, *The Production of Space*, trans. Donald Nicholson-Smith, Blackwell, 1994 [1974], p. 383; Guy Julier, *The Culture of Design*, Sage, 2000, p. 145.
13. David Lowenthal, *The Past Is a Foreign Country*, Cambridge University Press, 1990 [1985], p. 187.
14. Robert Hewison, *The Heritage Industry*, Methuen, 1987, pp. 131–146.
15. John Urry, ibid., p. 226.
16. Michael J. Chiarappa, 'Affirmed Objects in Affirmed Places: History, Geographic Sentiment and a Region's Crafts', *Journal of Design History*, Vol.

10, No. 4, pp. 399–415.

17. Ibid., p. 399.

18. Ibid., p. 400.

19. Mary Smith and Chris Bunyan, *A Shetland Knitter's Notebook*, The Shetland Times, Lerwick, 1991, p. 17.

20. David Chaney, *Lifestyles*, Routledge, 1996, p. 122.

21. Tanya Harrod, *The Crafts in Britain in the Twentieth Century*, pp. 412–13.

22. Christopher Frayling, 'The Crafts', in Boris Ford (ed.), *Modern Britain: The Cambridge Cultural History*, Cambridge, 1992, pp. 168–85.

23. Pennina Barnett, 'Making, Materiality and Memory', in Pamela Johnson (ed.), *Ideas in the Making*, p. 141.

24. M Gallagher, 'Gooden Gansey Sweaters', *Fiberarts*, November/ December, 1985, p. 12.

25. Simone de Beauvoir, *Old Age* (la Vieillesse), Gallimard, 1970, pp. 407–8, quoted in David Lowenthal, *The Past Is a Foreign Country*, Cambridge University Press, p. 195, p. 200.

26. Andrew Smith, 'Hampton Court Revisited: A Re-evaluation of the Consumer', in Gary Day (ed.), *Readings in Popular Culture: Trivial Pursuits?*, Macmillan, 1990, pp. 24–5; Patrick Wright, *On Living in an Old Country*, Verso, 1985, p. 5.

27. Rohana Darlington, *Irish Knitting: Patterns Inspired by Ireland*, A&C Black, London, 1991, p. 7.

28. S. McGregor, *The Complete Book of Traditional Fair Isle Knitting*, B. T. Batsford, London, 1981, pp. 13–14.

29. A Starmore, *Alice Starmore's Book of Fair Isle Knitting*, The Taunton Press, Newtown, CT, 1988, p. 28.

30. Shelagh Hollingworth, *The Complete Book of Traditional Aran Knitting*, B. T. Batsford, London, 1982, p. 11.

31. Margaret Bruzelius, 'Exploring a Knitting Pattern: Bohus Stickning Sweater Generates Diverse Designs Knit with Simple Stitches', *Threads Magazine*, Knitting Around the World Issue, The Taunton Press, Newtown CT, 1993, pp. 21–5; Sheila McGregor, *The Complete Book of Scandinavian Knitting*, B. T. Batsford, London, 1984; Nancy Bush, 'Two-Colour Knitting of Norway', *Piecework*, Jan/ Feb 1996, pp. 32–6; Britt-Marie Christoffersson, *Swedish Sweaters: New Designs from Historical Examples*, The Taunton Press, Newtown CT, 1990. Also, *Knitter's Magazine* ran a celebratory supplement in winter 1996 to commemorate 100 years of the Lopi (Icelandic) sweater.

32. Lily Chin, 'On Designing Austrian Avant-Garde', *Knitter's Magazine*, Fall 1991, pp. 40, 70–73.

33. Lizbeth Upitis, *Latvian Mittens: Traditional Designs and Techniques*, Dos Tejedoras, St Paul MN, 1981; Sigrid Piroch, 'A Woman's Cap: The Glory of Slovakia', *Piecework*, Jan/ Feb 1994; Sandra Messinger De Master, 'Messages

in Mittens: The Story of a Latvian Knitter', *Piecework*, Nov/ Dec 1995, pp. 31–49; Alexis Xenakis, 'From Russia With Love', *Knitter's Magazine*, Fall 1992, pp. 2–10.

34. Kate Martinson, 'Sweater Watching', Knitter's Magazine, Fall 1993, pp. 10–16.

35. Stephen Sheard, *Summer and Winter Knitting*, Century Hutchinson Ltd., 1987, press release.

36. Sam McMillan, 'George Brett: Webs of a Mad Spider', *Fiberarts*, November/ December 1981, pp. 33–5.

37. Interview with Shane Waltener, 24th September 2007.

38. Barbara Nappen, 'In the Web of Superstition: Myths and Folktales About Nets', *Fiberarts*, May/ June 1982, pp. 30–31.

39. Walter Benjamin, quoted in Patrick Wright, *On Living in an Old Country*, Verso, 1985, p. 1.

40. Examples of this include Cynthia Gravelle Le Count, *Andean Folk Knitting: Traditions and Techniques from Peru and Bolivia*, Dos Tejedoras, St Paul MN, 1990, pp. 1–4; Carol Rasmussen Noble, 'Peruvian Maquitos: Colourful Sleeves Knit Traditions Together', *Piecework*, Jan/ Feb 1995, pp. 43–7.

41. Priscilla A. Gibson-Roberts, *Salish Indian Sweaters: A Pacific Northwest Tradition*, Dos Tejedoras, St Paul MN, 1998, p. 14.

42. Galer Britton Barnes, 'Amish Wedding Stockings of the Nineteenth Century', *Piecework*, March/ April 1997, pp. 25–7.

43. Susan Strawn Bailey, 'Knitting in the Amanas', *Piecework*, September/ October 1997, pp. 19–21.

44. M. Wright, 'In Search of Cornish Guernseys and Knit-Frocks', *Piecework*, September/ October 1994, pp. 70–71.

45. Susanna Lewis, 'District of Ohio', *Knitters*, spring 1993, pp. 34–6.

46. Kate Martinson, *Knitters*, Fall 1993, p. 10.

47. Britt-Marie Christoffersson, *Swedish Sweaters: New Designs from Historical Examples*, The Taunton Press, Newtown CT, 1990, p. 9.

48. Ibid., p. 9.

49. R. Samuel, *Theatres of Memory*, Verso, London, 1994, p. 85.

50. Harold Pinter, quoted in David Lowenthal, ibid., p. 201.

51. Catherine McDermott, *Made in Britain*, Mitchell Beazley, 2002, pp. 70–74; Hugh Barty King, *Pringle of Scotland and the Hawick Knitwear Story*, JJG Publishing, 2006.

52. Sandy Black, *Knitwear in Fashion*, Thames and Hudson, 2002, p. 12.

53. T. Veblen, *The Theory of the Leisure Class*, Augustus M. Kelley, 1899.

54. Catherine McDermott, ibid., p. 11.

55. Peter York, 'Style Wars: Punk and Pageant', in John Thackara, *Design After Modernism: Beyond the Object*, Thames and Hudson, 1988.

56. Igor Kopytoff, 'The Cultural Biography of Things: Commoditization as

Process' in Arjun Appadurai, *The Social Life of Things: Commodities in Cultural Perspective*, Cambridge University Press, 1988, p. 67.

57. Ibid.

58. James Norbury, *Traditional Knitting Patterns: From Scandinavia, the British Isles, France, Italy and Other European Countries*, Dover Publications, NY, 1973, p. 9.

59. Heinz Edgar Kiewe, *The Sacred History of Knitting*, Art Needlework Industries Ltd., 1971.

60. Sally Harding (ed.), *Kaffe Fassett at the V&A: Knitting and Needlepoint*, Centium Hutchinson Ltd., 1988, p. 41.

61. Susanne Pagoldh, *Nordic Knitting: Thirty-One Patterns in the Scandinavian Tradition*, Interweave Press, 1st edition 1987, pp. 12–13. See also Nancy Bush, 'Two-Colour Knitting of Norway', *Piecework*, January/ February, 1996, pp. 32–3.

62. Nancy Bush, 'Two-Colour Knitting of Norway', *Piecework*, January/ February, 1996, p. 35.

63. Lizbeth Upitis, *Latvian Mittens: Traditional Designs and Techniques*, Dos Tejedoras, 1981, chapter 2.

64. Alice Stanmore, *Alice Stanmore's Book of Fair Isle Knitting*, The Taunton Press, 1988, pp. 33–4.

65. Michael Pearson, *Traditional Knitting: Aran, Fair Isle and Fisher Ganseys*, William Collins Sons and Co. Ltd., 1984, p. 112.

66. Priscilla A Gibson-Roberts, *Knitting in the Old Way*, Interweave Press, 1985, p. 80.

67. Nancy Bush, 'Two-Colour Knitting of Norway', *Piecework*, January/ February, 1996, p. 35.

68. Priscilla A Gibson-Roberts, ibid., p. 98.

69. Margaret Bruzelius, 'Exploring a Knitted Pattern', *Threads: Knitting Around the World*, The Taunton Press, 1993, p. 21.

70. Lopi is a type of yarn spun from the world's longest-fleeced sheep. It is extremely durable. See Alexis Xennnakis, 'An Icelandic Saga: 100 years of Lopi' in *Knitter's*, winter 1996, pp. 20–24; also Rae Compton, *The Complete Book of Traditional Knitting*, B. T. Batsford, 1983, p. 76.

71. Priscilla A. Gibson-Roberts, ibid., p. 111.

72. Michael Pearson, ibid., pp. 119–20.

73. Robert Louis Stevenson, 'Random Memories – The Coast of Fife', quoted in Mary Smith and Chris Bunyan, *A Shetland Knitter's Notebook*, The Shetland Times, Lerwick, 1991, p. 11.

74. Eliza Edmondston, *Sketches and Tales of the Shetland Isles*, 1856, quoted in Sheila McGregor, *The Complete Book of Traditional Fair Isle Knitting*, B. T. Batsford, 1981, p. 14.

75. There is some disagreement about the popularity of Fair Isle garments from

the 1850s to the 1920s, with authors debating the levels of trade during the period.

76. Michael Pearson, *Traditional Knitting: Aran, Fair Isle and Fisher Ganseys*, William Collins Sons and Co. Ltd., 1984, pp. 10–11.

77. Liz Gemmell, *Aussie Fair: Simple Fair Isle Knitting with Australian Motifs*, Lloyd O'Neil Pty Ltd., 1984.

78. Ibid., p. 27.

79. Patty Knox, *New Directions in Fair Isle Knitting*, Lark Books, 1985.

80. Caroline Evans, 'Yesterday's Emblems and Tomorrow's Commodities: The Return of the Repressed in Fashion Imagery Today' in Stella Bruzzi and Pamela Church-Gibson (eds.), *Fashion Cultures: Theories, Explorations, Analysis*, Routledge, 2000, p. 99.

81. Description of Edina Ronay's interest in Fair Isle. In Steven Sheard, *Summer and Winter Knitting*, Century Hutchinson Ltd., 1987, p. 48.

82. J. Barnett, *The American Christmas: A Study of National Culture*, Macmillan, 1954, referenced in Daniel Miller, 'A Theory of Christmas' in Daniel Miller (ed.), *Unwrapping Christmas*, Oxford University Press, 1995, p. 3.

83. Orvar Lofgren, 'The Great Christmas Quarrel and Other Swedish Traditions', in Daniel Miller (ed.), *Unwrapping Christmas*, Oxford University Press, 1995, p. 222.

84. Melissa Rayworth, 'Do it Yourself Toys', *Honolulu Advertiser*, 26th November 2007.

85. Ovar Lofgren, ibid., p. 232.

86. As in the novelty sweater worn by Mark Darcy (Colin Firth) in the film *Bridget Jones's Diary*, dir. Sharon Maguire, 2001.

87. *Girl on a Motorcycle*, dir. Jack Cardiff, 1968.

3 Twisted Yarns: Postmodern Knitting

1. Merryn Gates, 'Bronwen Sandland: Housecosy', *Artlink Magazine*, http://www.artlink.com.au/articles.cfm?id=2438.

2. Roland Barthes, 'The Death of the Author', *Image, Music, Text*, Fontana, 1977.

3. Simon Malpas, *Jean-Francois Lyotard*, Routledge, 2003, pp. 16–32.

4. Jean Baudrillard, *Simulations*, Semiotext(e), 1983; see also Guy Debord, *The Society of the Spectacle*, Black and Red, 1984.

5. This discourse is outlined by Tim Dant, *Material Culture in the Social World*, Open University Press, 1999, pp. 72–3.

6. Dick Hebdige, *Subculture: The Meaning of Style*, Methuen, 1979, p. 104.

7. Michel de Certeau, *The Practice of Everyday Life*, University of California Press, 1984.

8. Bruce Handy, 'A Spy Guide to Postmodern Everything', in A. A. Berger, *The Postmodern Presence*, ibid., p. 51.
9. Sandy Black, *Knitwear in Fashion*, Thames and Hudson, 2002, p. 42.
10. Frederick Jameson, *Marxism and Form*, Princeton University Press, 1971, pp. 104–5.
11. Jean Baudrillard, *For a Critique of the Political Economy of the Signs*, Telos Press Ltd., 1981, p. 66.
12. G. Arno Verhoeven, 'The Identity of Craft: Craft is Dead, Long Live Craft', in Georgina Follett and Louise Valentine (eds.), *New Craft: Future Voices*, Duncan of Jordanstone College of Art and Design, 2007, p. 191.
13. Gloria Hickey, 'Craft Within a Consuming Society', in Peter Dormer (ed.), *The Culture of Craft*, Manchester University Press, 1997, pp. 85–6.
14. http://www.loop.gb.com/designers/annettebugansky.html.
15. http://csw.art.pl/new/97/trockel_e.html.
16. *Observer Magazine*, 18th July 2004, p. 49.
17. http://theknittingmachine.com/.
18. Sabrina Gschwandtner, *KnitKnit: Profiles and Projects from Knitting's New Wave, Stewart*, Tabori and Chang, 2007, p. 41.
19. Interview with Arno Verhoeven, 12th December 2007.
20. Jason Rutter, 'Stepping into Wayne's World: Exploring Postmodern Comedy', in A. A. Berger (ed.), *The Postmodern Presence*, Altamira, 1998, p. 113.
21. Melissa Rayworth, 'Do it Yourself Toys', *Honolulu Advertiser*, 26th November 2007.
22. Mikhail Bakhtin, *Rabelais and His World*, Indiana University Press, 1984 [1965], trans. Helene Iswolsky.
23. Rachael Matthews, *Knitorama*, MQ Publications, 2005.
24. Alexandra Warwick and Dani Cavallaro, *Fashioning the Frame: Boundaries, Dress and the Body*, Berg, 1998.
25. Interview with Janet Morton, 10th October 2007.
26. Interview with Janet Morton, 10th October 2007.
27. Gaston Bachelard, *The Poetics of Space*, Beacon, 1994, p. 148.
28. Susan Stewart, *On Longing: Narrative of the Miniature, the Gigantic, the Souvenir, the Collection*, Duke University Press, 1993, p. 69.
29. Ross McGuinness, 'Knitting for Nits: Designer Mittens for Insects', *The Metro*, 31st October 2007, p. 3.
30. M. Abakanowicz, Magdalena Abakanowicz, Abbeville Press, 1983, p. 74.
31. Alexandra Warwick and Dani Cavallaro, *Fashioning the Frame: Boundaries, Dress and the Body*, Berg, 1998, p. 103.
32. Elizabeth Wilson, *Adorned in Dreams*, Virago, 1985, p. 3.
33. Henry Conway and Gail Downey, *Weardowney Knit Couture*, Collins and Brown, 2007, p. 50.
34. Andrew Bolton, *Anglomania*, Yale University Press, 2006.

35. Howard Sounes, *Seventies: The Sights, Sounds and Ideas of a Brilliant Decade*, Simon and Schuster, 2006, p. 296.

36. Sandy Black, *Knitwear in Fashion*, Thames and Hudson, 2005, p. 14.

37. Andrew Pemberton, 'John Lydon Lives Off the Past. He's a Buffoon', *Q* magazine, March 2006, p. 73.

38. Sandy Black, ibid., pp. 92–3.

39. Catherine Spooner, *Contemporary Gothic*, Reaktion Books, 2006, p. 133.

40. Dominic Cavendish, '*Why Knitting is the New Rock and Roll*', *Daily Telegraph*, 12th October 2002.

41. Interview with Celia Pym, 21st September 2007.

42. Knitta artist statement quoted in Sabrina Gschwandtner, *KnitKnit: Profiles and Projects from Knitting's New Wave*, Stewart, Tabori and Chang, 2007, p. 92.

43. Lesley Greaves, knitting club leader, Corsham, quoted in Ailya Frostick, 'It's Now Hip to Knit, So Get Out Those Needles', *The Bath Chronicle*, 12th October 2004, p. 9.

44. Su Holmes and Sean Redmond (eds.), *Framing Celebrity: New Directions in Celebrity Culture*, Routledge, 2006, p. 3.

45. Graeme Turner, *Understanding Celebrity*, Sage, 2004, p. 24.

46. Sean Redmond, 'Intimate Fame Everywhere', in Su Holmes and Sean Redmond (eds.), *Framing Celebrity: New Directions in Celebrity Culture*, Routledge, 2006, pp. 27–44.

47. Chris Rojek, *Celebrity*, Reaktion Books, 2001, p. 9.

48. Chris Rojek, *Celebrity*, Reaktion Books, 2001, p. 16.

49. Richard Dyer, *Stars*, BFI Publishing, 1979.

50. Su Holmes and Sean Redmond, 'Introduction: Understanding Celebrity Culture', in Su Holmes and Sean Redmond, *Framing Celebrity: New Directions in Celebrity Culture*, Routledge, 2006, p. 9.

51. Rachel Cooke, 'Saturday Night Fever', *The Observer*, 29th January 2006.

52. Interview with Sue Bradley, 25th September 2007. See also Patricia Roberts interviewed for the V&A website, http://www.vam.ac.uk/collections/fashion/features/knitting/designers/patricia_roberts/.

53. Ken Roberts, *Leisure*, Longman, 1981, p. 52, referenced in Deborah Philips and Alan Tomlinson, 'Homeward Bound: Leisure, Popular Culture and Consumer Capitalism', in Dominic Strinati and Stephen Wagg (eds.), *Come On Down? Popular Media Culture in Post-War Britain*, Routledge, 1992, p. 17.

54. Joanne Hollows, 'Can I Go Home Yet?', in Joanne Hollows and Rachel Moseley (eds.), *Feminism in Popular Culture*, Berg, 2006, p. 108.

55. Knitting has been described as the 'new yoga' and has been promoted as having therapeutic qualities, as outlined in texts such as Tara Jon Manning, *Mindful Knitting*, Tuttle Publishing, Boston, 2004.

56. Andrew Tolston, 'Being Yourself: The Pursuit of Authentic Celebrity', Discourse Studies, 3 (4), 2001, p. 452, quoted in Wendy Parkins, 'Celebrity Knitting and the Temporality of Postmodernity', *Fashion Theory*, Vol. 8, issue 4, 2004, p. 427.

57. Rosalind Coward, *Female Desire: Women's Sexuality Today*, Paladin Grafton Books, 1984, pp. 76–7.

58. Wendy Parkins, 'Celebrity Knitting and the Temporality of Postmodernity', *Fashion Theory*, Vol. 8, issue 4, 2004, pp. 425–41.

59. Ibid., p. 436.

60. This can be seen as part of the New Domesticity, which also includes 'Slow Food', and 'Slow Clothes' as exemplified by companies such as Keep and Share.

61. P. David Marshall, *Celebrity and Power: Fame in Contemporary Culture*, University of Minnesota, 1997, p. 57.

62. Roland Barthes, 'The Death of the Author' in Roland Barthes, *Image, Music, Text*, Fontana, 1977.

4 Unravelling the Surface: Unhomely Knitting

1. Alison Lurie, *The Language of Clothes*, Hamlyn, 1983.

2. Christopher Booker, *The Seventies: Portrait of a Decade*, Allen Lane, 1980, p. 6.

3. J. C. Flugel, *The Psychology of Clothes*, The Hogarth Press, 1930.

4. Ibid.

5. Ariel Levy, *Female Chauvinist Pigs: Women and the Rise of Raunch Culture*, Simon & Schuster, London, 2005.

6. Rebecca Arnold, *Fashion, Desire and Anxiety: Image and Morality in the 20th Century*, I. B. Tauris, & Co. Ltd., New York, 2001, p. 89.

7. Lorraine Gammon, 'Visual Seduction and Perverse Compliance: Reviewing Food Fantasies, Large Appetites and Grotesque Bodies', in Stella Bruzzi and Pamela Church-Gibson, *Fashion Cultures*, Routledge, London, pp. 61–78.

8. Clare Qualmann, quoted in Susan Mowery Kieffer, *Fiberarts Design Book 7*, Lark Books, New York, 2004, p. 179.

9. Françoise Dupré, quoted in Jac Scott, *Textile Perspectives in Mixed Media Sculpture*, D & N Publishing, Hungerford, 2003, p. 117.

10. Jacques Lacan, *The Four Fundamental Concepts of Psychoanalysis*, Penguin, London, 1977, p. 199.

11. Alexandra Warwick and Dani Cavallaro, *Fashioning the Frame*, Berg, Oxford, 1998, pp. 26–7.

12. Schelling quoted in Sigmund Freud, *The Uncanny, Part I*, Penguin, (reprint) 1971.

13. Renata Salecl, *On Anxiety*, Routledge, London, 2004, pp. 101–2.

14. Ibid., p. 102.

15. Roland Barthes, 'The Rhetoric of the Image', *Image, Music, Text*, Fontana, 1977, reproduced in A. Gray and J. McGuigan, *Studying Culture: An Introductory Reader*, Arnold, 1997, pp. 15–27.

16. Jean Paiget, *Play, Dreams and Imitation in Childhood*, Heinemann, first published 1946; Sigmund Freud, *On Metapsychology*, reprint, Penguin, 1984; and D. W. Winnicott, *Playing and Reality*, Tavistock Press, 1971.

17. Daniel Miller, Material Culture and Mass Consumption, Blackwell, 1994, p. 94

18. There is research that acknowledges that children rarely follow the play scenarios outlined by toy manufacturers, preferring to address their own issues and conflicts through the toys. Examples of these are Mary F. Rogers, *Barbie Culture*, Sage, 1999, pp. 29–33; Jonathan Bignell (University of Reading), 'Where is Action Man's Penis? Gender in Toys', unpublished paper, 'Anti-Bodies' conference, Buckinghamshire Chilterns University, High Wycombe, UK, 13th March 1999; and Guy Holder, 'Will It Go Outside', in Pamela Johnson (ed.), *Ideas in the Making*, Crafts Council, 1998, p. 79.

19. Sigmund Freud, *On Sexuality* [1927], reprint Penguin 1991, pp. 345–58; and Janis Jeffries, 'Text and Textiles: Reading Across the Borderlines' in Katy Deepwell (ed.), *New Feminist Art Criticism*, University of Manchester Press, 1995.

20. Peter Collingwood, 'Arts and Crafts Exhibition', *Quarterly Journal of the Guilds of Weavers, Spinners and Dyers*, No. 14, June 1955, quoted by Victoria Mitchell, 'Textiles, Text and Techne', in Tanya Harrod (ed.), *Obscure Objects of Desire: Reviewing the Crafts in the Twentieth Century*, Crafts Council, 1997, p. 328. The impulse to touch textile objects was studied by students at the Textile Conservation Centre, University of Southampton, in 2000, where students catalogued the tactile impulses of visitors in relation to historic textile wall hangings in National Trust properties.

21. Pennina Barnett, 'Making, Materiality and Memory', in Pamela Johnson (ed.), *Ideas in the Making: Practice in Theory*, Crafts Council, 1998, pp. 141–8; Jivan Asfalack-Prall, 'Semaphore', in Julian Stair (ed.), *The Body Politic: The Role of the Body and Contemporary Craft*, Crafts Council, 2000, pp. 134–40.

22. Karin Findeis, 'Atropos and the Consumable', in Julian Stair (ed.), *The Body Politic*, Blackwell, 1994, pp. 141–53.

23. Daniel Miller, *Material Culture and Mass Consumption*, Blackwell, 1994, p. 11.

24. D. W. Winnicott, *Playing and Reality*, Tavistock Press, 1971, quoted in Daniel Miller, *Material Culture and Mass Consumption*, Blackwell, 1994, p. 95; see also Maxine Bristow, 'Three Weeks to Turn 348, Three Years to Turn Intuition Towards Understanding', in Pamela Johnson (ed.), *Ideas in the Making*, Crafts

Council, 1999, pp. 114–21.

25. Pierre Bourdieu, *Distinction: Outline of a Theory of Practice*, Routledge, 1986, pp. 72–95.

26. Daniel Miller, *Material Culture and Mass Consumption*, Blackwell, 1994, p. 105; Peter Pels, 'The Spirit of Matter: On Fetish, Rarity, Fact and Fancy', in Patricia Spyer (ed.), *Border Fetishisms*, Routledge, 1998, pp. 91–121.

27. Anthony Vidler, *The Architectural Uncanny*; Christopher Reed, *Not At Home: The Supression of Domesticity in Modern Art and Architecture*, Thames and Hudson, 1996; Linda Sandino, 'Not at Home with Craft', (unpublished paper), 'Object and Idea' symposium held at the V&A, 17th November 2000.

28. Love Jonsson, '100 Ideas About Craft', exhibition review, *Crafts*, January/ February 2006, pp. 55–6.

29. Mario Perniola, 'Between Clothing and Nudity', in M. Feher, R. Naddaff and N. Tazi (eds.), *Fragments for a History of the Human Body, Part 2*, Zone, New York, 1989, p. 237, quoted in Rebecca Arnold, *Fashion, Desire and Anxiety*, I. B. Tauris, London, 2001, p. 67.

30. Jennifer Stafford, *Dominknitrix: Whip Your Knitting Into Shape*, North Light Books, Cincinnati, 2007, pp. 8–9.

31. Nikol Lohr, *Naughty Needles: Sexy, Saucy Knits for the Bedroom and Beyond*, Potter Style, 2007.

32. http://naughtyneedlesknitting.com/?page_id=2.

33. http://modblog.bmezine.com/2006/01/31/interesting-fetish-knitting-chastity/.

34. http://naughtyneedlesknitting.com/?page_id=2.

35. http://www.alternativeknitting.co.uk/knittingarchivemay23-3104.htm.

36. http://www.castoff.info/shop.asp; and http://www.theanticraft.com/archive/imbolc07/beanis.htm.

37. 'Craft Rocks', V&A, 2005.

38. Elizabeth Gross, 'The Body of Signification', in J. Fletcher (ed.), *Abjection, Melancholia and Love*, Routledge, London, 1990, p. 84, quoted in Alexandra Warwick and Dani Cavallaro, *Fashioning the Frame*, Berg, 1998, p. 38.

39. Julia Kristeva, 'Powers of Horror – Approaching Abjection' (1980), in Kelly Oliver (ed.), *The Portable Kristeva*, Columbia University Press, New York, 2002, p. 230.

40. Ibid., p. 231.

41. Ibid., p. 232.

42. Sasha Claire McInnes, 'The Political Is Personal: Or Why Have a Revolution (From Within or Without) When You Can Have Soma?', *Feminist Review* 6, 2001, pp. 160–80, referenced in Sara Mills, *Michel Foucault*, Routledge, London, 2003, p. 103.

43. John Prescott, quoted by India Knight, 'Let Them Wear Hoodies', *The Sunday Times*, 15th May, 2005, p. 5.

44. Gareth McLean, 'In the Hood', *The Guardian*, 13th May 2005.

45. Aileen Ribeiro, *Dress and Morality*, B. T. Batsford, 1986, p. 12.
46. Quentin Bell, *On Human Finery*, The Hogarth Press, 1947, quoted in Aileen Ribeiro, *Dress and Morality*, B. T. Batsford, 1986, p. 12.
47. India Knight, 'Let Them Wear Hoodies', *The Sunday Times*, 15th May 2005.
48. Vanessa Allen and Bob Roberts, 'Reclaim Our Streets: Hoodies and Baddies', *Daily Mirror*, 13th May 2005.
49. Andrew Stone, 'Boys in the Hoodies', *Socialist Review*, June 2005.
50. Gareth McLean, 'In the Hood', *The Guardian*, 13th May 2005.
51. Alexandra Warwick and Dani Cavallaro, *Fashioning the Frame: Boundaries, Dress and the Body*, Berg, Oxford, 1998, pp. 128–9.
52. Peter Schjeldahl, 'The Empty Body Part 2: Skin Has No Edges. Clothes Do', in Chris Townsend, *Rapture: Art's Seduction by Fashion*, Thames & Hudson, 2002, p. 78.
53. Julia Kristeva, ibid., p. 229.
54. Elizabeth Wilson, *Adorned in Dreams: Fashion and Modernity*, Virago, London 1985.
55. Samantha Holland, *Alternative Femininities: Body, Age and Identity*, Berg, Oxford, 2004, p. 74.
56. Juliet Ash, 'The Aesthetic Absence: Clothes Without People in Paintings', in Amy de la Haye and Elizabeth Wilson (eds.), *Defining Dress*, Manchester University Press, Manchester, 1999, p. 129.
57. Jennifer Craik, *The Face of Fashion*, Routledge, London, 1994, p. 1.
58. Polly Vernon, 'Don't Look Now: It's the Fashion Hoodies', *Observer Woman Magazine*, October 2006.

5 In the Loop? Knitting Narratives, Biographies and Identities

1. Patrizia Calefato, *The Clothed Body*, Berg, 2004, p. 87.
2. Igor Kopytoff, 'The Cultural Biography of Things: Commoditization as Process', in A. Appadurai, *The Social Life of Things*, pp. 64–91; Arjun Appadurai, 'Introduction: Commodities and the Politics of Value', in A. Appadurai, *The Social Life of Things*, pp. 3–63.
3. Emanuel Cooper, *People's Art: Working Class Art from 1750 to the Present Day*, Mainstream Publishing, 1994, pp. 159–75; Tanya Harod, *The Crafts in Britain in the Twentieth Century*, Yale University Press, 1999, pp. 27–8.
4. Zoe Williams, 'Close Knit', *The Guardian*, 8th January 2005.
5. Bruno Bettleheim, *The Uses of Enchantment: The Meaning and Importance of Fairy Tales*, Penguin, 1991.
6. Sue Rowley, 'There Once Lived … Craft and Narrative Traditions', in Sue Rowley (ed.), *Craft and Critical Theory*, Allen and Unwin, 1997, p. 77.
7. Interview with Celia Pym, 21st September 2007.

8. Interview with Celia Pym, 21st September 2007.

9. Interview with Celia Pym, 21st September 2007.

10. Similarly, the Cork-based Half/ angel project, *The Knitting Map*, was a large-scale durational installation, involving twenty knitters who knitted in a single space on every day for a year; their knitting pattern was generated by movement in the city, and the colour of yarn by the weather. Over the course of the year, more than 2,500 knitters from twenty-two countries were involved in the project.

11. Judy Attfield, *Wild Things*, Berg, 2000, pp. 256–61.

12. Ibid., p. 49.

13. Igor Kopytoff, ibid., pp. 64–91.

14. Arjun Appadurai, ibid., pp. 3–63.

15. Igor Kopytoff, ibid., p. 13.

16. Karl Marx, *Capital: Vol. 1*, Progress Publishers, 1973 [1887].

17. A. Appadurai, quoted in Tim Dant, *Material Culture in the Social World*, Open University Press, 1999, p. 24.

18. Tim Dant, *Material Culture in the Social World*, Open University Press, 1999, p. 24.

19. Igor Kopytoff, ibid., p. 65.

20. Daniel Miller, *Material Culture and Mass Consumption*, Blackwell, 1987, p. 190.

21. Igor Kopytpoff, ibid., p. 89.

22. Gail Williams, interviewed 6th April 2000.

23. Gail Williams, interviewed 6th April 2000.

24. Gail Williams, interviewed 6th April 2000.

25. Susan Stewart *On Longing: Narratives of the Miniature, the Gigantic, the Souvenir, the Collection*, Duke University Press, 1994, p. 135.

26. C Nadia Seremetakis, 'Memory of the Senses, Part I', in C. Nadia Seremetakis (ed.), *The Senses Still: Perception and Memory as Material Culture in Modernity*, University of Chicago Press, 1996, p. 7.

27. Jean Baudrillard, *Seduction*, Macmillan, 1990, p. 39; quoted in Peter Corrigan, *The Sociology of Consumption*, Sage, 1990, p. 48.

28. Kerry Wills, *The Close Knit Circle: American Knitters Today*, Praeger, 2007, p. 76.

29. Betsy Hosegood, *Not Tonight Darling, I'm Knitting*, David and Charles, 2006, p. 25.

30. Knitting in public was a particular vogue during the 1920s, escalating during wartime, but knitting specifically in groups and in public is a relatively new phenomenon.

31. Sharon Aris, *It's My Party and I'll Knit if I Want To*, Allen and Unwin, 2003, pp. 71–2.

32. Cast Off constitution http://www.castoff.info/.

33. Interview with Rachael Matthews, founder member of Cast Off, 1st October 2007.
34. Kerry Wills, ibid., pp. 78–84.
35. Stella Minahan and Julie Wolfram Cox, 'Stitch 'n' Bitch', *Journal of Material Culture*, Vol. 12, No. 1, 2007.
36. Interview with Shane Waltener, 24th September 2007.
37. Stella Minahan and Julie Wolfram Cox, 'Stitch 'n' Bitch', *Journal of Material Culture*, Vol. 12, No. 1, 2007.
38. R Mulgan notes: 'A world built on networks ... calls into question older conceptions of space and power. Where the early market economies grew out of the temporal and spatial regularities of city life, today's are built on the logical or "virtual" regularities of electronic communications, a new geography of nodes and hubs, processing and control centres. The nineteenth century's physical infrastructure of railways, canals and roads is now overshadowed by the network of computers, cables and radio links that govern where things go, how they are paid for, and who has access to what.' Quoted in David Cheal, *The Gift Economy*, Routledge, 1990, p. 34.
39. Similarly, the workplace is becoming increasingly private, with desk space compartmentalized in open-plan offices, stuck in the middle of industrial estates or in the depths of the countryside.
40. Sherry Turkle, 'Identity in the Age of the Internet', in Hugh Mackay and Tim O'Sullivan (eds.), *The Media Reader: Continuity and Transformation*, Sage, 1999, p. 287.
41. Howard Rheingold, 'The Virtual Community: Finding Connection in a Computerized World', in Hugh Mackay and Tim O'Sullivan (eds.), *The Media Reader: Continuity and Transformation*, Sage, 1999, p. 273.
42. Ibid., p. 274.
43. www.knitlist.com.
44. Anne, Knit List, February 2000.
45. Daniel Miller and Don Slater, *The Internet: An Ethnographic Approach*, Berg, 2000.
46. Ibid., p. 178.
47. Lion Brand Yarn Company, founded in New York in 1878, is America's oldest hand knitting yarn brand.
48. Lion Brand Yarn Survey, 2007; http://blogit.webirpr.com/?ReleaseID=7005.
49. Stephanie Pearl-McPhee, responding to the Lion Brand survey, ibid.
50. Mark Penn, Microtrends, quoted 10th October 2007, http://prudentpressagency.com/modules/news/article.php?storyid=942.
51. Stella Minaham and Julie Wolfram Cox, 'Stitch 'n' Bitch', *Journal of Material Culture*, Vol. 12. No. 1, 2007.
52. Tara Jon Manning, *Mindful Knitting*, Tuttle Publishing, Boston, 2004, p. 4.
53. Susan Gordon Lydon, *The Knitting Sutra: Craft as Spiritual Practice*, Harper,

San Francisco, 1998.

54. Tara Jon Manning, ibid., p. 4.

55. Bernadette Murphy, *Zen and the Art of Knitting*, Adams Media, 2002.

56. Tara Jon Manning, ibid., p. 4.

57. Ibid., p. 9.

58. Julian Stair, *The Body Politic: The Role of the Body and Contemporary Craft*, Crafts Council, 2000, p. 10.

59. Terence Hawkes, *Structuralism and Semiotics*, Methuen, 1977; and John Storey, *An Introductory Guide to Cultural Theory and Popular Culture*, Harvester Wheatsheaf, 1993, pp. 69–94.

60. Julia Kristeva, 'Revolution in Poetic Language', in Toril Moi (ed.), *The Kristeva Reader*, Blackwell, 1986, p. 13.

61. Pennina Barnett, 'Making, Materiality and Memory', in Pamela Johnson (ed.), *Ideas in the Making*, Crafts Council, 1998, p. 142.

62. Julia Kristeva, 'Revolution in Poetic Language', in Toril Moi (ed.), *The Kristeva Reader*, Blackwell, 1986, p. 13.

63. Mary Hughes, interviewed 12th September 1998.

64. Rosemary Deem, 'Leisure and the Household', in S. Jackson and S. Moores (eds.), *The Politics of Domestic Consumption*, Harvester Wheatsheaf, 1995, p. 138.

65. Alison Lloyd, interviewed 17th September 2002.

66. Pen Dalton, 'Housewives, Leisure Crafts and Ideology: De-skilling in Consumer Crafts', in G. Elinor (ed.), *Women and Craft*, Virago, 1987, p. 34.

67. Mrs Davis, interviewed 14th September 1998.

68. Renata Salecl, *On Anxiety*, Routledge, 2004, p. 5.

69. 'Occupational therapy is primarily rehabilitation through occupation, or activity, manipulation and employment, which facilitates and encourages mental and physical well-being in order to satisfy the demands of everyday living. The belief that mind and body are intrinsically linked encourages the combination of manual and mental processes to aid recovery. This means that activity facilitates the understanding of feelings, thoughts and emotions, which encourage a sense of achievement and in turn, well-being. This can be achieved by maintaining or creating a balance between intellectual and practical skills to meet the needs of everyday life, i.e. work, leisure and rest. Similarly, it is vital for the patient to understand the pain, which is associated with any illness, and want to rid themselves of it, whilst at the same time realizing that they are master of their own destiny i.e. "The person is the product of his or her own efforts, not the article made or the activity accomplished." ' (Bing 1971).

70. Bernadette Murphy, ibid., p. 98.

71. Ibid., p. 149.

72. James Tozer, 'Safety Police Outlaw NHS Knitters Over Fears of Accidents

With Needles', *Daily Mail*, 12th November 2007.

73. Alan Davies, interviewed 4th September 2002.

74. Interestingly, the dishcloth has been elevated from the boring and mundane as a result of featuring in Rachael Matthews's knitting book, *Knitorama*, and is now seen as a glamorous addition to the kitchen.

75. Adolph Meyer (1922), quoted in Christiansen and Baum, *Enabling Function and Well-Being*, Slack, 1997, chapter 2, p. 33.

76. Zygmunt Bauman, *Life in Fragments: Essays in Postmodern Morality*, Blackwell, 1995, pp. 86–8.

77. Claire LaZebnik, *Knitting Under the Influence*, Five Spot Publishing, New York, 2006, cover.

78. 'She held up the oft-neglected circular sweater and examined the rose-coloured yarn. Row after row of neat stockinette stitches. She was going to finish this sweater at last.' Maggie Sefton, *A Deadly Yarn*, Berkley Prime Crime, 2006, p. 257.

79. Maggie Sefton, *A Deadly Yarn*, Berkley Prime Crime, 2006, p. 32.

80. Monica Ferris, *Crewel World*, Berkley Publishing, 1999, p. 47.

81. Mary Kruger, *Died in the Wool*, Pocket Books, 2005, p. 1.

82. Mary Kruger, *Knit Fast Die Young*, Pocket Books, 2007.

83. Mary Kruger, *Died in the Wool*, Pocket Books, 2005, back cover.

84. Linda Mizejewski, *Hardboiled and High Heeled: The Woman Detective in Popular Culture*, Routledge, 2004, p. 23.

85. In Mary Kruger's books, the protagonist, Ariadne Evans, has a young daughter who often stays with her father, which enables periods of time devoid of family responsibility.

86. Maggie Sefton's main character is self-employed and works from home.

87. Monica Ferris, *Unravelled Sleeve*, Berkley Publishing, 2001, p. 5.

88. Naomi Wolf, *Promiscuities: A Secret History of Female Desire*, Vintage, 1998, pp. 67–94.

89. Michael J. Hayes, 'Recipes for Success', in Gary Day (ed.), *Readings in Popular Culture: Trivial Pursuits?*, Macmillan, 1990, pp. 75–83.

90. Loraine Gammon, 'Visual Seduction and Perverse Compliance: Reviewing Food Fantasies, Large Appetites and Grotesque Bodies', in Stella Bruzzi and Pamela Church Gibson (eds.), *Fashion Cultures: Theories, Explorations and Analysis*, Routledge, 2000, pp. 61–78.

91. Natasha Walter, *The New Feminism*, Virago, 1999, pp. 186–7.

92. Discussion with Marian Keyes, Kelly Gyenes. 'Chick Lit: Sex, Shoes … And Substance', CNN, 8th September 2006, see http://www.cnn.com/2006/SHOWBIZ/books/09/07/chick.lit/index.html and Gina Frangello, 'Is Chick Lit the Culprit?', 29th April 2006, see http://ginafrangello.blogs.com/gina_frangello/2006/04/is_chick_lit_th.html.

93. Olivia Goldsmith, *Wish Upon a Star*, Harper Collins, 2004.

94. Ibid. p. 355.
95. Gill McNeil, *Divas Don't Knit*, Bloomsbury, 2007; Kate Jacobs, *The Friday Night Knitting Club*, Hodder and Stoughton, 2007.
96. Olivia Goldsmith, *Wish Upon a Star*, Harper Collins, 2004; Claire Lezebnik, *Knitting Under the Influence*, Five Spot Publishing, 2006.
97. Ann Bartlett, *Knitting*, Penguin Books, 2005.
98. Imelda Whelehan, *Overloaded: Popular Culture and the Future of Feminism*, The Women's Press, 2000, p. 136.
99. Examples include John Gray, *Men Are From Mars, Women Are From Venus*, Harper Collins, 1992.
100. Claire Lazebnik, *Knitting Under the Influence*, Five Spot Publishing, 2006, p. 59.
101. Gill McNeil, *Divas Don't Knit*, Bloomsbury, 2007, p. 117.
102. Olivia Goldsmith, *Wish Upon a Star*, Harper Collins, 2004, pp. 201–2.
103. 'The Craft Yarn Council reports that in 2002, 13 per cent of women aged 25–34 knitted; by 2004, that figure had more than doubled to 33 per cent', Natalie Danford, 'The End of the Yarn?', *Publishers' Weekly*, 28th August 2006.
104. Ariel Levy, *Female Chauvinist Pigs: Women and the Rise of Raunch Culture*, Pocket Books, 2006, p. 172.
105. Walter Benjamin, referenced in Sue Rowley, 'There Once Lived ... Craft and Narrative Traditions', in Sue Rowley (ed.), *Craft and Critical Theory*, Allen and Unwin, 1997.
106. Sheila Rowbotham, *Hidden From History: 300 Years of Women's Oppression and the Fight Against It*, Pluto Press, 1977.
107. Paul Willis, 'Symbolic Creativity', in Ann Gray and Jim McGuigan, *Studying Culture: An Introductory Reader*, Arnold, 1997, pp. 206–9.
108. Ibid., p. 206.
109. Ibid., p. 209.

6 Knit Power: The Politics of Knitting

1. Lisa Anne Auerbach, quoted in Sabrina Gschwandtner, *KnitKnit: Profiles and Projects from Knitting's New Wave*, Harry N. Abrams Inc., 2007, p. 9.
2. M. M. Postan, *The Medieval Economy and Society*, Penguin, 1986, p. 242.
3. Christopher Hill, *Reformation to Industrial Revolution*, Penguin, 1967, p. 173.
4. The Statute of Artificers, 1563, and the Statute of Apprentices, 1563. Christopher Hill, *Reformation to Industrial Revolution*, Penguin, 1967, p. 57 and p. 92; Paul Greenhalgh, in Peter Dormer (ed.), *The Culture of Craft*, Manchester University Press, p. 23.
5. Karl Marx, 'Manuscripts of 1844', quoted in Richard Appignesi (ed.),

Introducing Marx, Icon Books, 2006, p. 79.

6. Vincent Geoghegan, *Utopianism and Marxism*, Methuen, 1987, p. 67.

7. Workers in the woollen industry, particularly those in Yorkshire, were the most active of all workers in the UK in protesting at legislation and the onslaught of industrialization in the seventeenth century.

8. Rachael Matthews quoted in Charlotte Higgins, 'Political Protest Turns to the Radical Art of Knitting', *The Guardian*, 31st January 2005.

9. http://knitting.activist.ca/manifesto.html.

10. www.microrevolt.org.

11. Christina Walkeley, *The Ghost in the Looking Glass*, Peter Owen, 1981.

12. N. McKendrick, J. Brewer, and J. Plumb, *The Birth of a Consumer Society*, Europa, 1982, quoted in Steven Miles, *Consumerism as a Way of Life*, Sage, 1998, p. 6; Penny Sparke, *An Introduction to Design and Culture in the Twentieth Century*, Allen and Unwin, 1986, p. 10.

13. M. J. Lee, *Consumer Culture Reborn*, Routledge, 1993, Preface, p.ix.

14. Colin Campbell, 'The Sociology of Consumption', in Daniel Miller (ed.), *Acknowledging Consumption*, Routledge, 1995, pp. 96–126; Tim Dant, *Material Culture in the Social World*, Open University Press, 1999, p. 36 and pp. 102–7.

15. David Chaney, *Lifestyles*, Routledge, 1996.

16. Ibid., p. 32.

17. Pierre Bourdieu, quoted in Tim Dant, *Material Culture in the Social World*, Open University Press, 1999, p. 29.

18. Gillian Elinor, 'Feminism and Craftwork', *Circa*, No. 47, September/October 1989.

19. Ibid.

20. Sue Rowley, 'There Once Lived … Narrative Traditions in the Crafts', in Sue Rowley (ed.), *Crafts and Contemporary Theory*, Allen and Unwin, Sydney, 1997, p. 77; and Paul Greenhalgh, 'The History of Craft', in Peter Dormer (ed.), *The Culture of Craft*, Manchester University Press, Manchester, 1997, pp. 20–52.

21. Documentaries, including *The Craft of the Potter* and *The Craft of the Weaver* (1980), and the film *Mud and Water Man*, (1973), based on the life of the potter Michael Cardew, who popularized craft as a way of life distinct to contemporary living.

22. The prevalence of suburbia in 1970s British television situation comedies, i.e. *The Rise and Fall of Reginald Perrin*, *Dad's Army*, *Love Thy Neighbour*, *George and Mildred* and *Terry and June*, emphasized the paradox of suburbia – garden and desert: both fertile and impotent – which offered an alternative to accepted and/ or normalized lifestyles. See Leon Hunt, *British Low Culture: From Safari Suits to Sexploitation*, Routledge, 1998, pp. 1–56. See also Andy Medhurst, 'Negotiating the Gnome Zone: Versions of Suburbia in

British Popular Culture', in Roger Silverstone (ed.), *Visions of Suburbia*, Routledge, 1997, pp. 240–68.

23. The show attracted between 5 million and 17 million viewers weekly, and was repeated every year or so, with the most recent reruns in 2001.

24. Richard Webber, *A Celebration of the Good Life*, Orion Books, 2000, pp. 144–54, which includes stories of people who emulated the Goods' lifestyle.

25. Mary Eddy, 'Talking Point', *How to Save Money with Sewing and Knitting*, September 1976, p. 3.

26. Advertisement for Sirdar's Majestic wool and pattern, *Pins and Needles*, March 1980.

27. Terence Conran's Habitat openly exhorted the positive potential of mixing and matching new goods with old. The combination of new with old found favour with bohemian types, who scoured the increasing plethora of flea markets for bargains and 'antiques'.

28. *Woman*, 25th February 1978, pp. 42–3.

29. 'People Are Getting Craftier', *Woman*, 11th March 1978, p. 27.

30. Leonore Davidoff, *Worlds Between: Historical Perspectives on Gender and Class*, Polity Press, 1995, p. 65.

31. Jean Baudrillard, *The Consumer Society*, Sage, 1998.

32. 'The Family Who Swapped Flowers for a Farm', *Woman*, 25th February 1978, p. 42.

33. June Freeman, *Knitting: A Common Art*, Minorities Art Gallery, 1986.

34. Anne L. Macdonald, *No Idle Hands: The Social History of American Knitting*, Ballantyne Books, 1988; Helen Reynolds, 'Your Clothes Are Materials of War', in Barbara Burman (ed.), *The Culture of Sewing*, Berg, 1999, pp. 327–40.

35. Design for society has a history that developed as an aspect of modernist doctrines emerging in the early twentieth century. Adages such as 'Form follows function' and 'Fitness for purpose' became synonymous with designed objects that adhered to a quest for truth and beauty, and a move away from the overt and unnecessary ornamentation prevalent in Victorian design. Pioneered by groups such as the Bauhaus, design was understood as a means of addressing social problems as well as utilizing new technologies and industrial processes.

36. Liz Linthicum, 'Acknowledging Disability Within Dress History', paper presented at 'Oral Historical Approaches to Fashion, Dress and Textiles' conference, London College of Fashion, 14th September 2007.

37. Mike Shamash, 'A Dedicated (Disabled) Follower of Fashion', paper presented at 'Oral Historical Approaches to Fashion, Dress and Textiles' conference, London College of Fashion, 14th September 2007.

38. Interview with Caterina Radvan, 15th October 2007.

39. Interview with Caterina Radvan, 15th October 2007.

40. Interview with Caterina Radvan, 15th October 2007.

41. Thistle and Broom press release, 26th April 2007.

42. Malachy Tallack, 'Knitwear: Our Heritage on the Cheap', *Shetland Life*, 7th September 2007.

43. Brian Donnelly, 'Knitters Turn to Fairtrade in a Bid to Save Their Tradition', *The Herald*, 14th May 2007, p. 3.

44. Ibid.

45. http://www.keepandshare.co.uk/index.html.

46. The interrelationship between embroidery and philanthropy is discussed in relation to the education of working-class children by Rozsika Parker in *The Subversive Stitch: Embroidery and the Making of the Feminine*, The Women's Press, 1984, pp. 173–8.

47. Helen Reynolds, 'Your Clothes are Materials of War': The British Government Promotion of Home Sewing During the Second World War', in Barbara Burman (ed.), *The Culture of Sewing*, Berg, 1999, pp. 327–40.

48. Penny Sparke, *As Long As It's Pink: The Sexual Politics of Taste*, Pandora Press, 1995. pp. 151–2.

49. Rozsika Parker, *The Subversive Stitch: Embroidery and the Making of the Feminine*, The Women's Press, 1984, p. 11.

50. Maggie Andrews, *The Acceptable Face of Feminism*, Lawrence and Wishart, 1997.

51. 'Planning a Bazaar', an article in *Woman's Weekly*, 1977.

52. MO respondent C115.

53. *Woman*, 23rd March 1985, p. 9.

54. 'Is There Still Time to Save the Dying Children?', *Woman*, 1st June 1985, pp. 34–6; 'Readers' Letters', *Woman*, 29th June 1985, p. 7; 'The Village Where Hope Survives', *Woman*, 3rd August 1985, pp. 46–7; a report from Ethiopia with photos of readers' blankets in use; 'Soap Box on Live Aid', *Woman*, 5th October 1985, p. 9; and 'Report from Ethiopia', *Woman*, 14th December 1985, p. 47.

55. Mrs Joan Buck, Chesterfield, 'Soap Box on Ethiopia', *Woman*, 13th July 1985, p. 9.

56. 'Knit Now for Romania', *Knitting Now*, April 1993, pp. 16–17.

57. 'Romanian Update', *Knitting Now*, July/ August 1993, p. 15.

58. 'Barnardo's: A Charity Moving With the Times', *Knitting Now*, September/ October 1993, p. 14.

59. Betty Christiansen, *Knitting for Peace: Make the World a Better Place One Stitch at a Time*, Harry N. Abrams Inc., 2006.

60. Doreen West, interviewed 18th May 1999.

61. Gill Morris interviewed 18th May 1999.

62. Daniel Miller, *A Theory of Shopping*, Blackwell Publishers Ltd., 1998, pp. 90–110.

63. Margaret Maynard, *Dress and Globalization*, Manchester University Press, 2004, p. 3.

64. Ibid., pp. 35–6, in which she draws attention to the ways in which transnational companies such as Benetton market their products to different groups by using concepts of lifestyle. Effectively, there is no differentiation in product, but the brand identity is used to distinguish consumer groups and by association, the product.

65. Jennifer Craik, *The Face of Fashion*, Routledge, 1994, p. 205; and Margaret Maynard, *Dress and Globalization*, Manchester University Press, 2004, pp. 33–4.

66. Naomi Klein, *No Logo*, Flamingo, 2000, p. 129.

67. Fred Davis, *Fashion Culture and Identity*, University of Chicago Press, 1994; Malcolm Barnard, *Fashion as Communication*, Routledge, 2002; and Alison Lurie, *The Language of Clothes*, Hamlyn, 1983, exemplify this approach to the study of fashion and dress.

68. Robert J. S. Ross, *Slaves to Fashion: Poverty and Abuse in the New Sweatshops*, The University of Michigan Press, 2004, pp. 105–7. See also Dan McDougall, 'Ethical Business', *The Observer*, 28th October 2007.

69. www.labourbehindthelabel.org, and www.waronewant.org.

70. Diana Kiernander, 'Ethical Chic', *The List*, 16th January 2007. See http://www.listco.uk/article/1127-ethical-chic/.

71. 'Adventures in Modern Craft', *The Guardian Guide to Craft*, in *The Guardian*, February 2007, p. 5.

72. Interview with Rachael Matthews, 1st October 2007.

73. Interview with Rachael Matthews, 1st October 2007.

74. Patrizia Calefato, *The Clothed Body*, Berg, 2004, p. 87.

75. Sylvia Cosh and James Walters, 'New Concepts for Knitting and Crochet', *Fashion and Craft*, No. 98, spring 1990, pp. 16–17.

76. Grant Neufeld, quoted in 'G8 Protesters Turn to Knitting Blankets to Needle Heavy Security Presence', CommonDreams.org News Center, 27th June 2002; see also Wes Lafortune. 'Activist Guide', FFWD, 6th March 2003.

77. Interview with Kimberley Elderton, 29th September 2007.

78. Vance Packard, *The Hidden Persuaders*, Penguin, 1960.

79. Jane Pavitt (ed.), *Brand:New*, V&A Publications, 2000.

80. Theodor Adorno and Max Horheimer, *Dialectic of Enlightenment*, Continuum Books 1972 [1944], pp. 120–4.

81. Amber Cowie, 'Everybody Needs More Fibre: How Knitting Will Save the World', http://www.aboutmyplanet.com/environment/everybody-needs-more-fibre-how-knitting-will-save-the-world/.

82. 'Knit Your Own Shopping Bag', Femail, *Daily Mail*, 25th April 2007; Fiona Macdonald, 'Think Outside the Bag', *The Metro*, 23rd April 2007, p. 17.

83. Amber Cowie, 'Everybody Needs More Fibre: How Knitting will Save the World', http://www.aboutmyplanet.com/everybody-needs-more-fibre-how-knitting-will-save-the-world/.

84. http://sewgreen.blogspot.com/2007/04/knit-green.html; http://www.ethicalknitting.co.uk/about.html.

85. http://www.wasteonline.org.uk/resources/InformationSheets/Textiles.htm.

86. Janet Wolff, *The Social Production of Art*, Macmillan, 1981, p. 9.

87. Mark Steel, *Vive La Revolution: A Stand-up History of the French Revolution*, Scribner, 2003, p. 5.

88. Baroness Emmuska Orczy, *The Scarlet Pimpernel*, Brockhampton Press 1961 [1905].

89. Paul Greenhagh, 'The History of Craft', in Peter Dormer (ed.), *The Culture of Craft*, Manchester University Press, 1997, pp. 21–5.

90. The first recorded examples of a women's knitting circle's involvement in direct action were The Daughters of Liberty and the Philadelphia-based George Washington's Sewing Circle, both founded in the eighteenth century. See Anne L. Macdonald, *No Idle Hands: The Social History of American Knitting*, Ballantine, 1985, pp. 29–35.

91. Janet Wolff, The Social Production of Art, Macmillan, 1981, p. 14

92. Betsy Greer, http://www.acechick.typepad.com/knitchicks_features/ and www.craftivism.com.

93. Nicole Bursch and Anthea Black, 'Craft Hard, Die Free: Radical Curatorial Strategies for Craftivism in Unruly Contexts', in Georgina Follett and Louise Valentine (eds.), *New Craft: Future Voices*, Duncan of Jordanstone College of Art and Design Publications, 2007, p. 135.

94. Revolutionary Knitting Circle Call to Action: Global Knit-In, http://g8.activist.ca/calltoaction/knit.html, 2002.

95. Marianne Joergensen, http://www.marianneart.dk/.

96. Jennifer Sabella 'Craftivism: Is Crafting the New Activism?', *The Columbia Chronicle*, http://www.columbiachronicle.com/paper/arts.php?id=2251.

97. Max Horkheimer, 'The End of Reason: Changes in the Structure of Political Compromise', *Studies in Philosophy and Social Sciences*, Vol. IX, 1941, reproduced in Andrew Arato and Eike Gebhardt (eds.), *The Essential Frankfurt School Reader*, Continuum Publishing, 1982, pp. 26–48.

98. Chris Shepherd, 'The Revolution Will Wear a Cardigan', Brock Press, 2nd July 2002.

99. Betsy Greer, http://craftivism.com/what.html.

100. Jean Baudrillard, *The Spirit of Terrorism*, trans. Chris Turner, Verso, 2002, pp. 87–89.

101. Jean Baudrillard, *The Spirit of Terrorism*, trans. Chris Turner, Verso, 2002, pp. 94–5.

102. Vincent Geoghegan, *Utopianism and Marxism*, Methuen, 1987, p. 107.

103. Jean Baudrillard, *Simulations*, trans. Paul Foss, Paul Patton and Philip Beitchman, Semiotext(e), 1983, p. 4.

104. Interview with Lisa Anne Auerbach, 4th November 2007.

105. Lisa Anne Auerbach quoted in Sabrina Gschwandtner, *KnitKnit: Profiles and Projects from Knitting's New Wave*, Stewart, Tabori and Chang, 2007, p. 11.

106. Interview with Lisa Anne Auerbach, 4th November 2007.

107. Interview with Janet Morton, 10th October 2007.

108. www.stealthissweater.com/patterns/mittenpattern.pdf.

109. Susan Chaityn Lebovits, 'Textile Artist Knitting War Protests', *The Boston Globe*, 2nd September 2007.

110. Renata Salecl, *On Anxiety*, Routledge, 2004, p. 7.

111. Katie Bevan, curator of 'Knit2gether' exhibition, Crafts Council, London, 24th February 2005, quoted in Charlotte Higgins, 'Political Protest Turns to the Radical Art of Knitting', *The Guardian*, 31st January 2005.

112. Kirsty Robertson, 'The Viral Knitting Project: An Ongoing Collaboration', www.kirstyrobertson.com/viral%20knitting.html.

113. Interview with Lisa Anne Auerbach, 4th November 2007.

Bibliography

Abakanowicz, M., *Magdalena Abakanowicz*, Abbeville Press, 1983.

Adorno, Theodor and Max Horheimer, *Dialectic of Enlightenment*, Continuum Books [1944] 1972.

Allen, Vanessa and Bob Roberts, 'Reclaim Our Streets: Hoodies and Baddies', *Daily Mirror,* 13th May 2005.

Andrews, Maggie, *The Acceptable Face of Feminism: The Women's Institute As a Social Movement*, Lawrence and Wishart, 1999.

Appadurai, Arjun, *The Social Life of Things*, Cambridge University Press, 1988.

Appignesi, Richard (ed.), *Introducing Marx*, Icon Books, 2006.

Aris, Sharon, *It's My Party and I'll Knit If I Want To!,* Allen and Unwin, 2003.

Arnold, Rebecca, *Fashion, Desire and Anxiety: Image and Morality in the Twentieth Century*, I. B. Tauris, New York, 2001.

Asfalack-Prall, Jivan, 'Semaphore', in Julian Stair (ed.), *The Body Politic: The Role of the Body and Contemporary Craft*, Crafts Council, 2000.

Ash, Juliet, 'The Aesthetic Absence: Clothes Without People in Paintings', in Amy de la Haye and Elizabeth Wilson (eds.), *Defining Dress*, Manchester University Press, 1999.

Attfield, Judy, *Wild Things*, Berg, 2000.

Attfield, Judy and Pat Kirkham, *A View From the Interior: Feminism, Women and Design*, The Women's Press, 1989.

Bachelard, Gaston, *The Poetics of Space*, Beacon, 1994.

Bakhtin, Mikhail, *Rabelais and His World*, trans. Helene Iswolsky, Indiana University Press, 1984 [1965].

Barnard, Malcolm, *Fashion as Communication,* Routledge, 2002.

Barnett, J., *The American Christmas: A Study of National Culture*, Macmillan, 1954.

Barnett, Pennina, 'Making, Materiality and Memory', in Pamela Johnson (ed.), *Ideas in the Making*, Crafts Council, 1998.

Barrett, M. and M. McIntosh, *The Antisocial Family*, Verso, 1982.

Barthes, Roland, *Image, Music, Text*, Fontana, 1977.

Bartlett, Anne, *Knitting,* Penguin Books, 2005.

Baudrillard, Jean, *Simulations*, trans. Paul Foss, Paul Patton and Philip Beitchman, Semiotext(e), 1983.

Baudrillard, Jean, *Seduction,* Macmillan, 1990.

Baudrillard, Jean, *The Consumer Society*, Sage, 1998.

Baudrilard, Jean, *The Spirit of Terrorism*, trans. Chris Turner, Verso, 2002.

Bauman, Zygmunt, *Life in Fragments: Essays in Postmodern Morality*, Blackwell, 1995.

de Beauvoir, Simone, *Old Age* (la Vieillesse), Gallimard, 1970.

Belford, Patricia, and Ruth Morrow, 'Girli Concrete: Bringing Together Concrete and Textile Technologies', in Georgina Follett and Louise Valentine (eds.), *New Craft: Future Voices*, Duncan of Jordanstone College of Art and Design, 2007.

Bell, Quentin, *On Human Finery*, The Hogarth Press, 1947.

Bettleheim, Bruno, *The Uses of Enchantment: The Meaning and Importance of Fairy Tales*, Penguin, 1991.

Binkley, Sam, 'Kitsch as a Repetitive System: A Problem for the Theory of Taste Hierarchy', *Journal of Material Culture*, Vol. 5, No. 2, July 2000.

Bird, John et al. (eds.), *Mapping the Futures: Local Cultures, Global Change*, Routledge,1990.

Black, Sandy, *Knitwear in Fashion*, Thames and Hudson, 2002.

Bocock, Robert, *Consumption*, Routledge, 1993.

Bolton, Andrew, *Anglomania*, Yale University Press, 2006.

Booker, Christopher, *The Seventies: Portrait of a Decade*, Allen Lane, 1980.

Bourdieu, Pierre, *Distinction: Outline of a Theory of Practice*, Routledge, 1986.

Bristow, Maxine, 'Three Weeks to Turn 348, Three Years to Turn Intuition Towards Understanding', in Pamela Johnson (ed.), *Ideas in the Making*, Crafts Council, 1998.

Britton Barnes, Galer, 'Amish Wedding Stockings of the Nineteenth Century', *Piecework*, March/April, 1997.

Bruzelius, Margaret, 'Exploring a Knitting Pattern: Bohus Stickning Sweater Generates Diverse Designs Knit with Simple Stitches', *Threads Magazine*, Knitting Around the World Issue, The Taunton Press, Newtown, 1993.

Buckley, Cheryl, 'Made in Patriarchy: Towards a Feminist Analysis of Women and Design', *Design Issues*, Vol. III, No. 2.

Burgess, Lesley and Kate Schofield, 'Shorting the Circuit', in Pamela Johnson (ed.), *Ideas in the Making,* Crafts Council, 1998.

Burman, Barbara, 'Made at Home With Clever Fingers', in Barbara Burman (ed.), *The Culture of Sewing*, Berg, 1999.

Bursch, Nicole, and Anthea Black, 'Craft Hard, Die Free: Radical Curatorial Strategies for Craftivism in Unruly Contexts', in Georgina Follett and Louise Valentine (eds.), *New Craft: Future Voices*, Duncan of Jordanstone College of Art and Design Publications, 2007, p.135.

Bush, Nancy, 'Two-Colour Knitting of Norway', *Piecework*, Jan/ Feb 1996.

Calefato, Patrizia, *The Clothed Body*, Berg, 2004.

Campbell, Colin, 'The Sociology of Consumption', in Daniel Miller (ed.),

Acknowledging Consumption, Routledge, 1995.

Cavendish, Dominic, 'Why Knitting is the New Rock and Roll', *Daily Telegraph*, 12th October 2002.

de Certeau, Michel, *The Practice of Everyday Life*, University of California Press, 1984.

Chaney, David, *Lifestyles*, Routledge, 1996.

Cheal, David, *The Gift Economy*, Routledge, 1990.

Chiarappa, Michael J., 'Affirmed Objects in Affirmed Places: History, Geographic Sentiment and a Region's Crafts', *Journal of Design History*, Vol. 10, No. 4.

Christiansen, Betty, *Knitting For Peace: Make the World a Better Place One Stitch at a Time*, Harry N. Abrams Inc., 2006.

Christiansen, C. and C. M. Baum, *Enabling Function and Well-Being*, Slack, 1997.

Christoffersson, Britt-Marie, *Swedish Sweaters: New Designs From Historical Examples*, The Taunton Press, Newtown CT, 1990.

Cockburn, Cynthia, 'Black and Decker Versus Moulinex', in S. Jackson and S. Moores (eds.), *The Politics of Domestic Consumption*, Harvester Wheatsheaf, 1995.

Collingwood, Peter, 'Arts and Crafts Exhibition', *Quarterly Journal of the Guilds of Weavers, Spinners and Dyers*, No.14, June 1955.

Compton, Rae, *The Complete Book of Traditional Knitting*, B. T. Batsford, 1983.

Conran, Shirley, *Superwoman*, Fontana, 1980.

Conway, Henry and Gail Downey, *Weardowney Knit Couture*, Collins and Brown, 2007.

Cooke, Rachel, 'Saturday Night Fever', *The Observer*, 29th January 2006.

Corrigan, Peter, *The Sociology of Consumption*, Sage, 1997.

Cosh, Sylvia, and James Walters, 'New Concepts for Knitting and Crochet', *Fashion and Craft*, No. 98, spring 1990.

Coward, Rosalind, *Female Desire: Women's Sexuality Today*, Paladin Grafton Books, 1984.

Craik, Jennifer, *The Face of Fashion*, Routledge, 1994.

Csikszentmihalyi, M. and E. Rochberg-Halton, *The Meaning of Things*, Cambridge University Press, 1975.

Dalton, Pen, 'Housewives, Leisure Crafts and Ideology', in G. Elinor et al. (eds.), *Women and Craft*, Virago, 1987.

Danford, Natalie, 'The End of the Yarn?', *Publishers' Weekly*, 28th August 2006.

Dant, Tim, *Material Culture in the Social World*, Open University Press, 1999.

Darlington, Rohana, *Irish Knitting: Patterns Inspired by Ireland*, A&C Black, 1991.

Davidoff, Leonore, *Worlds Between: Historical Perspectives on Gender and Class*, Polity Press, 1995.

Davis, Fred, *Fashion, Culture and Identity*, University of Chicago Press, 1994.

Debord, Guy, *The Society of the Spectacle*, Black and Red, 1984.

Deem, Rosemary, 'Leisure and the Household', in Stevi Jackson and Shaun Moores (eds.), *The Politics of Domestic Consumption*, Harvester Wheatsheaf, 1995.

Dentith, Simon, *Baktinnian Thought: An Introductory Reader*, Routledge, 1995.

Dissanayake, Ellen, 'The Pleasure and Meaning of Making', *American Craft*, Vol. 55, April/ May 1995.

Donnelly, Brian, 'Knitters Turn to Fairtrade in a Bid to Save Their Tradition', *The Herald*, 14th May 2007.

Dorfles, Gillo, *Kitsch: The World of Bad Taste*, Universe, 1969.

Durant, Judith, *Never Knit Your Man a Sweater Unless You've Got the Ring*, Storey Publishing, 2006.

Dyer, Richard, *Stars*, BFI Publishing, 1979.

Easthope, Anthony, *What a Man's Gotta Do: The Masculine Myth in Popular Culture*, Unwin Hyman, 1990.

Eddy, Mary, 'Talking Point', *How to Save Money With Sewing and Knitting*, September 1976.

Edwards, Adam, 'Absolutely Ethical, Darling', *Daily Telegraph*, 19th July 2006.

Edwards, Tim, *Men in the Mirror: Men's Fashion, Masculinity and Consumer Society*, Cassell, 1997.

Elinor, Gillian, 'Feminism and Craftwork', *Circa*, No.47, Sept/ Oct 1989.

Entwistle, Joanne, *The Fashioned Body*, Polity Press, 2000.

Evans, Caroline, 'Yesterday's Emblems and Tomorrow's Commodities: The Return of the Repressed in Fashion Imagery Today', in Stella Bruzzi and Pamela Church-Gibson (eds.), *Fashion Cultures: Theories, Explorations, Analysis*, Routledge, 2000.

Evans, Louise and Karen Lipton, 'A Woolly Affair', *Now*, 9th November 2005.

Ferris, Monica, *Crewel World*, Berkley Prime Crime Books, 1999.

Ferris, Monica, *Unravelled Sleeve*, Berkley Prime Crime Books, 2001.

Ferris, Monica, *A Murderous Yarn*, Berkley Prime Crime Books, 2002.

Ferris, Monica, *Hanging by a Thread*, Berkley Prime Crime Books, 2003.

Ferris, Monica, *Crewel Yule*, Berkley Prime Crime Books, 2004.

Findeis, Karin, 'Atropos and the Consumable', in Julian Stair (ed.), *The Body Politic: The Role of the Body and Contemporary Craft*, Crafts Council, 1999.

Flugel, J. C., *The Psychology of Clothes*, The Hogarth Press, 1930.

Forty, Adrian, *Objects of Desire: Design and Society 1750–1980*, Thames & Hudson, 1989.

Frayling, Christopher, 'The Crafts in the 1990s', *The Journal of Art and Design Education*, Vol. 9, No. 1, 1990.

Freeman, June, *Knitting: A Common Art*, Minorities, Colchester, 1986.

Freud, Sigmund, *Introductory Lectures on Psychoanalysis*, reprint, Penguin, 1991.

Freud, Sigmund, *On Metapsychology*, reprint, Penguin, 1984.

Friedan, Betty, *The Feminine Mystique, Penguin*, 1992.

Frostick, Ailya, 'It's Now Hip to Knit, So Get Out Those Needles', *The Bath Chronicle*, 12th October 2004.

Gallagher, M., 'Gooden Gansey Sweaters', *Fiberarts*, November/ December 1985.

Gammon, Larraine, 'Visual Seduction and Perverse Compliance: Reviewing Food Fantasies, Large Appetites and Grotesque Bodies', in Stella Bruzzi and Pamela Church-Gibson (eds.), *Fashion Cultures: Theories, Explorations and Analysis*, Routledge, 2000.

Gemmell, Liz, *Aussie Fair: Simple Fair Isle Knitting with Australian Motifs*, Lloyd O'Neil Pty Ltd., 1984.

Geoghegan, Vincent, *Utopianism and Marxism*, Methuen, 1987.

Gibson-Roberts, Priscilla A., *Knitting in the Old Way*, Interweave Press, 1985.

Gibson-Roberts, Priscilla A., *Salish Indian Sweaters: A Pacific Northwest Tradition*, Dos Tejedoras, St Paul MN, 1998.

Goldsmith, Olivia, *Wish Upon a Star*, Harper Collins, 2004.

Gordon Lydon, Susan, *The Knitting Sutra: Craft as Spiritual Practice*, HarperOne, 1998.

Gottdiener, M., *Postmodern Semiotics*, Blackwell, 1995.

Gravelle LeCount, Cynthia, *Andean Folk Knitting: Traditions and Techniques From Peru and Bolivia*, Dos Tejedoras, St Paul MN, 1990.

Gray, A. and J. McGuigan, *Studying Culture: An Introductory Reader*, Arnold, 1997.

Green, Nicholas, *The Spectacle of Nature: Landscape and Bourgeois Culture in Nineteenth-Century France,* Manchester University Press, 1990.

Greenhalgh, Paul, 'The History of Craft', in Peter Dormer (ed.), *The Culture of Craft*, Manchester University Press, 1997.

Gross, Elizabeth, 'The Body of Signification', in J. Fletcher (ed.), *Abjection, Melancholia and Love*, Routledge, 1990.

Gschwandtner, Sabrina, *KnitKnit: Profiles and Projects From Knitting's New Wave*, Stewart, Tabori and Chang, 2007.

Handy, Bruce, 'A Spy Guide to Postmodern Everything', in A. A .Berger (ed.), *The Postmodern Presence*, Altamira, 1998.

Harding, Sally (ed.), *Kaffe Fassett at the V&A: Knitting and Needlepoint*, Centium Hutchinson, 1988.

Harrod, Tanya, *The Crafts in Britain in the Twentieth Century*, Yale University Press, 1999.

Hartley, M. and J. Ingilby, *The Old Hand-Knitters of the Dales*, Dalesman Press, [1951] 1969.

Hawkes, Terence, *Structuralism and Semiotics*, Methuen, 1977.

Hayes, Michael J., 'Recipes for Success', in Gary Day (ed.), *Readings in Popular Culture: Trivial Pursuits?*, Macmillan, 1990.

Hebdige, Dick, *Subculture: The Meaning of Style*, Methuen, 1979.

Hecker, Carolyn, 'The Mother of Creative Knitting', *Fiberarts*, No. 1, 1980.

Hewison, Robert, *The Heritage Industry*, Methuen, 1987.

Hewitt, Paolo and Mark Baxter, *The Fashion of Football: From Best to Beckham, From Mod to Label Slave*, Mainstream Publishing Company, 2006.

Hickey, Gloria, 'Craft in a Consuming Society', in Peter Dormer (ed.), *The Culture of Craft*, Manchester University Press, 1997.

Higgins, Charlotte, 'Political Protest Turns to The Radical Art of Knitting', *The Guardian*, 31st January 2005.

Highmore, Ben, *Everyday Life and Cultural Theory*, Routledge, 2002.

Hill, Christopher, *Reformation to Industrial Revolution*, Penguin, 1967.

Hinchcliffe, Frances, *Knit One, Purl One: Historic and Contemporary Knitting from the V&A's Collection*, V&A Publishing, 1985.

Holder, Guy, 'Will It Go Outside', in Pamela Johnson (ed.), *Ideas in the Making*, Crafts Council, 1998.

Holland, Samantha, *Alternative Femininities: Body, Age and Identity*, Berg, 2004.

Hollingworth, Shelagh, *The Complete Book of Traditional Aran Knitting*, B. T. Batsford, 1982.

Hollows, Joanne, 'Can I Go Home Yet?', in Joanne Hollows and Rachel Moseley (eds.), *Feminism in Popular Culture*, Berg, 2006.

Holmes, Su and Sean Redmond (eds.), *Framing Celebrity: New Directions in Celebrity Culture*, Routledge, 2006.

Horkheimer, Max, 'The End of Reason: Changes in the Structure of Political Compromise', *Studies in Philosophy and Social Sciences*, Vol. IX, 1941, reproduced in Andrew Arato and Eike Gebhardt (eds.), *The Essential Frankfurt School Reader*, Continuum Publishing, 1982.

Hosegood, Betsy, *Not Tonight Darling, I'm Knitting*, David and Charles, 2006.

Hunt, Leon, *British Low Culture: From Safari Suits to Sexploitation*, Routledge, 1998.

Jackson, P. and N. Thrift, 'Geographies of Consumption', in Daniel Miller (ed.), *Acknowledging Consumption: A Review of New Studies*, Routledge, 1995.

Jackson, Stevi and Shaun Moores, *The Politics of Domestic Consumption*, Harvester Wheatsheaf, 1995.

Jacobs, Kate, *The Friday Night Knitting Club*, Hodder and Stoughton, 2007.

Jameson, Frederick, 'Postmodernism, or the Cultural Logic of Late Capitalism', *New Left Review*, 146, 1984.

Jeffries, Janis, 'Text and Textiles: Reading Across the Borderlines', in Katy Deepwell (ed.), *New Feminist Art Criticism*, University of Manchester Press, 1995.

Johnson, Pamela, 'Can Theory Damage Your Practice?', in Pamela Johnson (ed.), *Ideas in the Making: Practice in Theory*, Crafts Council, 1998.

Jonsson, Love, '100 Ideas About Craft', exhibition review, *Crafts*, January/February 2006.

Julier, Guy, *The Culture of Design*, Sage, 2000.

Kiewe, Heinz Edgar, *The Sacred History of Knitting*, Art Needlework Industries Ltd., 1971 [1967].

Kirkham, Pat, 'Women and the Inter-War Handicrafts Revival', in Judy Attfield and Pat Kirkham (eds.), *A View From the Interior*, The Women's Press, 1989.

Klein, Naomi, *No Logo*, Flamingo, 2000.

Knight, India, 'Let Them Wear Hoodies', *The Sunday Times*, 15th May 2005.

Knox, Patty, *New Directions in Fair Isle Knitting*, Lark Books, 1985.

Knox, P., 'The Restless Urban Landscape: Economic and Sociocultural Change and the Transformation of Metropolitan Washington DC', *Annals: Association of American Geographers*, 81, 1991.

Kopytoff, Igor, 'The Cultural Biography of Things: Commoditization as Process', in Arjun Appadurai, *The Social Life of Things: Commodities in Cultural Perspective*, Cambridge University Press, 1988.

Kristeva, Julia, 'Powers of Horror – Approaching Abjection' (1980), in Kelly Oliver (ed.), *The Portable Kristeva*, Columbia University Press, New York, 2002.

Kruger, Mary, *Died in the Wool*, Pocket Books, 2005.

Kruger, Mary, *Knit Fast Die Young*, Pocket Books, 2007.

Kuper, Adam, 'The English Christmas and the Family: Time Out and Alternative Realities', in Daniel Miller (ed.), *Unwrapping Christmas*, Oxford University Press, 1993.

Lacan, Jacques, *The Four Fundamental Concepts of Psychoanalysis*, Penguin, London, 1977.

LaZebnik, Claire, *Knitting Under the Influence*, Five Spot Publishing, New York, 2006.

Lebovits, Susan Chaityn, 'Textile Artist Knitting War Protests', *The Boston Globe*, 2nd September 2007.

Lee, M. J., *Consumer Culture Reborn*, Routledge, 1993.

Lefebvre, Henri, *The Production of Space*, trans. Donald Nicholson-Smith, Blackwell, 1994 [1974].

Lenor Larsen, Jack, 'Mary Walker Phillips', *Knitters*, spring/ summer, 1985.

Levy, Ariel, *Female Chauvinist Pigs: Women and the Rise of Raunch Culture*, Simon & Schuster, 2005.

Lewis, Susanna, 'District of Ohio', *Knitters*, spring 1993.

Lofgren, Orvar, 'The Great Christmas Quarrel and Other Swedish Traditions', in Daniel Miller (ed.), *Unwrapping Christmas*, Oxford University Press, 1995.

Lohr, Nikol, *Naughty Needles: Sexy, Saucy Knits for the Bedroom and Beyond*, Potter Style, 2007.

Lowenthal, David, *The Past is a Foreign Country*, Cambridge University Press, 1985.

Lucie-Smith, Edward, *The Story of Craft: The Craftsman's Role in Society*, Phaidon Press, 1981.

Lurie, Alison, *The Language of Clothes*, Hamlyn, 1983.

Macdonald, Anne L., *No Idle Hands: The Social History of American Knitting*, Ballantyne Books, 1988.

Macdonald, Fiona, 'Think Outside the Bag', *The Metro*, 23rd April 2007.

Mackay, Hugh and Tim O'Sullivan (eds.), *The Media Reader: Continuity and Transformation*, Sage and OUP, 1999.

Malpas, Simon, *Jean-Francois Lyotard*, Routledge, 2003.

Manning, Tara Jon, *Mindful Knitting*, Tuttle Publishing, Boston MA, 2004.

Manning, Tara Jon, *Men in Knits: Sweaters to Knit That He WILL Wear*, Interweave Press Inc., 2004.

Marshall, P. David, *Celebrity and Power: Fame in Contemporary Culture*, University of Minnesota, 1997.

Martin, Richard and Harold Koda, *Jocks and Nerds: Men's Style in the Twentieth Century*, Rizzoli, 1989.

Martinson, Kate, 'Sweater Watching', *Knitter's Magazine*, fall 1993.

Marx, Karl, *Capital: Vol. 1*, Progress Publishers, 1973 [1887].

Matthews, Rachael, *Knitorama*, MQ Publications, 2005.

Maynard, Margaret, *Dress and Globalization*, Manchester University Press, 2004.

Mazza, Cris, 'Who's Laughing Now? A Short History of Chick Lit and the Perversion of a Genre', in Suzanne Ferriss and Mallory Young (eds.), *Chick Lit: The New Woman's Fiction*, Routledge, 2005.

McDermott, Catherine, *Made in Britain*, Mitchell Beazley, 2002.

McDougall, Dan, 'Ethical Business', *The Observer*, 28th October 2007.

McGregor, S., *The Complete Book of Traditional Fair Isle Knitting*, B. T. Batsford, 1981.

McGregor, Sheila, *The Complete Book of Scandinavian Knitting*, B. T. Batsford, 1984.

McGuinness, Ross, 'Knitting for Nits: Designer Mittens for Insects', *The Metro*, 31st October 2007.

McInnes, Sasha Claire, 'The Political is Personal: Or Why Have a Revolution (From Within Or Without) When You Can Have Soma?', *Feminist Review*, 6, 2001.

McKendrick, N., J. Brewer and J. Plumb, *The Birth of a Consumer Society*, Europa, 1982.

McLean, Gareth, 'In the Hood', *The Guardian*, 13th May 2005.

McMillan, Sam, 'George Brett: Webs of a Mad Spider', *Fiberarts*, November/ December 1981.

McNeil, Gill, *Divas Don't Knit*, Bloomsbury 2007.

Medhurst, Andy, 'Negotiating the Gnome Zone: Versions of Suburbia in British Popular Culture', in Roger Silverstone (ed.), *Visions of Suburbia*, Routledge, 1997.

Messinger De Master, Sandra, 'Messages in Mittens: The Story of a Latvian

Knitter', *Piecework*, Nov/ Dec 1995.

Meyrowitz, Joshua, 'No Sense of Place: The Impact of Electronic Media on Social Behaviour', in Hugh Mackay and Tim O'Sullivan (eds.), *The Media Reader: Continuity and Transformation*, Sage and OUP, 1999.

Mierendorff, Vida, 'Craft From the Past Brings New Meaning to Needlework', *Sixth Annual Australian Craft and Design Showcase*, Vol. 72, April 2003.

Miles, Stephen, *Consumerism – As a Way of Life*, Sage, 1998.

Miller, Daniel, *Material Culture and Mass Consumption*, Blackwell, 1994.

Miller, Daniel, 'A Theory of Christmas', in Daniel Miller (ed.), *Unwrapping Christmas*, Oxford University Press, 1995.

Miller, Daniel, *A Theory of Shopping*, Blackwell, 1998.

Miller, Daniel and Don Slater, *The Internet: An Ethnographic Approach*, Berg, 2000.

Millett, Kate, *Sexual Politics*, Virago, 1977.

Mills, Sara, *Michel Foucault*, Routledge, 2003.

Minahan, Stella and Julie Wolfram Cox, 'Stitch 'n' Bitch', *Journal of Material Culture*, Vol. 12, No. 1, 2007.

Mitchell, Victoria, 'Textiles, Text and Techne', in Tanya Harrod (ed.), *Obscure Objects of Desire: Reviewing the Crafts in the Twentieth Century*, Crafts Council, 1997.

Mizejewski, Linda, *Hardboiled and High Heeled: The Woman Detective in Popular Culture*, Routledge, 2004.

Moore, Henrietta L., *Feminism and Anthropology*, Blackwell, 1988.

Mort, Frank, *Cultures of Consumption: Masculinities and Social Space in Twentieth-Century Britain*, Routledge, 1996.

Mowery Kieffer, Susan, *Fiberarts Design Book 7*, Lark Books, New York, 2004.

Murphy, Bernadette, *Zen and the Art of Knitting*, Adams Media, 2002.

Nappen, Barbara, 'In the Web of Superstition: Myths and Folktales about Nets', *Fiberarts*, May/ June 1982.

Nead, Lynda, *Myths of Sexuality*, Blackwell, 1980.

Nixon, Sean, *Hard Looks: Masculinities, Spectatorship and Contemporary Consumption*, Routledge, 1996.

Norbury, James, *Traditional Knitting Patterns: From Scandinavia, the British Isles, France, Italy and Other European Countries*, Dover Publications, 1973.

Orczy, Baroness Emmuska, *The Scarlet Pimpernel*, Brockhampton Press, 1961 [1905].

Packard, Vance, *The Hidden Persuaders*, Penguin, 1960.

Pagoldh, Susanne, *Nordic Knitting: Thirty-One Patterns in the Scandinavian Tradition*, Interweave Press, Loveland CO, 1st edition, 1987.

Paiget, Jean, *Play, Dreams and Imitation in Childhood*, Heinemann, [1946] 1951.

Papanek, Victor, *Design for the Real World*, Thames and Hudson, 1971.

Parker, Roszika, *The Subversive Stitch*, The Women's Press, 1996.

Parkins, Wendy, 'Celebrity Knitting and the Temporality of Postmodernity', *Fashion Theory*, Vol. 8, issue 4, 2004.

Pavitt, Jane (ed.), *Brand: New*, V&A Publications, 2000.

Pearce, Susan M., *Museums, Objects and Collections*, Leicester University Press, 1992.

Pearson, Michael, *Traditional Knitting: Aran, Fair Isle and Fisher Ganseys*, William Collins Sons and Co. Ltd., 1984.

Pels, Peter, 'The Spirit of Matter: On Fetish, Rarity, Fact and Fancy', in Patricia Spyer (ed.), *Border Fetishisms*, Routledge, 1998.

Pemberton, Andrew, 'John Lydon Lives Off the Past. He's a Buffoon', *Q* magazine, March 2006.

Perniola, Mario, 'Between Clothing and Nudity', in M. Feher, R. Naddaff and N. Tazi (eds.), *Fragments for a History of the Human Body, Part 2*, Zone, New York, 1989.

Phillips, D., *Exhibiting Authenticity*, Manchester University Press, 1997.

Philips, Deborah and Alan Tomlinson, 'Homeward Bound: Leisure, Popular Culture and Consumer Capitalism', in Dominic Strinati and Stephen Wagg (eds.), *Come On Down? Popular Media Culture in Post-War Britain*, Routledge, 1992.

Piroch, Sigrid, 'A Woman's Cap: The Glory of Slovakia', *Piecework*, Jan/ Feb 1994.

Postan, M. M., *The Medieval Economy and Society*, Penguin, 1986.

Proops, Margie, *Fresh Start: A Guide to Training Opportunities*, Equal Opportunities Commission, 1978.

Pumphrey, M., 'Why Do Cowboys Wear Hats in the Bath? Style Politics for the Older Man', *Critical Quarterly*, 31, 3, autumn.

Radway, Janice, *Reading the Romance: Women, Patriarchy and Popular Literature*, Verso, 1987.

Rasmussen Noble, Carol, 'Peruvian Maquitos: Colourful Sleeves Knit Traditions Together', *Piecework*, Jan/ Feb 1995.

Rayworth, Melissa, 'Do it Yourself Toys', *Honolulu Advertiser*, 26th November 2007.

Read, Herbert, *Art and Industry*, Faber and Faber, 1934.

Redmond, Sean, 'Intimate Fame Everywhere', in Su Holmes and Sean Redmond (eds.), *Framing Celebrity: New Directions in Celebrity Culture*, Routledge, 2006.

Reed, Christopher, *Not at Home: The Suppression of Domesticity in Modern Art and Architecture,* Thames and Hudson, 1996.

Reuter, Lauren, *Machiko Agano*, Telos, 2003.

Rew, Christine, *Bill Gibb: The Golden History of Fashion,* Aberdeen City Council, 2003.

Rheingold, Howard, 'The Virtual Community: Finding Connection in a

Computerized World', in Hugh Mackay and Tim O'Sullivan (eds.), *The Media Reader: Continuity and Transformation*, Sage and OUP, 1999.

Ribeiro, Aileen, *Dress and Morality*, B. T. Batsford, 1986.

Roberts, Gwyneth, 'A Thing of Beauty and a Source of Wonderment: Ornaments for the Home as Cultural Status Markers', in Gary Day (ed.), *Trivial Pursuits? Readings in Popular Culture*, Macmillan, 1990.

Roberts, Ken, *Leisure*, Longman, 1981.

Robins, Freddie, 'Woolly Wedding', *Real People*, 30th August 2007.

Rogers, Mary F., *Barbie Culture*, Sage, 1999.

Rojek, Chris, *Celebrity,* Reaktion Books, 2001.

Ross, M., 'The Last Twenty-Five Years: The Arts in Education, 1963–1988', in M. Ross (ed.), *The Claims of Feeling: Readings in Aesthetic Education*, The Falmer Press, 1989.

Ross, Robert J. S., *Slaves to Fashion: Poverty and Abuse in the New Sweatshops*, University of Michigan Press, 2004.

Rowley, Sue, 'There Once Lived … Craft and Narrative Traditions', in Sue Rowley (ed.), *Craft and Critical Theory*, Allen and Unwin, 1997.

Rutt, Richard, *A History of Hand Knitting*, Interweave Press, 2003.

Rutter, Jason, 'Stepping Into Wayne's World: Exploring Postmodern Comedy', in A. A. Berger (ed.), *The Postmodern Presence*, Altamira, 1998.

Sabo, Donald F. Jr. and Ross Rinfola, *Jock: Sports and Male Identity*, Prentice Hall Inc., 1980.

Salecl, Renata, *On Anxiety*, Routledge, London, 2004.

Samuel, Raphael, *Theatres of Memory*, Verso, 1996.

Schjeldhal, Peter, 'The Empty Body Part 2: Skin Has No Edges. Clothes Do', in Chris Townsend, *Rapture: Art's Seduction by Fashion*, Thames & Hudson, 2002.

Schumacher, E. F., *Small Is Beautiful: A Study of Economics As If People Mattered*, Abacus, 1974.

Scott, Jac, *Textile Perspectives in Mixed Media Sculpture*, D & N Publishing, Hungerford, 2003.

Sefton, Maggie, *A Deadly Yarn*, Berkley Prime Crime, 2006.

Seremetakis, C. Nadia, 'Memory of the Senses, Part I', in C. Nadia Seremetakis (ed.), *The Senses Still: Perception and Memory as Material Culture in Modernity*, University of Chicago Press, 1996.

Sheard, Stephen, *Summer and Winter Knitting*, Century Hutchinson, 1987.

Silverstone, Roger, *Why Study the Media?,* Sage, 1999.

Smith, Andrew, 'Hampton Court Revisited: A Re-evaluation of the Consumer', in Gary Day (ed.), *Readings in Popular Culture: Trivial Pursuits?*, Macmillan, 1990.

Smith, Mary and Chris Bunyan, *A Shetland Knitter's Notebook*, The Shetland Times, Lerwick, 1991.

Soloman, Jack, 'Our Decentred Culture', in A. A. Berger, *The Postmodern*

Presence, Altamira Press, 1998.

Sorenson, Crolin, 'Theme Parks and Time Machines', in Peter Vergo (ed.), *The New Museology*, Reaktion Books, 1989.

Sounes, Howard, *Seventies: The Sights, Sounds and Ideas of a Brilliant Decade*, Simon and Schuster, 2006.

Sparke, Penny, *An Introduction to Design and Culture in the Twentieth Century*, Allen and Unwin, 1986.

Sparke, Penny, *As Long As It's Pink: The Sexual Politics of Taste*, Pandora, 1995.

Spencer, David J., *Knitting Technology*, Woodhead Publishing, 1998 (3rd edition).

Spencer, Neil, 'Is Hip Hop Really Responsible for Britain's Rampant Knife Culture', *The Observer*, 11th June 2006.

Spooner, Catherine, *Contemporary Gothic*, Reaktion Books, 2006.

Stafford, Jennifer, *Dominknitrix: Whip Your Knitting Into Shape*, North Light Books, Cincinnati, 2007.

Stair, Julian, *The Body Politic: The Role of the Body and Contemporary Craft*, Crafts Council, 1999.

Stanley, Montse, 'Jumpers That Drive You Quite Insane: Colour, Structure and Form in Knitted Objects', in Mary Schoeser and Chrstine Boydell (eds.), *Disentangling Textiles*, Middlesex University Press, 2002.

Starmore, A., *Alice Starmore's Book of Fair Isle Knitting*, The Taunton Press, Newtown CT, 1988.

Steel, Mark, *Vive La Revolution: A Stand-Up History of the French Revolution*, Scribner, 2003.

Steele, Valerie, 'Clothing and Sexuality', in C. Kidwell and V. Steele (eds.), *Men and Women: Dressing the Part*, Smithsonian Institute Press, 1989.

Stewart, Richard, *Design and British Industry*, John Murray, 1987.

Stewart, Susan, *On Longing: Narrative of the Miniature, the Gigantic, the Souvenir, the Collection*, Duke University Press, 1993.

Stone, Andrew, 'Boys in the Hoodies', *Socialist Review*, June 2005.

Storey, John, *An Introductory Guide to Cultural Theory and Popular Culture*, Harvester Wheatsheaf, 1993.

Strawn Bailey, Susan, 'Knitting in the Amanas', *Piecework*, September/ October 1997.

Strinati, Dominic, *An Introduction to Theories of Popular Culture*, Routledge, 1995.

Tallack, Malachy, 'Knitwear: Our Heritage on the Cheap', *Shetland Life*, 7th September 2007.

Taylor, Joan (ed.), *The Knitwear Revue: Exhibition Catalogue and Knitter's Sourcebook*, British Crafts Centre, 1983.

Thomas, Ruth, *Things to Make and Mend*, Faber and Faber, 2007.

Thornton, Phil, *Casuals: Football, Fighting and Fashion – the Story of a Terrace Cult*, Milo Books, 2003.

Tolston, Andrew, 'Being Yourself: The Pursuit of Authentic Celebrity', *Discourse Studies*, 3 (4), 2001.

Tozer, James, 'Safety Police Outlaw NHS Knitters Over Fears of Accidents With Needles', *Daily Mail*, 12th November 2007.

Turkle, Sherry, 'Identity in the Age of the Internet', in Hugh Mackay and Tim O'Sullivan (eds.), *The Media Reader: Continuity and Transformation*, Sage and OUP, 1999.

Turner, Graeme, *Understanding Celebrity*, Sage, 2004.

Upitis, Lizbeth, *Latvian Mittens: Traditional Designs and Techniques*, Dos Tejedoras, St Paul MN, 1981.

Urry, John, *Consuming Places*, Routledge, 1995.

Veblen, Thorstein, *Theory of the Leisure Class*, Augustus M. Kelley, 1899.

Vernon, Polly, 'Don't Look Now: It's the Fashion Hoodies', *Observer Woman Magazine*, October 2006.

Vidler, Anthony, *The Architectural Uncanny*, MIT Press, 1994.

Wagg, Stephen, 'Here's One I Made Earlier', in Dominic Strinati and Stephen Wagg, *Come On Down? Popular Media Culture in Post-War Britain*, Routledge, 1992.

Walker, Barbara, *A Treasury of Knitting Patterns*, Schoolhouse Press, 1998.

Walker Phillips, Mary, *Creative Knitting: A New Art Form*, Van Nostrand Reinhold Company, New York, 1971.

Walkley, Cristina, *The Ghost in the Looking Glass*, Peter Owen, 1981.

Walter, Natasha, *The New Feminism*, Virago, 1999.

Warwick, Alexandra and Dani Cavallaro, *Fashioning the Frame*, Berg, 1998.

Wearing, Betsy, *Leisure and Feminist Theory*, Sage, 1998.

Webber, Richard, *A Celebration of the Good Life*, Orion Books, 2000.

Whannel, Garry, *Media Sports Stars: Masculinities and Moralities*, Routledge, 2002.

Whelehan, Imelda, *Overloaded: Popular Culture and the Future of Feminism*, The Women's Press, 2000.

Whiteley, Nigel, *Design for Society*, Reaktion Books, 1993.

Williams, P. H. M., *Teaching Craft, Design and Technology*, Routledge, 1990.

Williams, Zoe, 'Close Knit', *The Guardian*, 8th January 2005.

Willis, Paul, 'Symbolic Creativity', in Ann Gray and Jim McGuigan, *Studying Culture: An Introductory Reader*, Arnold, 1997.

Wills, Kerry, *The Close Knit Circle: American Knitters Today*, Praeger, 2007.

Wilson, Elizabeth, *Adorned in Dreams: Fashion and Modernity*, Virago, 1985.

Winnicott, D. W., *Playing and Reality*, Tavistock Press, 1971.

Winship, Janice, 'The Impossibility of Best: Enterprise Meets Domesticity in the Practical Women's Magazines of the 1980s', in Dominic Strinati and Stephen Wagg, *Come On Down? Popular Media Culture*, Routledge, 1992.

Wolf, Naomi, *Promiscuities: A Secret History of Female Desire*, Chatto and Windus, 1997.

Wolff, Janet, *The Social Production of Art*, Macmillan, 1981.

Woodham, J. M., 'Managing British Design Reform I: Fresh Perspectives of the Early Years of the Council of Industrial Design', *Journal of Design History*, Vol. 9, No. 1, 1996.

Woodham, J. M., 'Managing British Design Reform II: The Film Deadly Lampshade – An Ill-Fated Episode in the Politics of Good Taste', *Journal of Design History*, Vol. 9, No. 2, 1996.

Wright, Mary, *Cornish Guernseys and Knit-Frocks*, Ethnographica, 1979.

Wright, Mary, 'In Search of Cornish Guernseys and Knit-Frocks', *Piecework*, September/October 1994.

Wright, Patrick, *On Living in an Old Country*, Verso, 1985.

Xenakis, Alexis, 'From Russia With Love', *Knitter's Magazine*, Fall 1992.

Xenakis, Alexis, 'An Icelandic Saga: 100 Years of Lopi', *Knitter's Magazine*, winter 1996.

York, Peter, 'Style Wars: Punk and Pageant', in John Thackara, *Design After Modernism: Beyond the Object*, Thames and Hudson, 1988.

Zimmerman, Elizabeth, *Knitting Without Tears*, Simon and Schuster, 1973.

Index

Made in the USA
San Bernardino, CA
13 September 2019